D0118784

SHOEMAKER

The jockeys' room.

SHOEMAKER

Bill Shoemaker
and Barney Nagler

Doubleday
NEW YORK
1988

PHOTO CREDITS: R. Wenkham Photo, Frontis; Santa Anita Photo, pp. 4–5, 10, 15, 45, 116–17, 124, 150–51, 171; Kentucky Derby Photo, pp. 24, 29, 185, 192; N.Y.R.A. Photos, pp. 52, 79, 97, 106–7, 144, 159; Turfotos, pp. 36, 61, 164; Hollywood Park, p. 72; Maryland Jockey Club of Baltimore City, Inc., p. 88; Del Mar Thoroughbred Club, p. 137; Stidham Photo, p. 199.

DESIGNED BY PETER R. KRUZAN

Library of Congress Cataloging-in-Publication Data
Shoemaker, Willie.
Shoemaker: the autobiography of the world's greatest jockey/Bill Shoemaker and Barney Nagler.
p. cm.
1. Shoemaker, Willie. 2. Jockeys—United States—Biography.
I. Nagler, Barney. II. Title.
SF336.S47A3 1988
798.4'3'0924—dc19
[B] 87-28743
CIP

ISBN 0-385-23945-9

PRINTED IN THE UNITED STATES OF AMERICA
FIRST EDITION

This is dedicated to my darling daughter Amanda,
who has given me more happiness
than ten thousand winners ever could.
—Bill Shoemaker

For my grandchildren:
Kate, Ross, Craig, and Keith
—Barney Nagler

ACKNOWLEDGMENTS

We are grateful for the assistance, cooperation and advice from many people, an an especially indebted to the following:

To Jane Goldstein, publicity director, Los Angeles Turf Club, Santa Anita Park, for allowing us to search in the racetrack's archives and for providing many of the photographs from Santa Anita.

To the press department of the New York Racing Association for information and encouragement.

To Mr. Michael Sandler, publisher, and Mr. Fred Grossman, editor of the *Daily Racing Form*, for generously opening their files.

To the staff of the Thoroughbred Racing Association for their assistance.

To Mr. Steven Haskin, librarian of the *Daily Racing Form*, for his invaluable statistical assistance.

To Mrs. Marjorie L. Everett, chairman of the board and CEO of Hollywood Park, for much time and trouble, and guidance.

To Frances Goldin, my literary agent, for much hard work and patience.

To Fara Bushnell for allowing the use of the photograph of both authors in the winner's circle at Pimlico Race Course.

To Mr. Frank J. De Francis, president and chairman of the board; to Linda J. O'Dey, director of marketing, and Mr. Jeffrey Weissman, director of media relations, the Maryland Jockey Club, for their help in making available photographs of various events at Pimlico Race Course.

To Mr. Allen Gutterman, director of development and public relations, and Mr. James Raftery, track photographer for the New Jersey Sports and Exposition Authority, for making available photographs of races at Monmouth Park and the Meadowlands.

To Mr. Charlie Whittingham, a great trainer who proved to be a mine of information.

To Dr. Robert Kerlan for assistance and guidance.

To Mr. Jim Fitzgerald, my editor at Doubleday, for conceiving this book and much hard work and guidance.

To Mr. Tom Meeker, president, and Mr. Edgar Allen, director of media relations, Churchill Downs, for information and encouragement.

To Mr. William Rubin for being a squirrel in racing's archives, and for his considerable work in compiling the year-by-year record of a great rider's achievements.

To Christopher Scherf of the Thoroughbred Racing Association for his help in keeping things accurate.

To Mrs. Cindy Shoemaker for information and encouragement.

To Dr. Leonard J. Garrett, class of '50, United States Military Academy, for his help.

To Harry, Teresa, and Tom Meyerhoff for information relating to Spectacular Bid's career.

To Mr. John Nerud for his assistance.

To all the others who lent moral support. They are too numerous to mention, but they know who they are.

List of Illustrations

Introduction

The three-year-olds were going to the gate, sixteen of them running for the roses. I was up on one of them called Ferdinand and thinking, Hey, I'm fifty-four years old and here I am with a bunch of kids, some of them young enough to be my sons, and I'm going to ride against them in the biggest race of them all—the Kentucky Derby.

The Derby wasn't a new thing for me. No sir. This was my 24th Derby, more rides than anyone in history. I had been on three winners before and should have had another on Gallant Man, but I made the terrible mistake of standing up on him in the stirrups before the finish line just when I had a real shot. A shot for the roses. Now it was the 112th Derby and, yeah, 120,000 people were singing "My Old Kentucky Home," and if you've never been to the Derby, if you've never heard them singing, you don't know how it feels to be on a colt, going toward the gate, walking slowly, maybe even cantering, and if you're sitting chilly, well, then, you don't have any blood in you at all.

I was riding Ferdinand and I think he knew this was his big day. Maybe he knew, from the talk around the barn back in California, that Charlie Whittingham, his trainer, hadn't had a Derby horse in twenty-six years. "Only time I'm going back," Charlie said, "is if I have a real Derby horse," and now Charlie was seventy-three and he was back in Louisville and I was on Charlie's Derby horse.

Charlie and I go back a lot of years. We once tried to remember the name of the first horse I rode for him, but he couldn't remember. Neither could I. It's so long ago, old guys can't remember. Charlie's trained thousands of winners and now here I am up on his horse Ferdinand and it's a long way from Fabens, Texas, where I was born in scrubby cotton country back on August 19, 1931. It is May 1986 now, and if I could make as much money doing something else, I probably wouldn't be here at Churchill Downs riding a horse. But, I am.

Riding is a big thing to me. It always has been. I think the public doesn't understand it. The public thinks a jockey is somebody who just sits on top of a horse while the horse does the running. To be a top jockey, you not only have to be a good athlete, but you have to have pride in what you are doing. I get mad when I hear anything about jockeys throwing races. I love the game. It brought me a lot of fame and money, and I'll protect racing every way I can.

Just being in the Derby is a big lift. It is twenty-one years since my last victory in this mile-and-a-quarter race. If a man hasn't won on the first Saturday in May in twenty-one years, chances are he is never going to win another. He is really lucky even to get another mount in the Run for the Roses. At my age I was getting a shot that I never thought I'd get again.

But first, I've got to tell you about my agent and this horse Ferdinand. I used to talk a lot about him with Harry Silbert. Harry was my agent. He got me my first mounts in 1949. Until he died in 1987, he had booked me on almost every mount I ever

rode. He was like a father to me. We never had a contract and we never had an argument. He took me on as a kid and made me a man, and I'm going to remember him for the rest of my life. I even cried a little when he died.

When we talked about Ferdinand, Harry would say, "Hey, Bill, let's be honest. This big good-looking dude, he goofs off. We rode him when he was two and he didn't put out. Too many times, when he's going to win galloping, he'd prick his ears and ease up. When he gets to the front of the heap, he thinks it's over."

"You bet," I used to say, knowing anyway that this was going to be our Derby horse, if wise old Charlie would only decide to take him to Louisville.

We're at Churchill Downs now and I'm thinking only about the race. I'm thinking of Charlie and what he said before he threw me up on the horse, saying he knew I knew all about the colt and I should remember to take the horse inside the other horses when I got the chance.

Charlie loved Ferdinand. If he hadn't, we wouldn't have been in Louisville. I knew that much. What I didn't know going into the first slot in the gate, closest to the rail, was that the ABC-TV people were isolating Ferdinand on camera and taping us in the race.

What they do is pick three horses out of the sixteen in the race and isolate each horse on camera all the way around the track. They tape this and then they play it back, and Charlie says that if they didn't do that, if they hadn't isolated Ferdinand and two other horses in the race, Snow Chief and Badger Land, nobody

would have clearly seen how I was almost put over the fence twice in the run to the first turn.

It's a good thing they isolated Ferdinand. Otherwise, Charlie might not have seen the race the way it was really run; with me getting pinched back coming out of the gate. In the race, we are fighting for position and I'm on the rail, and my big gold colt is almost clipping the heels of the other horses. During the actual race, Charlie didn't see this very clearly. His binoculars were back in his hotel room, where he had forgotten them. He was so nervous. So there he was in the stands squinting at the track, trying to see the horses charging out of the gate.

I've never seen anything like this bunch at the start. Sixteen jockeys fighting for position, and I start to think, Hell, we're all crazy, we're all jockeys. And now the others are streaming away toward the first turn and I start calling on my own experience. I'm running last, but in my heart, I know I'm not going to chase them. If I do, I'll use up my horse early. Some call it patience and some call it sitting chilly.

I'm going to take my time. Let them run out, and then I will just pick them up. You learn that as you go along. All those years of experience always come out at the right time. Rush Ferdinand early, and he dies in the stretch.

Not that I'm bragging or anything, I'm just telling you the facts. Going into the first turn, I've got a real good hold on Ferdinand. It's then that we start picking up horses, turning into the backstretch.

We're in the upper stretch now. I'm moving between horses,

knowing I have to get back to the rail again. There are three horses in front of me and I'm on the outside shoulders of two others on the rail. It's then that I see my chance.

It's like a guy driving a car trying to cut over from the middle lane to the outside lane. He's got to be going faster than cars he's trying to pass. I duck in and I hear the noise from the crowd. I'm on the rail and I'm hitting Ferdinand with the whip in my left hand. Now I'm really digging in with the whip.

I've got Ferdinand right where I want him now, inside horses, and I'm saying to myself, "Look at this, I'm going . . . I'm going to win." I'm sure of it by then, and I have two-and-a-quarter lengths on the English horse Bold Arrangement going under the wire first.

I'm patting Ferdinand on the withers and taking him down a way, when the outriders come up to me. There is Charlsie Cantey on horseback, broadcasting for ABC-TV, and she asks me if this is the greatest Derby victory of my four. I say, "This is as good as any of the others. I'm just happy for Charlie and happy for myself."

They take me to the winner's circle then and my wife, Cindy, is there and so is Charlie. Charlie is so nervous, he can't speak. My wife is crying and she bends down and throws her arms around me and kisses me. She has to bend to kiss me because she's five feet, ten inches tall. I'm four feet, eleven inches. Now while I'm in the winner's circle here at Churchill Downs, in the thirty-eighth year of my career as a rider, I start thinking what a great feeling this all is. I think about my little daughter, Amanda, who is six years old. I know she has seen me win on television, but I wish then that we had brought her with us for this race from California.

When I get home to San Marino the next day, there's a big sign on the door of our garage. I LOVE YOU, DADDY, it says. I kiss Amanda and talk to her for a while, then I have to head for more work at Hollywood Park. I'm running lucky these days. I ride Charlie's French horse, Palace Music, in the John Henry Handicap and win again. How sweet it is. How sweet it is.

SHOEMAKER

1

People sometimes ask me, "Shoe, when you were a kid in Texas, living poor, did you ever think you'd have a nice house and be comfortably rich and have a beautiful family?"

I tell them, "I couldn't think that big then. When I got up in racing, I knew I was doing all right, but I never dreamed I would do as well as they say I have. Once, when I was getting ready to leave my apprenticeship, I told Harry, "Harry, I'm going to lose my bug soon. You'd better try to find yourself a new jockey. You know, you have a family to take care of. I might not do any good after I lose my apprenticeship, and you have those kids. Better take care of yourself." He said, "Don't you worry about it, Bill, you'll do all right." I didn't want to leave Harry. I didn't consider him an employee, like a lot of jockeys feel about their agents. I don't want anybody guessing about that and maybe making wrong guesses. Whatever Harry got out of my riding, he had every right to it. When I was new in the business, I lived with Harry and his family down in La Jolla. We were riding at Del

Mar then. He used to rent a house there, Harry and his wife, Thelma, and their kids.

Harry was Jewish, out of Brooklyn, and I didn't know his wife kept a kosher house. I didn't know anything about such things, being brought up Baptist in Texas. One day I'm having dinner, some sort of steak, I think. I say to Harry, "Hey, I got to have some milk and butter." He says, "You can't," and I don't get it, I'm not making weight or anything. So he explains that the house is kosher and you don't mix meat and dairy products. That ain't kosher. I say, "Hey, Harry, you eat ham and eggs when we're out. How come I can't have milk and butter with my meat?" Harry says, "In the house, I keep kosher."

When I got up in racing, newspaper writers put a lot of words in my mouth. I knew they were wrong, but I didn't think it was important to set them straight. Harry always said, "Shoe, if they spell your name right, it's all for the best."

A lot of things they wrote about me got to be like gospel. One thing that became like a legend about me and came to be taken for granted, but was wrong, was that I was put into a shoe box and shoved into the stove in my grandmother's house when I was born. I weighed one and a half pounds.

They wrote this so often that people believed it. A few years ago I went down to Fabens, which is on the Rio Grande, thirty miles downriver from El Paso, and found out the real truth about when I was born.

My grandmother, Maud Harris, was ninety-two years old then, and she could remember just about everything that ever hap-

pened to our family. We sat around in her old house and the people who were shooting a television show—that's why I was there in Fabens—asked her to tell the story of how she put me in a shoe box. My mother said, "Momma, tell them the story about when you put him in the shoe box and the doctor said he wouldn't live through the night."

Grandma Harris said, "I already told them the story," and I said, "Grandma, they want you to tell it again," and she said, "The doctor just laid you down on the bed and said there were no chance for you at all. So I got up and sat down in front of the stove and got some wraps, warmed them, and put them around you. No, I didn't stick you in no oven. I just got some pillows and put you on the stove door, that's what I did."

The heat coming out of the oven kept me warm, and I lived. My Aunt Effie—she's my mother's older sister—she says, "When I saw him when he was two months old, I said, 'You mean that's a baby? Oh, my God! He looks like a little rat.' "

My mother told me, "You had such black long hair and you was so tiny, your little fingers looked like pencil stubs. You was almost a blue baby. I felt terrible."

My father wasn't home the night I was born. It was his birthday and he was out celebrating with the boys. In those days he was a tough old guy, hardworking and a drinker, but now he's a church-going Baptist who doesn't touch a drop. He lives in California, but back then when I was born, he was a tenant farmer cutting cotton and just making enough money for all of us to get by.

My first $100,000 stakes race victory, riding Great Circle on February 3, 1951, in the Santa Anita Maturity.

Picking cotton wasn't an easy job. I remember how hard the work was, going up and down a row. You first picked the cotton then you stuck it in your sack. At the end of your row, you'd pull your sack around and then start down the other side of the row. I wasn't very smart, but I knew there was an easier way to make a living. There was many a cotton row and when I left Texas I swore to myself that I didn't ever want to go back to doing that again. My mother says now, years later, that every time she sees a cotton row she wants to cry, the memory is so tough.

Cotton was king in Fabens when I was a kid. There used to be a sign near the railroad tracks that said it was the world's greatest cotton-producing region, but when I went back there, I could see it was one Texas town that had seen better days. The sign was broken and the words were faded, and the Farmers Gin Company wasn't there anymore. The house where I was born was gone. I stood there on the spot with my mother and she said, "This is where you were born, son. We really wasn't expecting you for another whole month. That's why your father was out celebrating his birthday the day you arrived."

Then she drew a sketch in the hard ground to show me how the house was laid out. She pointed to a spot and said, "This is the stove where Momma says she warmed you when you was born. You weighed about two-and-a-half pounds, maybe even less. The bedroom was down a way from where the stove was." I said, "It feels just like home, Mother." We had a big laugh. Then we went over to the school I started in when I was six years old. My mother pointed to the two-story building and said, "You went to

school there and it's the same school I went to more than sixty years ago." I said, "In 1937, I was in the first grade, and in 1938, I was in the second grade in this school. It's amazing the school is still standing." My mother said, "Your daddy and I was going to school here when we first met. Then we had you." I looked up at my mom and I said, "That's nice. I'm sure glad you did."

When I was three years old, my father and mother got divorced. By then my brother, Lonnie, was born. I stayed living with my mother, right there in Fabens, and then we went to live part-time with my grandfather. He was called "Big Ed" Harris and he was the foreman of a ranch in Winters. That's about thirty miles southwest of Abilene, in central Texas. "Big Ed" had a son named Earl who was only a few years older than me. I kind of grew up with my Uncle Earl. We learned all about the sheep on the ranch, and cattle, too, and that is where I rode my first horse.

How it happened was that my mother left me alone in the corral one day. I must have been four or five then, and when she wasn't looking, I climbed up on a fence near this old horse. Then I grabbed the horse's mane and kind of slipped over on the horse and sat on it. I kicked the horse a little bit, and he started away from the fence but he didn't run. He just kind of walked around the corral. My mother says everybody was scared when they came out of the house and saw me up on that old horse. It made me feel ten feet tall. Years later, my mother said she was half scared to death when I had a few falls on the tracks in California. She said she couldn't help thinking back to when I got on a horse for the very first time in Texas.

That first ride, the writers said later, made me believe that I could be a jockey. That wasn't true. When I did become a jockey, that was learned. It wasn't a born thing. Back then in Texas, I didn't dream of being a jockey, not then anyway. I didn't even know about racetracks.

We were church-going people. I had an aunt—my mother's sister—who was church-minded, and she had a big influence on me. But going to church didn't make me happy. Don't get me wrong. I was as happy as a kid could be from a broken home. The fun I had with my Uncle Earl was part of the reason I wasn't unhappy. Uncle Earl taught me how to roll cigarettes, you see. We'd go behind the house in Winters and smoke. Nobody knew we smoked, but how we came to get caught was because my grandmother got suspicious when the chickens she had in the backyard weren't laying enough eggs. Instead of finding a couple of dozen eggs in the morning, she'd find two or three in the henhouse.

My Uncle Earl was stealing the eggs and then going to the store and turning them in for tobacco and paper. One morning my grandmother hid out near the chickens, waiting to catch the egg thief. She caught Uncle Earl in the act and he told her the truth. I think I hollered louder than my uncle when we got whipped.

Before I get to telling you how I got to California, I must tell you that it was when I first went to school in Fabens that I realized I was smaller than all of the other kids. I was first in line in my class. No one ever talked about it, as I can remember, but I knew then that I was a runt. My Aunt Effie was very small and I

always said she was the only one in the family I could look straight in the eye. My father, B. B. Shoemaker, was five feet, eleven inches, and my mom was just under five feet, four inches. She still towers over me and she's seventy-three years old. But height didn't bother me when I was around the ranch in Winters. I guess it was because I liked the horses. I'd ride bareback and go out into the pasture looking for sheep they couldn't find. One day I was riding bareback when a bird—I think it was a crow—flew up and landed in my lap. It spooked the horse and I went flying into a briar patch. The horse just took off and ran all the way home. I had to walk two miles and I was only five or six years old. I sure didn't take that as a sign that I would become a jockey someday.

The kids who lived down there in that part of the country didn't have much, but they kept happy anyway. The best times we had was around the horses. I don't think I even realized we were poor. We didn't have much, but I kept happy. I wasn't so happy, though, the day I almost drowned on the ranch. What happened was that they had these watering tanks for the cattle. The cattle would come to the tanks and drink, and then one day I lifted myself to the top of a tank and just fell in. I can hardly remember the feeling. I couldn't swim and I didn't know what to do. Water filled my eyes and throat and got into my lungs. I was drowning. I screamed and one of my aunts heard me and came running. It was a close call and when they were getting the water out of my lungs, I didn't cry. I just knew I had been very lucky.

Things were tough in Texas during the Depression. My father

In the winner's circle after the Santa Anita Maturity, 1951. Yolo Stable owner Charles deBlois Wack received the winner's cup, left, and trainer Warren Stute stands behind the groom at rear.

was tied to cotton. When he wasn't picking it, he was working in the cotton gin. But then he heard about new jobs opening up in California. He had remarried and his new wife's name was Vivian.

They had four children, so besides my brother, Lonnie, I had four little half-brothers. I was ten and Lonnie was almost nine when we went to California to stay with my father and Vivian. They lived in a town called El Monte in the San Gabriel Valley. The town is east of Los Angeles and when my dad first came there from Texas, it was big in the manufacturing of planes and electronic equipment. He was there because he could get work. Back home in Texas it was hard getting a job, but in El Monte he worked in a tire factory. By then, World War II was on in Europe and anybody could find work if they wanted it, and at good pay.

El Monte is maybe eight miles from San Marino, where I now live with my family. That's a funny thing, only eight miles. In my race-riding career I've been all over the world, riding in Japan and Australia and France and Ireland and England and South Africa and Argentina. Yet, when I think of it, I've gone only eight miles, from El Monte to San Marino.

I liked El Monte, but Lonnie didn't. He was homesick for Texas, and after a while, he went back to stay with my mother. I remember a lot of good times in El Monte. I went to Baldwin Park grade school, and when I graduated, I entered El Monte Union High School. It was a nice building, but I heard recently that it had been torn down. People make jokes that they had to burn the school down to get me out, but that wasn't the case. I'll tell you about that later.

When I got to high school, I was still a scrawny-looking runt. I realized that the girls didn't want to be around a guy like me. I don't remember if it bothered me, but I think it did. Maybe that's why I hung around with the big football players. They had all the girls. Or maybe it was because I liked sports.

I weighed maybe eighty pounds, but I sure wanted to be a member of a team, any team. I want to confess something here. I liked sports so much, I even went out for the football team. Years later when I got to be a successful race-rider, the writers made a lot out of how good an all-around athlete I was. I have to say it was near the truth, but it was real funny that I even tried to play football. They didn't have shoes that would fit me and the shoulder pads made me look funny. When the coach took a look at me, he just turned away. I guess he was too polite to laugh in my face. If he did laugh, it never got to me.

Next I tried basketball. I would go in against kids a head taller than me. They towered over me, but I tried. I tried real hard. I got a lot of fatherly talk from the coach, but when it came time to cut the squad, he told me I was finished.

People always ask me if I was pushed around by the other kids. I didn't fight very much, but I want you to know I was never a crybaby. If I had to take my lumps, I took them. And I could really lay it in there when I had to, with both fists.

That's why I went out for the boxing and wrestling teams at El Monte High. The lightest class in boxing and wrestling was

ninety-five pounds. I made the weight easy, maybe by fifteen pounds, and they fixed it for me to box and wrestle the guys in that division. I beat them all.

I really got interested in boxing. I put on the gloves with anybody who came along, and I even entered the Golden Gloves—the Los Angeles Gloves—when they were held at Legion Stadium in El Monte. I knew I had the stuff to go all the way. Because I was so small, I had no real power in my punches, but I was real fast. Speed in the ring—in both boxing and wrestling—is a great asset, like having patience and a sense of pace in race-riding.

I learned a lot about boxing. I worked hard in the gymnasium, and when I went into the ring in the final bout of the Golden Gloves tournament, I was ready for this big skinny kid who stood between me and a title. He was a head taller than me and I realized I couldn't beat him with a jab because he had longer arms and I just couldn't reach him. He wasn't dumb. He knew he could beat me with the jab and hook, and he kept whacking me pretty good until I moved inside the jab and pounded his midsection. I got the decision after three rounds. I thought it was the best night of my life.

There was talk that I had considered going into professional boxing, but that simply wasn't true. It never crossed my mind to turn pro. When I did become a professional athlete, it was when I went into racing. And that, too, started at El Monte High. There was this girl at El Monte High. If you were to ask me her whole name, I can't remember, except that her first name was Joyce. I was only a freshman at El Monte High when I met her. She was

dating some little jock and he was working at Santa Anita Park. Later, I learned his name was Wallace (Bud) Bailey. One day, in class, she said she thought that I ought to become a jockey. I didn't know what a jockey was. She said, "You ride the horses at the track." She talked about it some more and I got interested. I said it sounded good and that I thought I might like to try it. I never learned why Bailey ever listened to this girl, but soon after that he took me to this ranch in La Puente, which wasn't too far from El Monte. I had never seen a place like that before. It was a ranch where they trained thoroughbreds. I was fourteen years old, maybe closer to fifteen, and it was the best thing that could have happened to me. I decided right then and there that it was better to educate my hands than my head.

As I said, being at that ranch was the best thing that had happened to me up to that point in my life. When I got there, I knew that was what I wanted to do. I used to go to school in El Monte in the mornings and after school I'd rush over to the ranch and go to work. One day I decided I didn't like this situation and that I was going to fool my father. I wrote out a transfer from El Monte High to La Puente High, and I put my father's name on it. I forged his name and then I transferred. I never went to school another day. It wasn't that I was a bad student. I could do the work, I was smart enough for that, but I felt I didn't have any future in school. I believed that then and I don't know why to this day.

Now I was into horses all the way. I was on my own too. My father thought I was still going to high school. I used to go to the

Holding a plaque commemorating my then-record 485 winners ridden in 1953.

ranch every morning and work all day, and then come home at night and pretend like I'd been at school. My father and Vivian didn't know what I was doing. It took them almost a whole year before they caught on to my situation. After they learned everything, I just told my father straight out that I was leaving home to live at the ranch, where they had quarters for the kids. I was making $75 a month, which was a lot of money considering I got my room and board for nothing. I felt like a big man.

2

Tom Simmons, who owned the ranch, was also the president of Hollywood Park. I didn't get to know much about him. Once in a while he'd come around to the ranch and all the kids working there would kind of stand up tall. That's a funny thing to say because most of the kids were real short, some taller than me, but still short. It was a nice feeling being around short guys for a change, instead of those big high school football players. Living and working at the ranch made me feel right at home.

It worked out real good. The two years I was there were about as good as any in my life. We spent a lot of time talking about horses and about the jockeys, and how much they got for riding winners in big races. I didn't know if I'd ever get to be anybody in racing, but I sure liked being around horses. I learned a lot at the Suzy Q Ranch. It didn't come easy, but as I went along, I picked up a lot of good information.

People around the place showed me how to muck out stalls. Cleaning a stall isn't easy work. Some kids never did get the hang

of it. That was because they really didn't like what they were doing. But I did. I learned to take care of horses. I rubbed them and I walked them. They had a training track at the ranch and we took care of it too. We harrowed the track and watered it. We practically did everything around the place. We carted hay in from fields to feed the horses and after being there for a while I was even beginning to break in yearlings.

If you've never been on a horse, you don't know how it feels, a little guy up on a big horse weighing maybe nine hundred or a thousand pounds. It makes you feel like a king. It's a funny thing about learning how to break yearlings. You're a little nervous, but after a while it comes to you, the feel of the horse. You're hoping the horse throws you, bucks you to the ground, because that way, the other kids realize you have the stuff you need to be a rider. But I had good balance on a horse, almost from the start. Even when I hoped a horse would buck me off, he didn't. I finally got thrown. I fell hard and I liked the feel, and after that, every time I was tossed by a horse at the ranch, I got a kick out of it.

I was eating three square meals a day and I was putting on weight. I got over 100 pounds, maybe 102. Now I could talk like a real jockey. When jockeys talk about their weight, they usually say they weigh '12 or '13, something like that, and throw away the 100. Not that I thought I was a real jockey. I dreamed about it, you bet I did, but I knew it wasn't the truth.

There were a lot of characters around the Suzy Q, guys that had been in racing for a thousand years, some still hoping to make it big, others just working out their years. The old guys on the

Suzy Q treated the kids real good. One old guy who had been a jockey showed me how to cross the reins and how to sit on a horse right. When I was just starting out, I didn't know how to get down in the irons. What I did was I used to stand in the irons but the wrong way, but an old rider helped me out. He showed me how to set down on the horse. I guess he taught me everything he knew. It's funny, I don't remember his name, but whatever he told me to do on a horse, I did it, and it was right.

What I learned on the ranch was the feel of a horse. The most important thing to learn is to get your balance. This old guy kept drilling me on that and after a while I was comfortable in the saddle. He was a great old guy and we got along swell. I learned right off that a rider couldn't ride any faster than the horse could run, but I knew there were tricks and there was an ability that made one rider different than other riders. Pretty soon I had the feeling I could be one of those really good riders.

You can't keep all the things straight that happen to you when you are a kid. They come so fast. In 1948 this fellow Bill Roland, who was my buddy, said, "Hey, how about getting out of here? They're running at Bay Meadows." That's in San Mateo, up by San Francisco, and we spent the first night in a cheap hotel. The next morning we walked around the barn area at the track. It's a funny thing in racing. Racing is a small world. Everybody gets to know almost everybody else in it, no matter where you go. We knew a lot of the kids around Bay Meadows. One of the kids we met told us to go see a trainer named Hurst Philpot who had Charles S. Howard's string. Howard was important in California

racing. He was a rich auto dealer and he owned the great horse Seabiscuit and another real good one named Noor. He had a lot of horses training with Philpot when I got to Bay Meadows in 1948. Philpot was a busy fellow, but he always seemed to have time for a little fun.

I walked up to him one day and asked him for a job. He asked, "Can you gallop a horse?" I said I could ride and he said, "I'll try you." So he put me on a filly and took me out to the track and told me to gallop her once around and then to pull her up and bring her back.

She was a tough gal, that one. She was a lady with her own mind. I galloped her once around and she started running off with me. I couldn't stop her. We went by Philpot and he was making noises like a crazy man. "Hey, pull her up!" I heard him scream. "I thought you knew how to ride, you lying bum." I thought, What the hell do you think I'm trying to do, you dumb son of a bitch? I yanked hard on the reins and I pulled her up. I was dead tired. When I got off the horse, I found out that Philpot was just having fun with me. He knew this filly would run off. It wasn't long before he told me that he thought I was a good exercise boy.

Buddy Heacock and Jimmy Hood were two other riders in Philpot's barn. The trainer paid more attention to them than to me. It didn't bother me at first, but after a while I got to realize that Philpot was favoring them over me. He thought I was too small to become a rider. He let me gallop some of his good horses, but somehow I knew my days with him were numbered. I stayed

on until Philpot moved his stock to Hollywood Park for the meeting there. When the meeting was over, I walked away.

I knew it took two, maybe three, years before a kid like me would get the feel of riding, but I was willing to put my time in. There is no such thing as a natural rider. Some guys have a knack. Horses run better for them. They sit on them differently, and if you have the knack, it comes easier for you. I felt I had the knack and I knew I had the feel and touch to be a good rider.

A lot of people took my relationship with Hurst Philpot wrong. They got things totally out of context. They even swore that one of the two kids working with Philpot when I was in the barn actually got to the races. They said the first time Buddy Heacock got on a horse on the California fair circuit he stood up in the saddle to look back and fell off. The truth is that he had a bad accident while working horses one morning and got all crippled up. I don't even know if he's still alive.

The other kid they're mistaken about was Jimmy Hood. He is now my valet in the jocks' room. He tried to ride but he just got too big. I've tried to tell everybody the truth of the story, but I haven't succeeded to this day. When a story gets told over the years, they start to add on to it to make it better. It's wrong, dead wrong, but it never goes away.

There's one thing I forgot to tell you about my time with Philpot. I did get one break with him. He had this jockey named Johnny Adams riding for him and every morning, Adams came out to the track to work horses for the trainer. By watching him, I got a good idea about what they meant when they talked about pace and rating a horse. What I learned most of all was how much a jockey could do with his hands. Until this day, I have good hands and that's important. A rider with good hands sends a message to his horse through the reins. A horse knows kind hands from rough, insensitive hands.

I went to Del Mar to find work after I quit working for Philpot. And it was a big move. I was my own man, though. I went down there alone and walked around in the backstretch until I got a job with George Reeves. He was an old racetracker and a good horseman. Old John Barleycorn got to him over the years but when I went to work for him, he was at the top of his game. I owe a lot to him. He didn't have many horses in his barn, maybe a dozen, and he was free to pay more attention to me than Philpot ever had.

What George Reeves recognized in me was that I was an athlete. I could play all the games and I was fast. Another guy around there at the time was Bob Cass, who was a bloodstock agent and owned horses. He took a shine to me from the start. It began when I just came and hung around the track, and when they had running match races between the boys. I used to win a lot of bets for Cass. What they did was they pitted one kid against another and they made bets on the races, which were sprints of about fifty yards. One time Cass bet a couple of hundred on one of these races. He won so much off of me that he bought me a watch. It was the first watch I ever owned.

Early in the winter of 1949, I was in Santa Anita with Mr. Reeves. I was walking a horse on the tow ring one morning when an agent named Harry Silbert came around to visit with Mr.

Reeves. It wasn't exactly a visit because jocks' agents don't visit. When they come around, they're usually looking for business. Harry wasn't any different. He was a jocks' agent like all the others, out on one of his hustle mornings. That morning something different happened. Harry told me about it later. Mr. Reeves said to him, "Hey, Harry, I want to use your bug boy to win a bet. I want to get some weight off my horse." Harry said, "George, my boy ain't been riding good lately. Get some other boy." And that's the way Harry felt about the whole thing.

Mr. Reeves liked that about Harry. Another agent might have said, "Sure, George, use my boy any way you want to." So right there, Mr. Reeves showed how he liked Harry being truthful. He pointed at me and said, "See that boy over there. He's going to be a good one. You've got his book when I start him up at Golden Gate." Then he called me over and introduced me to Harry. "He's your agent from now on," Mr. Reeves said. The reason he acted the way he did was that he had an apprentice's contract on me.

We went up to Golden Gate Fields a few weeks later. Mr. Reeves got an apartment for us in Oakland, close to the track. He lived in the apartment and so did all the boys that exercised horses for him. It was cheaper that way for everybody concerned. Mr. Reeves could hit the bottle pretty good, but when it came to the kids living with him, he was strict.

I was working hard at Golden Gate Fields, galloping horses in the mornings. If they needed somebody to muck out a stall, I'd do that, too, just to help out. One morning it rained. I remember the

In the winner's circle, Kentucky Derby, 1955. The horse, Swaps, was a 3–10 favorite and I won handily by one-and-a-half lengths.

date, which was March 19, 1949, and the reason I remember it is that it was the day I rode my first race. I should have been nervous, but I wasn't, not the way I thought I would be. In six months I would be eighteen years of age and here I was, a kid out of cotton country in Texas, going up on my first mount on a big-time California track. It was the third race of the day, claiming horses running six furlongs for $5,000.

I was lucky with my first mount. She was a four-year-old mare named Waxahachie. I used to gallop her mornings and knew just how she moved. When it came time to ride her in my first race as a bug rider, I felt at home in the saddle.

As I said, that morning it rained. When a track is muddy, a jockey wears not one pair of goggles, but sometimes as many as four, depending on how deep the slop is. That way, when his first pair of goggles gets smeared by flying mud, he can flip it down and the next pair is clear for him to see through. But on that day in March 1949, when I was going to the paddock to mount Waxahachie, I was so nervous that I forgot and I wore only one pair of goggles.

Harry didn't come up to Golden Gate Fields to see me ride my first horse. Mr. Reeves called him on the phone to tell him I was going to ride. Harry said he couldn't come up, because his wife, Thelma, was sick and needed an operation. When I got to know Thelma and lived with the Silberts in LaJolla, I learned to call her "Temmie," the name everybody called her.

There were eight horses in the race that day, the third race on the program, and there were some good jockeys in it, too. Here I

was, a bug boy making his first start, going up against people like Johnny Longden on a horse called Grand Canal. Longden was one of the greatest jockeys around. He set all sorts of records during his riding days and figured a lot in my career.

What happened was that Waxahachie didn't have much speed, which proved a real handicap. The mud kept flying back into my face and I couldn't see when my goggles got dirty. I pulled down my goggles and then I realized I didn't have another pair on. Waxahachie had been around and she knew her way. She brought me home, but I was in real trouble. Longden won it on Grand Canal. After the race, I heard Longden and Gordon Glisson arguing. I didn't know what they were arguing about, but then I realized what had happened. Glisson was accusing Longden of shutting me off coming out of the gate. Longden copped a plea. "I didn't do it on purpose," he said. "I didn't even know it was happening." They almost got into a real fight over me.

Looking back on it now, I understand the whole incident. Longden always took his best shot in a race. He rode to win, and when he was at the top of his game, he would shut off his best friend to get home first. We're friends now, now that I'm as old as I am and Longden is past eighty, but one time we almost came to blows.

Why nothing happened is that I learned early to keep my temper. I don't do silly things when I'm angry, like yelling and screaming at people. I came close a couple of times to hitting other riders in the jocks' room, but it never happened. One time I

came close to putting up my fists was with Longden. That's why I'm telling it now.

When Longden was going good, when he was still a young man, he was a tough guy on the track. You couldn't get by him in the old days. But one day I stayed right behind him, where he couldn't see me. Then he moved his horse out and opened a hole, not realizing I was behind him. Before he could close the hole, I came through that hole and beat him. He was so mad, he couldn't hardly talk. He screamed at me. "Don't ever do that again, or I'll run you over the fence," Longden shouted. I said, "You can take your best shot, because the racetrack is big enough for all of us. You want the whole track. You don't want anybody else to have any part of it."

I didn't really like him because of the way he did things. I thought one could be competitive and not be a jerk about it. Later, I came to respect him and like him a lot because he was a great competitor, but then, maybe about thirty years ago, I didn't have much respect for him.

I don't remember whether or not Longden was in the race when Mr. Reeves put me on my second mount, but it didn't matter. Mr. Reeves had me on a 90–1 shot named Soonuseeme, and we finished fourth. Only a month after my first mount, Mr. Reeves gave me a real shot. He put me on Shafter V. The date was April 20, 1949. The week before, Shafter V had won a race with a veteran rider named R. J. Martin. She was a 4–5 shot in that race, and when Mr. Reeves gave me the mount the next time out, he got a call from the stewards at Golden Gate. One steward asked,

"Hey, who is this kid Shoemaker, anyway? You can't put this kid on the favorite. The public won't like it." Mr. Reeves said, "I think this kid can do it. He's my kid and I'm going to keep him on. That's it!"

The public didn't like it. When they saw that I was riding Shafter V, they gave the three-year-old filly 9–1 odds in the six-furlong race. The track was fast. I didn't really know what I was doing but I just hoped that I wouldn't fall off. We won by two-and-a-quarter lengths, and when I jumped off the horse in the winner's circle, my knees almost buckled under me. I was very tired but was really excited too. Shafter V paid $21 to win and the stable got rich. Everybody had a bet on Shafter V. I didn't because I didn't know anything about betting.

Everybody was slapping me on the back and congratulating me, but I had no special feeling. To be honest, I didn't know what the hell had happened. It was a good feeling, I knew that, but when I tried to figure out why I won and how I won, I couldn't. The filly just laid second and took the lead and got there first. I didn't even celebrate. I went back to the jocks' room, changed into my regular clothes, and then went to the barn to cool out Shafter V. I was a contract rider, and that's the way they did things those days. I was still walking hots.

For winning, Shafter V returned a purse of $1,800, or 60 percent of the $3,000 purse. My 10 percent would have come to $180, but I don't remember if I got paid at all. In those days, apprentice jockeys got "if" money. "If" you got paid, you were lucky. But I

Here I am on Tomy Lee, a horse I didn't think was going to make it, after winning the 1959 Kentucky Derby.

didn't care. I was getting my room and board for nothing anyway.

Harry was with me at Golden Gate Fields the next week. Mr. Reeves had some other jocks' agent handle my book until Harry could make it up there. His wife was feeling better after her operation. Harry came out to the track mornings and got me mounts, and the next week we won seven races.

I was winning, but I didn't feel like a rider yet. That comes to you in maybe three years. By then you have the feel of the horse. Right from the start I found that I sat a horse differently than most of the other riders. Instead of moving around in the saddle, I sat still. Horsemen said I'd be a better rider if I moved on the horse. I didn't whip or slash, and I didn't jump around in the irons the way other riders did. What I was doing seemed to work. By the end of 1949, I had 219 winners, and only Górdon Glisson had more in the whole country. That didn't make me mad, because I liked Glisson. He was a full-fledged rider and was a good guy. He proved that the way he went after Longden for shutting me off coming out of the gate the first time I rode in a real race. I didn't make much of it, but Glisson had a head start on me in 1949. He rode the entire year. I didn't have my first ride until March of that year.

I was very happy. My career was breaking good and I had another reason to be happy. We were at Bay Meadows, down the San Francisco Peninsula from Golden Gate Fields, and I was riding regularly and winning races. A kid I knew around the racetrack asked me one day if I wanted to go out on a double date. I

said sure. My girl was Virginia McLaughlin. She was not yet sixteen years old, I think, and still going to high school. She was very pretty and we went to a drive-in movie on our first date. We got along good. You bet.

3

I began seeing a lot of Virginia McLaughlin. I was not eighteen yet and still wet behind the ears, but I felt good in her company. I still didn't talk a lot. People wondered about that. They thought I was shy. The writers began calling me "Silent Shoe." What caused me to be quiet was that I was self-conscious about my teeth. They were bucked. My upper teeth overlapped my lower lip. I had what some people called "wolf teeth." My mouth was very small, and my teeth distorted it and gave me a funny look. I knew that. I could see it in the mirror.

This didn't bother Virginia, though. I was happy about that. I called her Ginny, like everybody else, and I knew she was my girl. I got to know quickly that I was going to marry her. She was a head taller than me, but she used to sit on my lap and kiss my face. I was very happy. I was doing good in my career and I felt I could handle marriage. Harry was doing a great job as my agent and I was winning my share of races.

I was still a bug boy—an apprentice—and Harry thought I

needed some more schooling in riding. He said he saw the other jockeys always taking advantage of me on the track. He said I needed to learn how to give as well as take.

They were running Sundays down in Agua Caliente. That was a track south of the border, not far from San Diego, and Harry booked me into riding down there.

I was riding weekdays in California and Sundays at Caliente. Some weeks I'd ride nine races each day during the week and then go to Mexico on Sunday to ride twelve races at Agua Caliente. I was at Caliente for about six or seven Sundays and it was a rough place. A rider had to learn to whip and slash, and to protect himself at all times. I got some good experience down there. Finally, Harry told me one Sunday that we were finished at Caliente. I said, "Thank God, I've had enough of that place."

Harry and his wife, Temmie, were very good to me. One time they gave me a birthday party. It was the first birthday party I ever had. I invited a few racetrack friends and Temmie Silbert made some delicious food. She was a great cook. One of the things she made was chopped liver. I looked at the pâté and asked Harry, "What the hell is that?" He looked at me like I was crazy. He said, "That's chopped liver. It's delicious. Try it." I said, "Hey, not me." Now, I like chopped liver. Living with Harry, I learned to like things like the liver pâté and salami and eggs. Down in Texas we had never heard of such things.

I was still an apprentice in the early part of 1950. Those days it took about a year, or forty winners, to become a journeyman rider. As a bug rider you got certain advantages, ranging from ten

pounds at the beginning to five pounds toward the end of the apprenticeship, depending on the number of winners you rode. What this meant was that if a horse was slated to carry, say, 120 pounds, he would go in at 115 pounds because I as a bug was riding him.

I was one of three apprentices at Santa Anita that year. The others were Bill Boland and Glen Lasswell. I got to know Boland real good when I went East, but when he came out to California, I hardly knew anything about him except that he was a nice guy. I knew a lot about Lasswell. He looked beautiful on a horse. A lot better than I did. I looked at him and the way he sat a horse and said, "He's the best of the three. I'm going to work like hell to get as good as he is." I kept my eye on him and what I saw helped me pull things together pretty quickly. Instead of sitting a horse quietly, I began pushing on him and chirping to him. The more I rode, the more the feeling came. Pretty soon I was chirping to myself. I felt that I knew how to ride.

In April 1950, I lost my bug. That meant that from then on I didn't have the five-pound allowance. I was on even terms with the other riders. I kept winning races and I was very happy. I was married by then and living in a mobile home with Ginny. Later on, we would move to a big house on a one-acre plot in Arcadia.

I was locked in a close race once with Joe Culmone for the national riding championship and Harry said, "Shoe, we got to catch him. He's going to Bowie in Maryland to ride and we're going to follow him." So off we went to Bowie. It was my first trip East, and it was so cold, you had to bring in the brass mon-

On the scale with my tack after winning $2,001,165 in purse money, 1956.

keys. It was early spring, but I remember there was snow on the ground. The first horse I rode at Bowie was in front all the way. Everybody was surprised, because front-running horses weren't winning in the snow. The track was deep and cuppy. I felt good after winning the first race, but that good feeling didn't last long. For the rest of the day I chased other horses. Culmone won six races. We even had a match race, Shoemaker against Culmone. Would you believe that I lost that one, too? Bowie was a disaster in one way, but in another, it was a good thing. I got to know a lot of Eastern people, guys in the press box and others who said they appreciated the way I conducted myself. That way, I knew I could go back East any time and do some good for myself.

I was doing all right in California. I knew it and Harry knew it, but we didn't talk much about it. There were stories in all the papers about how I was neck-and-neck with Culmone for the most winning rides. That wasn't for the most winners in California. It was for the most winners in the whole country. Culmone did most of his riding in the East and I did most of my riding in the West, so the competition became an East-West rivalry. Harry said, "Shoe, we're going for the whole pot." I was in front of Culmone for many weeks, but one day I looked up and there was Culmone tied with me. It was the last day of 1950, my second year riding, and here I was tied for the title. The last day of the year was a Sunday. Harry said, "Shoe, we need some wins." In those days there was no Sunday racing in the United States. So Harry said, "We're going to Caliente to ride." Culmone's agent wasn't letting the title get away from his jock. He took Culmone to Havana to ride the last day of the year.

At the track in Caliente, they ran twelve races a day. On that last Sunday of 1950, I was on the favorite in every race. I won only three and finished with 388 winners. In Cuba, Culmone won three, too. That gave him a total of 388, same as mine. We finished in a dead heat for the riding title. I was very proud. Not since 1906 had an American jockey had so many winners in one year.

When it turned to 1951, I went right back to work. That was one thing about Harry. If you went out to the track mornings, there he was, talking to trainers, looking at the horses, figuring out which horses he wanted me to be on. Jocks' agents are like the riders themselves. In their game, it's every man for himself. Harry didn't tell me how to ride and I didn't tell him what horse to put me on. But when he spoke about my rides, he would say "I." An agent always says it like that: "I ride" this and "I ride" that.

Jockeys don't mind. I didn't. I knew Harry was with me all the way. We had a lot of fun together. One time, I remember, Harry put me on a horse and we finished up the track at big odds. So Harry put me right back on the horse the next time the horse ran. We still finished up the track. We got nothing. We rode him again. Again, we finished last. When I got off the horse, I said to Harry, "Hey, do you know something about this horse that I don't know?" We had a good laugh.

Harry knew how I felt about him. I never praised him straight out, but when he would do something I liked, like putting me on

a real good mount, I wouldn't say a word. I'd kind of nudge him —give him a little punch on the arm—and this way he knew I was happy. That was the way I praised him. In our business, he knew that the only thing that counted was winners.

Harry was something to see going through the barn area in the morning. He carried a condition book in his back pocket, a cigar in his mouth, and a smile. He went out after the best mounts he could get for me and most of the time he succeeded.

I start off 1951 in good shape. The year is just twenty days old when I win the Santa Margarita Handicap on a horse called Special Touch. That's at Santa Anita. By August, I win ten more stakes races in California, winding up with the Del Mar Derby. I'm married by now and for the Del Mar meet we're living near the Pacific Ocean. It's great at Del Mar. That's the track Bing Crosby and some other Hollywood film guys built. Everybody in the jocks' colony likes to ride there because it's so near the ocean and you can swim a couple of times a day.

Harry and Temmie liked Del Mar, too. Being there was like being on a vacation. We took walks on the beach and looked out at the ocean, and it was nice. Around this time, Harry got a call from a judge in Los Angeles named A. A. Scott. Judge Scott wanted to know why Harry was getting 20 percent of my earnings while other jocks' agents were working for 10 percent. You see, in California, minors were protected by something called the Coogan Law. How come that law was on the books went back all the way to the time Jackie Coogan was a great kid actor in Hollywood. A law was passed in Sacramento appointing the court to protect young actors and actresses from people who might want to take advantage of them. I was nineteen years old and married, but I was still a ward of the court.

The judge said to Harry, "How is it that you are getting 20 percent of Shoemaker's earnings on the track, while Johnny Longden's agent is only getting 10 percent?" Harry told Judge Scott, "I want to tell you something. I took Bill before he knew what a horse really was. Now he's riding three hundred winners a year. Judge, if you had a business and you were paying a man 10 percent, would you let him go or would you give him 20? I started with 20 percent with Bill. With all the good he's doing, don't you think I'm still entitled to the same 20 percent, or should I take a cut?"

The judge ruled in Harry's favor. I always paid him 20 percent and, like I said, I never begrudged him a cent of the money he earned. Mind you, everything wasn't smooth all the time. Not for Harry it wasn't. One day George Reeves turned my riding contract over to a woman named Thelma Snead. They were good friends, the way I understood it, and he owed her some money. He settled up by selling her the contract on me. They could do things like that in those days.

That was about the time Harry signed with the stable of William Goetz to give the stable first call on my services. That meant that if the stable wanted me to ride a horse in a certain race, I had to handle the horse. I couldn't take off and ride another horse in the same race. At the time Harry Daniels was training for Mr.

Goetz, who was a major movie producer in Hollywood and a son-in-law of Louis B. Mayer.

Harry got a call from Thelma Snead. She said, "I don't want you to give Harry Daniels first call on Shoe. You ride for me first." Harry couldn't figure it out. He said, "Look, you got only claiming horses and this guy Goetz has stakes horses." Thelma Snead stood tough. She said, "We'll see about that!" The next thing you know she went to the stewards and told them the story. And the stewards called Harry in. In those days, the stewards had all the power around the racetrack. Jim Tunney was one of the stewards and one of the best. He asked Harry to tell him his side of the story. Harry said he had given "first call" to Mr. Goetz but that Thelma Snead was against it. Jim Tunney told Harry, "Thelma not only wants first call on Shoemaker, she doesn't want you to have his book either."

I was in the room with Harry. I told the stewards, "If Harry doesn't have my book, I don't have to ride here." They weren't pleased. Jim Tunney said, "Don't fly off the handle. Let's see if we can straighten this thing out." The contract had only a couple or three months to run. Harry said to me, "Listen, Bill, you'll get another agent until the contract runs out. I'll help the other guy out." I said, "No, no, no. If you don't have my book, I don't want to ride here." Jim Tunney said, "Let's work on this thing." He spoke to Thelma Snead. He asked her how much she wanted for my contract. She wanted $15,000.

Because of the Coogan Law, Harry went to see Judge Scott. The court had to approve any deal Harry made for me if it involved money. Judge Scott was fair but tough. He said he wouldn't allow me to draw more than $10,000. Harry said, "Bill, let's do it this way. You put up $10,000, I'll put up the extra $5,000, and we'll get rid of her." I said that was all right with me. We paid off Thelma Snead.

I later talked to Harry over at his place. I threw $5,000 on the bed and said, "Here's your $5,000 back." Harry said, "No, no, no, no." I convinced him to take the money.

4

My tie with Culmone for the national riding championship brought me attention that I hadn't had until then. Trainers started coming to Harry to ask for my services. One of them was Robert Hyatt (Red) McDaniel. He was a hot trainer around California and he was smart. He could read a condition book better than anybody I knew. The condition book is put out by the racing secretary and handicapper at each track. It sets up the conditions of each race—the distance, the purse, the age bracket, the allowances for races won, the allowances for money won, and things like that.

Some trainers never learn to read a condition book, but McDaniel, he was a whiz at it. He could claim a horse and figure out that the horse was going to win a certain race thirty days later. The way it worked with Mac—everybody called McDaniel "Mac"—was if one of his claims didn't do well, he'd drop him down in class. He would wait the legal time and then try a $7,500 claimer in a $5,000 race. This sounds easy to do, but take my word

for it, it isn't. In the paddock Mac was a man of few words. I liked that. He'd say, "Ride him, he'll win." His confidence was not misplaced most of the time. When one of his horses didn't win, he'd just shrug his shoulders.

Charlie Whittingham knew Mac from the times when they were kids together and hung around the racetrack. Charlie said Mac always acted a little strange, especially when he was hitting the bottle. He'd have a few and become some sort of screwball. Mac was a little guy, very wiry. He could stand flat-footed and jump up and hit the ceiling with his head. When they first brought liquor back, after Prohibition, a little bar opened up on Broadway in Burlingame, up by San Francisco. Mac and Charlie were sitting around in the back there, and they had a few shooters and Mac got drunk. As they were leaving the place, Mac vaulted right over the bar and swept all the glasses off the bar with his arm and ran like hell.

There was a red-headed gal Mac was living with, Charlie told me, and they were in this place and one day they were having spaghetti. Mac was jealous of Charlie. He said Charlie was making a pass at the redheaded gal. Mac picked up a bottle and tried to hit Charlie with it. Charlie towered over him. It was almost like me picking a fight with Wilt Chamberlain. Charles got up to defend himself and Mac ran under the bar. Charlie couldn't get him out to slow him down.

It's a strange thing what happened to Mac. One day he drove his car up on the San Francisco–Oakland Bay Bridge. He parked, got out, and jumped over the side of the bridge. When they fished

With two of my longtime rivals, Johnny Longdon and Eddie Arcaro, in 1958 at Santa Anita.

him out of San Francisco Bay twenty-four minutes later, he was dead. It was a sad day in racing.

Red McDaniel wasn't a trainer of claiming horses only; he had stakes horses, too. One was Poona II. I rode the horse for Mac in the San Fernando Stakes in 1955. Poona II ran a big race and we got first in record time. I forgot to tell you that I won my first stakes race at Bay Meadows in 1949, in my first year as a rider. I was on a horse called Al—just plain Al—and we took the George Marshall Claiming Handicap. That was up at Bay Meadows. I remember the date. It was October 26, 1949. Since then I've won hundreds of stakes, but I'll never forget that one because it was my first.

When I won the San Fernando Stakes for Red McDaniel, it was almost automatic that I would ride the horse in the Santa Anita Handicap six weeks later. But before the Santa Anita Handicap, I got beat on Poona II. One racing columnist from New York wrote about Mac, "This guy knows something about claiming horses, but he doesn't know anything about how to train a good horse." Mac was burned up. He said, "That writer from New York has one problem. He doesn't know which end of a horse he's looking at." I rode Poona II in the San Fernando and won. Mac said, "Where's that New York guy who said I couldn't train good horses?" By then, the columnist was safely back East.

The reason I'm telling you about this New York columnist and how he took a rap at McDaniel is that there was a great rivalry between the East and West in racing. People said the racetrackers in New York looked down on California racing. They said it was

bush league stuff. I talked a lot about that to Harry. He was a New Yorker who had come to California with Sammy Renick, a rider, back in 1938. I got to know Renick later, but when Harry first told me about him, he said Sammy rode for Alfred Vanderbilt and then rode for Harry Warner and Mervyn LeRoy, who had the WL Ranch.

What Harry told me was that Renick came to him one day and told him that he had split with WL Ranch. Renick wanted to go home to New York. Harry said, "Sam, I like you, but I'm not going back to New York. This is God's country out here. I'm staying. I got a wife and three kids. I ain't going back to Brooklyn. I'd rather look at orange groves here than fruit on pushcarts in Brownsville."

Harry used to tell me about Brownsville. That's where he met his wife, Thelma. They were neighbors on Amboy Street. The reason I remember Amboy Street is from the book *The Amboy Dukes.* Brownsville was in Brooklyn, Harry told me, and was close to Aqueduct and the old Jamaica track. Harry went to the track when he was still a kid in high school.

In 1951 I won my first $100,000 race, the Santa Anita Maturity, on Great Circle. It was one of fifteen stakes races I won that year. After Del Mar closed, Harry said, "We're going to New York to ride." I asked Harry, "Why should we go to New York?" Harry explained that if we wanted to get on better horses, maybe Derby horses, we had to go to New York to let people back there know about me. I understood and said it was all right with me.

It was my first trip to New York. We went in Harry's Buick

and Ginny went with us. She was still a kid, not yet eighteen years of age, and bug-eyed. The chance to be in New York and to see Broadway was a big deal to her. When Harry first told me we were going to drive across the country, I didn't realize what a big country it was. Now I laugh about it. It's funny because since then I've made hundreds of cross-country trips, always by plane, many times on the red-eye. The trip in Harry's Buick was like the red-eye, only tougher.

When we got to New York, the horses were running at Aqueduct. The first day I rode there was September 22, 1951, a Saturday. That was the day they ran the Beldame. Harry wanted me to get the feel of the track so he booked me on more than one mount. I won two races before the Beldame, a $50,000 race for fillies and mares at a mile and one eighth. It was one of the most important races for female horses in the country and I was riding a filly called Thelma Burger. When I saw the name of the filly, I smiled. I wondered if she was named after Thelma, Harry's wife. She wasn't, of course.

In the Beldame I got good position coming out of the gate. All the way around I felt I had a lot of horse under me. Then, according to the *Daily Racing Form* chart, I "forged between the leaders to reach the lead past the furlong post" and drew away to win by two lengths. Alfred Vanderbilt's great filly Bed o' Roses was second and Walter Jefford's Kiss Me Kate was third. The next year I rode Bed o' Roses in the Santa Margarita Handicap at Santa Anita. I won on her.

What impressed me most about the Beldame was that one of

the riders in the race was Eddie Arcaro. He was as good a loser as he was a winner, and he may have been the greatest rider in America in 1951. Later we became good friends, and he took me around and said, "Meet the new champ." I was shy, but I liked that because it came from a really great rider like Arcaro. It was a wonderful compliment.

Starting out like that in New York should have made me appreciate the place. I didn't cotton to it at all. It was fall and it was cold, and I had to wear gloves when I was riding. I put my hands in hot water to get the chill out. I have to tell you right here that I always felt blessed with good hands, soft and sensitive. In a way, this sends a certain good feeling to horses. I believe that, and that's why racetrackers, when they talk about jockeys they say, "He has good hands."

I moved over to Belmont Park when they finished running at Aqueduct. I won the Vosburgh Handicap on War King and the Champagne Stakes on Armageddon. I was impressed by Belmont Park. In California, the tracks I rode on were one mile around. Belmont Park was a mile and one half. That made it tough on riders. Each horse didn't have a pony, the way they did in California. A rider had to gallop his mount to the gate without the help of a pony. This made riding at Belmont Park tiring, especially if a jockey had three or four mounts in one day. It didn't bother me. I was fit. I felt good about it, because it made me a better horseman.

One of the great trainers in New York—in the world, I guess—was Preston Burch. He was so good, they said he wrote the book. In fact, he did. His book on training horses became a bible for

trainers. He trained for Mrs. Isabel Dodge Sloane's Brookmeade Stable. That was, at the time, one of the finest racing stables in the country.

Mr. Burch was a gentleman through and through. He was respected by everybody because of his ability and his style. One day he told Harry that he wanted to buy my contract for Brookmeade. It was a compliment, but Harry didn't like the idea. Like I said, the thought of leaving California bothered him. And he knew how I felt about California. I was a kid out of the West. I like the lifestyle in California. When I was in New York it was all right, but California was where I belonged.

So Harry told Mr. Burch, "You know, this jock weighs only 96 pounds." Harry was cheating a little bit. I really weighed about 98. He said to Mr. Burch, "You don't want a jockey this small." They believed then that "dead" weight was a bigger burden to a horse than "live" weight. They wanted riders as close as possible to a horse's assigned weight. Let's say I was riding a horse assigned 126 pounds. That meant that if I weighed 96 pounds, I would have to have an additional 30 pounds of lead in my saddlebag to add up to 126 pounds. They called the lead in the saddlebag "dead" weight. The rider was "live" weight.

Mr. Burch said, "Harry, you listen to me. That dead-weight theory is wrong. If you take a soldier and put a pack on his back and don't tie it down, he isn't going to go as far as the soldier in back of him who has the same weight on his back but it is tied down."

When Harry heard this, he told me later, he thought, "Aw, shit,

this is going to be bad for me." So Harry put in a call to George Reeves and told him the story. "What are you guys going to do?" Reeves asked. Harry said, "George, to tell you the truth, Shoe wants to go home." George said that was all right with him, and that is what Harry told Mr. Burch.

Nineteen fifty-two was my first year without the "bug." I lost the weight allowance apprentices had—five pounds in those days—and I won more races than in 1951, but I rode in more races. And the amount of purses won dropped by about $300,000, from about $1.3 million to a little more than $1 million. That was because in 1952 I won only five stakes races.

When I was around New York, I started going to the best joints in town. I found Toots Shor's old joint—the one on Fifty-first Street, and I liked hanging out there. We drank there and had a lot of fun. Arcaro was around and it was one laugh after another. One time there was a fight in Shor's. It was long past midnight and this big guy was causing a disturbance at the bar. That might have been the best bar in the world, with the best bartenders and the greatest guys hanging out there. Anyway, pretty soon, there was Arcaro out on the sidewalk taking on this big guy. I was feeling good by now. I said, pulling off my jacket, "Let me take care of the guy for you, Eddie." That was enough to break up the party. There was a lot of laughter, seeing me take off my jacket to challenge the big guy.

In 1953, I rode over 1,600 races and won 485. No rider had ever had so many winners in one year. I guess I could have finished with at least 500 winners, but I took two weeks off in December.

In the winner's circle after my first Belmont victory in 1957, riding Gallant Man.

The holiday spirit got me. I wanted to enjoy Christmas, and I needed a rest before Santa Anita opened in a few weeks.

Around that time, Ginny and I moved into a new house in Santa Anita Oaks, near Arcadia. It was a beautiful place and Ginny tried to make it livable. She just wasn't experienced enough for the job, but she had common sense. She said one time that she would like to open a string of frankfurter stands with my name on them. I was dumb. I laughed. Ginny was ahead of her time. I should have syndicated my name later, when I was getting up in racing.

We were trying to have a baby, but we just couldn't. Temmie Silbert recommended a doctor to Ginny. We went to see him. The doctor said there was nothing wrong with either of us, we just couldn't have a baby together. We talked about adopting children. Later on we did. We got a boy first—Johnny Lee Shoemaker. When he was about two and one half, we got a little girl, Sheryl Lee Shoemaker. They both had my middle name. I want to straighten something out about that. I was really baptized Billie Lee Shoemaker, but when I started riding, they began writing me down as Willie. I never said anything because it made no difference to me, but I'm really Billie and not William or Willie.

The kids helped make our family complete. I remember the first Christmas. We had Sheryl Lee then and she was six months old, and we had put up a Christmas tree in our living room. A photographer came out from one of the papers in Los Angeles and posed us in front of the tree, with Sheryl Lee cradled in Ginny's lap and Johnny Lee sitting alongside me. And what do

you think I was doing? I was reading Clement Clarke Moore's "A Visit from St. Nicholas" to the kids. It was a nice family scene.

Ginny and I were married for eight years before our marriage started to go wrong. That was my fault. I goofed. She was a good girl and I cared about her. Later, when I was paying her alimony after our divorce, I never resented it. She deserved every penny she got.

5

A breeder named Rex Ellsworth was making a splash in California. At one time he controlled 600 Thoroughbreds and turned out more than 120 foals a year. Mesch Tenney was his trainer. One day, Eddie Arcaro was going up to Boston by train to ride in a race. On the train he met Mr. Ellsworth, who told him, "My barns are full and I got John Burton and Britt Layton riding for me and I can't win a thing." Eddie said something like, "Hell, that's the trouble. If you don't get a guy like Shoemaker riding your horses, you're going to get beat in the races you should be winning."

Eddie had great influence over horse owners. He had more to do with making race-riding respectable than anybody in the game. Before he came around, jockeys' first names weren't listed. They would be E. Arcaro or W. Shoemaker. Eddie changed all that. He knew how to be warm and friendly, and he was the first jockey to romance the whole horse industry. He didn't bother with the middleman. He went straight to the owner. He got a lot of work and a lot of respect, and it helped all jockeys. So Ellsworth listened to him when he suggested that he go get Shoemaker.

When Ellsworth got back to California, he called Harry. "I want to use Shoemaker," he said. Harry liked calls like that. They meant business. He said Mr. Ellsworth and Mr. Tenney could have my services whenever I was available, but they couldn't have first call. "That's fair enough," Mr. Ellsworth said.

That was a big break. If Eddie hadn't met Ellsworth on the train from New York to Boston, I might never have had a chance to ride Swaps. He was a chestnut colt bred by Mr. Ellsworth. When he was a two-year-old, Swaps won only two of five races. I rode him in one of these early in 1954. It was an allowance race at Santa Anita and he won it, but I wasn't impressed with him. Early the next year, I got another call on Swaps in the San Vicente Stakes at Santa Anita. I liked the way he ran. That day we beat Calumet Farm's Trentonian. The Santa Anita Derby was coming up. Mesch Tenney asked Harry for my services. "I can't give you Shoe," Harry said. "He's riding Blue Ruler." Tenney said all right, he would let Longden ride Swaps in the Santa Anita Derby, but he wanted me for the Kentucky Derby. "You betcha," Harry said. I don't know who used "you betcha" first, Harry or me, but we both used it a lot. Longden won the Santa Anita Derby on Swaps. He thought that would give him the ride on Swaps in the Derby. He discussed it with Mesch Tenney and got the bad news. "We promised the ride to Shoe," the trainer said. So I went to Kentucky and Longden stayed home.

That wasn't my first Derby. Remember how Harry insisted that we go to New York in 1951 if we wanted to get mounts in the big races? The way things worked out, he was right. In New York I got to know Jack Amiel. He was a big jolly guy who owned the Turf Restaurant on Broadway. He got hooked on racing and bought a Count Fleet yearling at the Saratoga sales for $4,500. It didn't figure to be much. Amiel named the horse Count Turf. The colt turned out to be a dude with big muscles in his chest and shoulders, and he could run. Amiel entered him in the 1951 Derby and put Conn McCreary on him, and wouldn't you know, Count Turf won and paid $31.20.

Now the 1952 Derby was coming up and Amiel had something called Count Flame going to Louisville. He wanted McCreary to ride Count Flame, but McCreary was booked on Blue Moon in the race. So Harry took the call on Count Flame. I was a few months short of my twenty-first birthday and in my third year as a jockey, and I had my first ride in Louisville on the first Saturday in May.

Eddie Arcaro was riding Hill Gail in the race. He was going after his fifth Derby victory. I was trying to win my first. What happened was that Count Flame wouldn't run for me early. When he decided to fire in the stretch, it was too late. He moved past horses, but could get no better than fifth. If I couldn't win, I'm glad Eddie did.

In the next Derby, Harry got me a ride on another outsider named Invigorator. There was an unbeaten gray colt named Native Dancer in the race. He was the talk of America. I think that happened because they were just beginning to televise races across the country and people watched Native Dancer and got to know him. He was by Polynesian out of Geisha, and was owned by Alfred Vanderbilt. Vanderbilt had a knack for names. He had a foal out of his mare Pansy. The sire was Shut Out, so he named the foal Social Outcast. The way it turned out, Social Outcast was coupled with Native Dancer in the 1953 Kentucky Derby. The entry was a heavy favorite, mostly because of Native Dancer. He had cleaned up in the East and was undefeated. It turned out to be the only race Native Dancer ever lost. He won twenty-one of twenty-two before he was retired to stud.

What happened in the Derby was that Native Dancer got knocked wide by Money Broker in the first turn. Great colt that he was, he ran his heart out in the stretch, but even with Eric Guerin pushing most of the way, Native Dancer was beaten a head by Dark Star. I went after the leaders in the stretch but could get no better than third, beaten a little more than five lengths. Social Outcast, Native Dancer's stablemate, finished seventh.

For the 1954 Derby, Harry got a real good mount for me. Correlation was the favorite going into the gate, but the best he could get was sixth. I got to tell you I was disappointed. I thought I would never win a Derby. The winner that year was a good colt named Determine.

A year later I was sitting pretty. I got Swaps for the Derby and I was doing all right riding at Golden Gate Fields in April. I had been lucky. I hadn't had a serious accident. But on this day in

April, at the track near San Francisco, I was thrown by a horse leaving the gate. I lay on the track and another horse kicked me in the knee. When they took me to the hospital, Harry was there. He was always there when I needed him. He twirled his cigar between two fingers and looked like he was going to cry. The doctor told Harry, "Mr. Silbert, this young man will be in no condition to ride for at least three, maybe four, weeks." Harry's expression changed. He looked like an undertaker. But he was thinking. So was I. I thought, Here I have a real live horse in the Derby and I get knocked out of the box.

They were running the Jefferson Purse at Churchill Downs in a few days. The Jefferson Purse later became known as the Stepping Stone, but then, in 1955, it was a $5,000 race over six furlongs. Derby runners used to go into the Jefferson Purse to test themselves for the big race coming up. Ellsworth and Tenney were using it to give Swaps a race over the track before the Derby. Harry said, "We gotta go. Mesch ain't going to like having another boy on the horse one day and another boy on him for the Derby." That night Harry came back to the hospital, helped me pull my clothes on, and smuggled me out of the place. We caught a plane for Louisville. In those days, before the jets, the trip took ten hours. We got there the next morning. My knee was swollen three times its size. Harry had to carry me off the plane. We got to a hotel and Harry tried to get a doctor. He couldn't find one, so we found a health club instead. The guy running the club put me in a whirlpool. When I got out of the whirlpool, he started massaging my knee. It wasn't helping a damn bit.

A fellow getting a rubdown on the next table saw what was happening. He turned out to be the trainer of the University of Louisville football team. He said I could come to their training room and get treatment. It might help. So off we went to the University of Louisville campus. Everybody in the training room couldn't get over seeing me there, this little guy among all those football players. The trainer put me in a whirlpool, and while he was treating me, one of the young football players came up and talked to me. He said his name was Johnny Unitas. He turned out to be a hell of a football player.

I get lucky again. The whirlpool helps, and when we go to the gate in the Jefferson Purse, Swaps is the 3–10 favorite. We win by nine lengths in 1:10.2 and the horse pays $2.60 to win. Right after the race, instead of taking Swaps back to the barn to be cooled out, Tenney tells me to work him a mile. That's something new on me, but Tenney is the trainer. Do it now and people will talk, but back then they did things their own way, especially Mesch Tenney. He always had a lot of his own ideas about training horses.

So now I work Swaps a mile and he covers the distance in 1:36.2 and that's pretty good time. A little guy with the funny name of Roscoe Goose comes up to me. In 1913, eighteen years before I was born, Roscoe Goose rode Donerail in the Kentucky Derby. The horse went off at 90–1 and paid $184.90 to win. That made Roscoe Goose a hero around Louisville. No Derby winners had ever come close to such an upset. So now Mr. Goose comes up to me and says, "Kid, you've got the winner. No Nashua is

Here I am looking pretty serious before a race at Santa Anita in 1961.

gonna beat your horse. What you just did is the greatest thing I ever saw." I'm thinking, Thank you, Mr. Goose, but that doesn't mean I got the Derby laid away in my saddlebag.

The favorite in the Derby has to be Nashua, the big horse from the East, with Eddie Arcaro on him. Eddie won with him in the Florida Derby and the Flamingo, and the colt, under Ted Atkinson, won the Wood Memorial in New York. With Eddie on him, he figured to be a tiger. The next Saturday, just before he throws me up on Swaps, Mr. Ellsworth says, "The reason you're on Swaps today is that Mr. Ellsworth and I think you are a good rider. Now prove it. I want you to lay second or third, but if you can't, use your own judgment. Go get 'em."

When he says that, I try to make myself believe it's just another horse race. I know it isn't. It's the biggest horse race in America and I have a shot, and even if they say I have ice water in my veins, I know better.

We break out of the eight hole and get away with the others, going kind of easy past the stands the first time. I have a good hold on Swaps. Everybody else is taking strong holds on their horses, too. So I let Swaps ease into the lead. We're moving and I think, Well, look at this. If they let me go on like this, they'll never catch me. And that's how the race is run. Turning for home, Nashua moves up to within a neck. I'm in a little trouble. Swaps spots the gate parked off to his right, off the track, and he kind of props, sticking his toes into the ground. That slows us up some, but I push Swaps and now we're in the straightaway, going for home. I cluck to Swaps. Then I whack him with the whip. He

shoots away from Nashua by a length, and going toward the wire, we're still pulling away. We have the best of it by a length and a half.

Swaps was a great horse. He was race-wise and he was easy to ride, and going to the winner's circle at Churchill Downs, I felt he was my good friend. When I think about it, I remember I thought, This horse did most of what had to be done. All I did was kind of sit up there and steer him around the track. He stored a lot of energy and he gave it to me when I asked for it.

Going to the winner's circle, Rex Ellsworth held the bridle on the right side and Mesch Tenney held it on the left side, and their smiles were as broad as Texas. They stopped Swaps in front of the porch in the infield and the cameramen came running. I posed waving my jockey's cap. I got off the horse and they rushed me back to the jocks' room. The reporters were waiting for me. That was in the old jocks' room at Churchill Downs. It was small and crowded, and it was a mob scene. Arcaro was the first one to congratulate me. He was dressed by then, dressed up in a dark suit and a white shirt and a dark tie, and his hair was combed. He had dark black hair and it glistened. When you ride a winner, you're the last guy back in the room. The losers are there ahead of you. I have a picture of Eddie congratulating me, and when I look at myself, I see that my teeth are still not the way they should have been. But at the time, in the jockeys' room after my first Derby win, I wasn't thinking about teeth. I was happy, maybe a little surprised, and maybe Arcaro was a little surprised, too.

Before the race, Eddie had thought Summer Tan was the horse

to watch. Maybe, in the race, he had his eye on Summer Tan and forgot about Swaps. Anyway, we had the roses and we went back to California. Nashua headed East and ran in the Preakness and the Belmont, and won both. Swaps was at the top of his game too. After the Derby he won three races at Hollywood Park and then went to Chicago and won the American Derby at Washington Park. People started talking up a match race between Swaps and Nashua. The papers were full of it. Ben Lindheimer had Washington Park and he went out to book the race, knowing it would be a big attraction. He got it for August 31, 1955.

Here's where I ought to tell you about the track at Washington Park. When it rained, the track didn't dry out evenly. This became important going against Nashua. There was another thing. Swaps wasn't fit. I'm not making excuses, but the day after the race it came out that Swaps could hardly get out of his stall the morning of the race. He had an infection in his right front foot, and when Mesch Tenney put him through a work the day before the race, he put a leather pad around the bad foot to protect it. The track came up muddy, after a heavy rain, and some mud got up inside the leather pad and made the infection worse.

Mesch Tenney went to see Ben Lindheimer. He told him the story. Mr. Lindheimer listened and then told Mesch that he couldn't call the race off, too much was involved. The papers were calling it the "dream race" and the public was all excited. Lindheimer said, "We can't disappoint these people." Mr. Ellsworth went along with the deal. Tenney called Harry and told him not to tell me about Swaps' sore foot. They figured that if I

knew, I would pull up the first time Swaps took a bad step. As it was, I did pull up Swaps in the stretch, but that was when I knew he was beat. I think Ellsworth and Tenney thought Swaps could handle the situation even with a bad foot. When I was warming up Swaps before the race, I felt that his action wasn't right, but I thought it was because the track was muddy in spots.

In the draw for posts, Nashua got the inside. Arcaro liked that. He was smart and knew it would be an advantage to get to the best part of the track. When the gate opened, Eddie popped out and got Nashua running in the dry part of the track. Swaps wasn't ready. He was almost turned sideways when the gate swung open and he began bearing out from the start. Me and Swaps were in the wet part of the track. Nashua, in the dry alley, outran us to the first turn. I had no strategy. Arcaro was in the driver's seat. Smart guy that he was, he knew that when a horse is laying second in a match race, the jockey has to use his horse more than the leader. Otherwise, if he starts saving his horse, the jockey leading the way doesn't have to put pressure on his own mount. Arcaro rode like the champ he was, and even if he hadn't, I'm not sure that Swaps could have beat Nashua anyway. The mistake was mine. I made no excuses because Eddie Arcaro, the master, just gave me a lesson.

6

The writers made up my nicknames for me right from the start. First it was Silent Shoe, then plain Shoe. Somebody began writing me up as Wee Willie and that stuck for a while. Next they came up with Will the Shoe. My friends called me Bill or Shoe. The win on Swaps in the 1955 Derby put these nicknames on a lot of lips. I liked that. If I said I didn't, I'd be lying. I was flying high. I set three world records on Swaps: a mile, a mile and a sixteenth, and a mile and five eighths. I was walking around with a lot of money in my pocket. This wasn't easy. My pants pockets were very small and we didn't have credit cards those days. I bet $5,000 on a horse I was riding at Santa Anita and got beat a nose. It cured me, you betcha. Eddie Arcaro always said he could be a rich man if they gave him the bookmaking concession in the jockeys' room.

Three years after I tied Culmone for the riding title, I led every jockey in the country again. That was 1953 and I had 485 winners. The winning horses produced $1,784,187 for their owners. My

end came to more than $200,000. That summer we were living in a house trailer at Del Mar and I had been working hard and I was tired. Midway in the Del Mar meeting I had more than 300 winners for the year. I was shooting for the record of 390 set by Tony DeSpirito the year before. I remember taking a walk along the beach one morning. I looked out at the ocean and it was nice and peaceful, and it made me think about a couple of friends of mine, one vacationing in Hawaii, the other in Europe. I thought, What the hell am I doing here, working my ass off? When I got back to the trailer, I said to Ginny, "I'm tired. We're going on a vacation." Ginny looked at me. She thought I was crazy. She said, "Vacation? You're riding great. You have more than 300 winners. No vacation. I'm not going on any vacation and you're not going."

I thought about Ginny's beef all day. I couldn't sleep that night and at midnight I got out of bed, got dressed, and went for a ride, all the while thinking about Hawaii and Europe and the long rest I thought I deserved. I drove back to the house and by the time I got there I knew Ginny had won. I wasn't going on any vacation.

I had 323 winners by the end of the Del Mar meeting. By October, at Golden Gate Fields, I had 389 winners. The newspapers and radio stations got all excited and sent reporters to write me up. They thought I was going to break the record the next day and everywhere I went the reporters and cameramen followed me. What happened was that I had eight mounts that day and didn't win on one. I was feeling tired again. The pressure was getting to me.

"You'll get it tomorrow," Ginny told me.

The next day I struck out again on six horses. I wasn't worried, because I knew it was only a matter of time. I got my 391st victory the very next day on a horse called The Hoop. By the time the year ended, I had 485 winners. Bill Hartack was second in the standings with 350 winners.

Charlie always said that Hartack rode like a cowhand roping a calf. I didn't agree. Hartack was a great rider. He had five Kentucky Derby winners. He got things done. In the old days, racetrackers said I sat too quiet on a horse, that I didn't push and scrub. That was my style. Hartack had his own. I sat a horse one way, his seat was different. Hartack was a rival, but I had a lot of respect for him as a competitor. He didn't like being called Willie, but it never bothered me.

In 1954, I beat Hartack again for the riding title. I had 380 winners and he had 323. He was getting closer. Our careers were hooked up and in 1957 I ran into him in the Kentucky Derby. I might as well come right out with it. That was the Derby I bobbled. I was riding Gallant Man and I mistook the finish line and stood up in the irons. It probably cost me the race. Hartack beat me by a nose on Iron Liege. People never forget to remind me about my mistake. Wherever I go, they ask me to tell them about the time I goofed on Gallant Man. When they ask, I tell it straight. I made a horrible mistake.

The funny thing is that I wasn't supposed to be on Gallant Man in the first place. The owner was Ralph Lowe and he wanted me to ride the colt, but John Nerud picked John Choquette to ride Gallant Man. Mr. Nerud told Mr. Lowe, "You want

another jockey, you can get another trainer, too." Mr. Lowe was a Texas oil man, a hell of a guy, and he didn't like to argue. So he went right along with his trainer, and when Gallant Man went into the gate in the Hibiscus Stakes at Hialeah, Choquette had the ride. He rode good enough to win the Hibiscus, and when the Wood Memorial came up at Jamaica, Choquette was on Gallant Man again.

I rode Ambehaving in the race. Ambehaving figured to be my Derby horse, but in the Wood he barreled into the gate at the start and hurt his stifle. That's the joint of a horse's hind leg. Ambehaving's action was gone and I eased him up. Bold Ruler beat Gallant Man a nose. Eddie Arcaro gave Bold Ruler a real good ride. He outdueled Choquette to the wire and Mr. Lowe told Nerud he should have had me on the colt. They had words, but Mr. Nerud stood his ground. He was one of the best trainers around and a good friend of Harry's, but he wouldn't change his mind. He said Choquette still had the call on Gallant Man in the Derby.

A few days later, Choquette got days for rough riding. In those days, when the stewards suspended a jockey, he stayed suspended. These days the stewards are different. When they take action against a rider, the rider goes to court and gets an injunction and keeps riding. This might be a good thing in some cases, but it weakens the power of the stewards. It isn't easy for me to say that, because I'm the national president of the Jockeys' Guild. I'll fight for a jockey's rights all the way, but there are some things I can't see. Weakening the authority of the stewards is one of them. If old Marshall Cassidy was still around, it wouldn't be happen-

ing. When he was a steward, all the way back to the old days at Agua Caliente, he helped clean up racing. He had a strong will and loved the game, and he knew that the cleaner the game got, the better off it was.

Now when Nerud got word that Choquette had been grounded, he went looking for another rider. He was mad. Early in Gallant Man's three-year-old season, agents for the top riders turned up their noses at Gallant Man as a stakes horse. Nerud had a long memory. So when he needed a rider for Gallant Man for the 1957 Derby, he went right to the phone and called the jocks' room at Hollywood Park and asked me if I was available to ride Gallant Man. "Betcha I am," I said, "if it's all right with Harry." Nerud said, "Harry's my friend. We'll get along." That's how I got to ride Gallant Man. When Mr. Lowe got the news, he was happy. He said he had wanted me on his colt in the first place.

I went out to Louisville and checked into the Brown Hotel. Mr. Lowe and Mr. Nerud were staying in the same hotel. The night before the Derby, the three of us had dinner together. We had a few shooters and some laughs, and Mr. Lowe told me he had a dream about a jockey on one of his horses misjudging the finish line. "Not me," I said. John Nerud didn't like the idea of Mr. Lowe telling me about his dream. I guess he was superstitious. You find a lot of that around the racetrack.

I wanted to get the feel of the track the day of the Derby, but Harry couldn't book a single ride for me. It was too late. What happened was that the finish line at Churchill Downs was a sixteenth of a mile farther toward the first turn than it was at other

Receiving a special award from Hollywood Turf Club's president, Mervyn LeRoy, after winning my 1,000th race at Hollywood Park, riding Jesse's Invader, June 12, 1962.

tracks in the country. And I hadn't had a ride over a track like that in a year. The year before, my Derby horse had been Ter-rang and he had finished twelfth, and when your horse finishes twelfth, you hardly notice where the wire is.

In the early stretch, I got close to Iron Liege. Then at the end, I stood up in the irons. Hartack was digging into his horse and Iron Liege was charging, and by the time I got my colt back in stride, I couldn't catch them. I knew I had made a big, big booboo. It happened so fast, a lot of people didn't realize it, but the other jockeys in the race knew it happened. It wasn't the first time a jock misjudged the finish line, but this was the Kentucky Derby and there I was looking like a fool in front of a national television audience and maybe a hundred thousand fans in the stands. I didn't make any excuses. Gallant Man might have hung a little, but I didn't cop a plea the day I made the mistake and I'm not doing it now.

I got a call from the stewards right after the race. They asked me what had happened. I said, "I goofed. I misjudged the finish line." The steward I was talking to was very nice. I said, "I'm sorry." He said, "We feel the same way. It was an honest mis-take."

After the race, I went to Dallas. I had some friends there, and three days later I got a telegram from the stewards at Churchill Downs. It said that under the circumstances they had to suspend me for fifteen days. I got pissy. So did John Nerud. The suspen-sion itself didn't bother me. After all, I was a pro and pros

weren't supposed to goof. What bothered me was the way they did it.

The suspension didn't put me out of the Preakness. The way it was, Gallant Man wasn't going to Baltimore anyway. Mr. Lowe wanted to go, but Mr. Nerud didn't. John had a theory that there are very few horses that can dance the three dances—the Derby, the Preakness, and the Belmont—in five weeks. The people in Baltimore put a lot of pressure on Mr. Nerud. He said Gallant Man would fit the Belmont better, because it was a mile and a half, a quarter of a mile longer than the Derby, and Gallant Man needed the distance to do his best.

Mr. Lowe was disappointed, but he hid it. Instead of blaming me, he sent me a new Chrysler, one of those long jobs they had back then thirty years ago. I'll never forget his kindness. Not that I was happy with what had happened, with easing Gallant Man too soon. But what stuck with me was that Mr. Lowe took my mistake like a real gentleman. When he died, I put up money to pay for a trophy they award each year to honor him. It's the Ralph Lowe Trophy for sportsmanship in racing. What the hell! I couldn't hide my mistake. The least I could do was to take it the way Mr. Lowe did, like a gentleman.

The public was mostly sympathetic to me, too. Maybe that's because the public always stays on the side of the underdog. I tried to keep my sense of humor about the whole thing. I told the papers in jest that Eddie Arcaro should have thanked me for making my booboo. After all, after the race, Arcaro told the press that he had made a mistake, just like me, by not letting Bold Ruler run

his race. I said, "Eddie was on the 8–5 shot and nobody said a word about him because they were paying so much attention to me. He should write me a letter and thank me."

That wasn't my first mistake in a big race, and it certainly wasn't going to be my last. The year before I was riding Swaps in the California Stakes at Hollywood Park. When I got out in front, I forgot to ride Swaps out, and the result was that Porterhouse passed me at the wire and the chalk players blew $178,000 on Swaps' nose. The stewards didn't suspend me. They called it a "regrettable error in judgment." In Kentucky, they said I was guilty of "gross carelessness."

Five weeks after my blooper in the Kentucky Derby, I rode Gallant Man in the Belmont Stakes in New York. The spectators near the walking ring had the needle out for me. "Don't close your eyes, Willie," an apprentice rider named Oscar Wildes yelled at me. "Wait for the alarm, Willie. Don't go to sleep, Willie." The other jocks in the Belmont heard him. They laughed. I didn't say a word. In the race, I passed Arcaro, on Bold Ruler, with five eighths of a mile to go. I couldn't help gloating a little bit. "Look at the hold I got on this horse," I yelled to Eddie. Then I was gone. If I had wanted to take a nap, I could have had the time right then. Gallant Man and I got home eight lengths in front, with Bold Ruler a tiring third, four lengths behind Inside Tract.

Gallant Man's net purse for winning the Belmont was $77,300. Out of this came 10 percent for John Nerud, 10 percent for me, and 5 for John Choquette. John Nerud wanted Choquette to get that money because the rider was supposed to be on Gallant Man in the Derby before he got suspended. Mr. Lowe agreed. He was a good man all the way.

Gallant Man set all kinds of records in the Belmont. His time of 2:26.6 for a mile and a half broke Citation's stakes record and knocked a second off the Belmont Park and the American records. Winning the Belmont was great. It didn't wipe out my mistake in the Derby, but I sure felt better. It was the goof I pulled in the Derby that started people asking me if I was a fatalist. I told them it was destined to be this way. I believed that whatever happened, happened for the best. I still believe that.

After the Derby, the big race for three-year-olds was the Travers at Saratoga. We went up there and won that historic race, which was first run in 1864. The Jockey Club Gold Cup was next for Gallant Man. I had a good trip in the Gold Cup. In the last half mile, I saved ground and then went out a little going into the stretch. Gallant Man got whacked a couple of times with my stick and he picked up speed with an eighth of a mile to go. We had a length on Third Brother going under the wire. By that time the mistake in Louisville was ancient history.

7

It's fun to look at old pictures. In an album at home there's one of me taken in 1958. It shows me wearing a flattop haircut and I'm standing next to a life-size statue of Swaps at Hollywood Park. I'm riding Swaps to nowhere, the "California Comet" just standing there head high. When I looked at the picture of the statue the last time, I thought of 1958 and what a year it was. It was the year I got elected to the Hall of Fame at Saratoga. It was the year I got my 3,000th winner and it was the year I won the national riding championship for the fourth time. I rode 300 winners and beat out Howard Grant for the title. The horses I rode that year won almost $3,000,000 in purses. That was in 1958 dollars. It was peanuts compared to 1987 standards, but it was a fortune in those days. Also, 1958 was the year I got my teeth fixed. My new teeth gave me a new look. Now, when I look at the picture of me taken next to the statue of Swaps, I think, Hey, I wasn't a mutt after all. The new teeth made a difference, you bet.

Why I got my teeth fixed for good in 1958 was that Jackie Westrope finally sent me to the right dentist. You had to know Westrope to appreciate him. He was one of the best riders around and all the way back in 1933, only two years after I was born, he won the national riding title. He might have been as good as Arcaro, but he was a little wilder and more stubborn than Eddie. I remember he used to ride acey-deucy all the way, with his left stirrup dropped so low, he had to extend his left leg to get his foot into the iron. I think maybe that started after he broke his leg. Anyway, you better believe me when I say Westrope was a great rider.

I've been telling a story about him for years and it still sounds good. I'm still a kid and I'm riding against Westrope, riding a horse for Red McDaniel. Westrope is on a horse behind me and he is whipping left-handed. I don't know it's Westrope. He's making up ground on me and I stick my whip out. Westrope's stick hits mine and he loses it, and I beat him a nose. He is hot. If looks could kill, I'm dead and buried. When we go to look at the movies of the race, the stewards are there and Westrope is burning up. He says to the stewards, "Look at that little son of a bitch. You can't let him get away with that." One of the stewards says, "I don't think Shoe's a son of a bitch. He's doing nothing. You stuck your whip out. You hit his whip and lost yours. Nothing wrong. Nothing we can see." Later Westrope told me I cost him a bet. He liked his horse so much, he had a bet on him. No wonder Westrope got pissy. I couldn't blame him. We were pals, but he let his emotions run him against me. When it was over, we were still pals.

Aboard Jaipur at the Gotham Stakes in 1962. I went on to win the Withers, Belmont Stakes, and Travers on Jaipur.

He had a nice broad smile and a wide mouth, and he had a sense of humor. We did a lot of drinking together. I liked the taste of whiskey when I was younger. Now I can't handle it the way I did. I'm down to two drinks a day, something like that. Back then, in 1958, I could handle a lot of things, and did. One thing I wasn't handling very well those days was my teeth. That's where Westrope comes in.

In the jockeys' room one day he told me, "Shoe, I got the greatest dentist. Dr. Peter K. Thomas over in Beverly Hills. You ought to go see the guy. He's great." Dentists scared me. The first one I went to yanked some of my teeth and gave me a partial set of uppers. I went swimming in the ocean down at Del Mar and they came out of my mouth. So when Westrope told me about Dr. Thomas I was cautious. Then I figured, "What the hell!" and I went to see Dr. Thomas.

I invested $10,000 in my teeth. That was Dr. Thomas' fee, but what he did was worth it. He was an expert and he had his own technique. It worked fine for me. The job was so good that Harry used to say, "Hey, Shoe's teeth are so great now, you can't shove a sheet of paper between the uppers and lowers. He's got a real bite."

That was the best $10,000 I ever spent. Until then, my bite was worse than my bark. I didn't eat the right way. I'd take liquids with my food to wash it down, because I really couldn't chew. I owe it all to Jackie Westrope. He discovered Dr. Thomas and sent me to him. The job Dr. Thomas did would cost $50,000 today. For the first time in my life I was happy with my teeth. I began

smiling my way through life. I smiled so much that Arcaro used to say, "Hey, don't you know how to do anything but smile?" Eddie remembered the time they called me Silent Shoe. He told me, "You had such bum teeth, you were too scared to open your trap."

In 1958 I rode Silky Sullivan. He was a colt that got a lot of attention in California. People wrote letters to him. He had his own radio show. The Irish were so proud of him, they called him "Himself," as if he was the head man in the family. Silky Sullivan practically walked out of the gate. He'd fall thirty lengths behind and make a late run. One time, at Santa Anita, he dropped back so far that he was thirty-five lengths in back of the eighth horse in a nine-horse field. I was on this big good-looking dude and I couldn't see the horses in the lead. There was no dirt or anything hitting me in the face, but I couldn't get a gander at the leaders. I was all by myself, and I started talking to Silky, calling the big sucker a son of a bitch. Maybe my talking to him did him some good. By the half-mile pole, he was moving closer to the pack.

I thought, Well, he'll beat somebody, anyway. We might get fourth or fifth. In the straightaway, I wheeled him out from behind the field. He started running and I thought, I'll be a son of a bitch! He was really running and we got the win in this six-and-a-half furlong race. That was the only time riding that I made up so much ground. We won by half a length. No wonder there was a crowd of sixty-one thousand on hand for the Santa Anita Derby that year. There was Silky Sullivan in the parade to the gate, "Himself" one of the favorites in the race. On the far turn Silky

Sullivan was thirty lengths back. I thought, Hell, here we go again. This dude can't make it up. Wouldn't you know that I moved on him in the stretch and got the win by three and a half lengths.

By the time we got to Louisville for the Kentucky Derby, Silky was the talk of the country. They were selling sundaes and Irish whiskey named for "Himself" and everybody looked forward to the Stepping Stone, the prep race for the Derby. In that race, Silky Sullivan was out of it by 32 lengths, but at the wire he was beaten only two and a quarter lengths. Nobody believed in him but the public. In the Derby betting, Churchill Downs sold more $2.00 tickets on Silky than on any other horse ever. He went off as the second co-favorite, bet down to $2.10 to $1.00.

The television people were all excited and CBS-TV split the screen so they could show the leader and show Silky Sullivan at the same time. It was a good thing they did, because Silky was so far out of it, they would have had to grind the biggest wide-angle lens in the world to get the leader and Silky Sullivan on the screen at the same time. It turned out Silky Sullivan could beat only two horses in the fourteen-horse field. He lost by more than 20 lengths to Calumet Farm's Tim Tan.

I was riding a lot around Chicago about that time. How Harry explained this was that one day, he got a call from a guy in Chicago. The guy told Harry that the public was tired of Bill Hartack riding all those $2.40, $2.60, and $2.80 winners. They needed and really wanted some competition for Hartack. So we went out to Chicago and rode at Ben Lindheimer's track. It was a

great place, run by a great man. Mr. Lindheimer was the one who made the Swaps-Nashua match after Swaps won the Kentucky Derby in 1955. He was one of the finest men I ever met in racing. The way Harry set it up, we'd always find room for Chicago, maybe even skipping Del Mar. And I had a lot of luck in Chicago. In 1958, I won the Arlington Futurity there on Restless Wind and three weeks later also won the Washington Park Futurity on him. Restless Wind was a real speedball. Two months later I was back in Chicago to ride Clem in the Hawthorne Gold Cup. He got home first.

Later, after Mr. Lindheimer retired, I continued to ride a lot at Arlington Park. Marje Lindheimer Everett ran the place later. She was Ben's daughter and she runs Hollywood Park now, but back then, she operated Arlington Park with a strong hand and great kindness. She was a great hostess. I stayed in her house at the track and got treated like royalty. Everybody who ever had the good luck to be Marje's guest was treated the same way. Marje entertained with a lavish hand. Her Saturday night poker games were fast and furious, but I never got hurt in any of them. I held my own and enjoyed every minute of the competition.

By then I had split with Ginny and was seeing a lady from Texas named Babbs Bayer. She was a divorcee and had an adopted son, Mitchell, who I adopted later when we got married. A friend of mine in Dallas named Fritz Reckenberg introduced us. He knew Babbs very well and told me I would like her and I did. She was six months younger than me and so different from Ginny, it was a case of day and night. Ginny was sweet and straightforward. Babbs was flashy and sophisticated, and beautiful. She had dark hair and dark eyes, and wherever she went, people gave her the eye. I kind of liked that. Later, I heard people say that Babbs' trouble was that she couldn't remember who the star of the family was, but back then, at the beginning of our time together, I was a very happy little man.

Not everything went right for me in 1958. I went to New Jersey to ride Tomy Lee in the Garden State Stakes. The two-year-old colt was owned by a Californian named Fred Turner, Jr. What I learned while riding Tomy Lee in New Jersey was that it was tough to make him change leads. A horse should be on his right lead in the straightaway and on his left lead on turns. What that means is that a horse in the straightaway should be leading with his right leg. On the turns, the left leg should lead the way. It's like changing gears in an automobile.

The Garden State Stakes in 1958 had the great colt First Landing as one of its runners. Tomy Lee could have outrun First Landing if he had run the kind of race I wanted him to. The track came up muddy on the day of the Garden State and we drew the tenth hole out of the gate. Tomy Lee kept running out, trying to get to the outside of the track all the way. He wouldn't switch leads and I had to fight him. Finally, when I got him to switch leads, I moved him toward the rail, but all the wrestling around had tired him out. Tomy Lee got beat a neck by First Landing and I thought, getting off the colt, Hell, we could have won if my horse had been more relaxed and had run kindly.

Tomy Lee's trainer was Frank Childs. He was one of the nicest

men around and a good friend of Harry's. The 1959 Kentucky Derby was coming up and Childs asked Harry if I would ride Tomy Lee at Churchill Downs. Harry said that it was all right with him, providing the colt won the Blue Grass Stakes at Keeneland with me in the irons. Around that same time, Elliott Burch called me from New York. He asked if I would ride Sword Dancer for him in the Stepping Stone before the Derby. I said that was all right with me. I had won on Sword Dancer and felt that he had a real shot in the Derby. I wanted to ride him.

Harry said, "Shoe, we can't do that. I gave Frank Childs my word that we would ride his colt in the Derby." I was angry. I said, "Okay, but let me tell you, Harry, Sword Dancer is going to win the Derby." Harry said, "Hey, Shoe, you know what a good guy Frank Childs is, and I gave him my word."

Going to the gate in the 1959 Derby, I thought that I was on the wrong horse. In my mind, Tomy Lee was not a mile-and-a-quarter horse but that Sword Dancer was.

When we told Elliott Burch that I couldn't ride Sword Dancer for him, it wasn't easy. Harry and I liked Elliott. His father was Preston Burch, the trainer who wanted to buy my contract the first time I rode in New York. Elliott had become one of the country's best trainers. He really wanted me for Sword Dancer, but when he couldn't get me, he gave the mount to Bill Boland. In the 1950 Kentucky Derby, Boland rode the winner, Middleground. He was only sixteen years old, the only apprentice to ride a Derby winner. Now he was up on Sword Dancer in the 1959 Derby, and I was riding Tomy Lee.

After the first mile at Churchill Downs, Tomy Lee and I had things pretty much to ourselves. Rounding the far turn into the stretch, we were just about head to head. I looked over at Boland and he seemed to be going good, with a lot of horse left under him. I thought, He's going to win it. He pulled up beside me and I yelled, "Good luck, Bill, go ahead. You got it won." I really thought that, I was serious. Boland thought I was trying to trick him. He smelled a rat. He didn't move away on Sword Dancer. My horse bore out and made contact with Sword Dancer.

Boland thought I was doing it on purpose, but I wasn't. If he'd have given Sword Dancer the whip and had gone on, he'd have won it. But he must have said to himself, "I'll give it right back to Shoe." So he got to riding me. My horse was on his left lead, and I couldn't get him to switch. Tomy Lee was all confused. At the eighth pole, Sword Dancer bumped Tomy Lee again. This made Tomy Lee switch to his right lead. He just had enough left to go on and win by a nose. If he hadn't been bumped, he never would have switched his lead. And he never would have won the race. Even then, I wasn't sure that he had won. Bill Boland claimed foul against me. The stewards looked at the film and said both of us were guilty of bumping. Tomy Lee's number stayed up. It was my second Derby win.

Fred Turner was a real sore winner. He was still angry because I said I would rather ride Sword Dancer than Tomy Lee. He told the papers, "Well, the bookmakers had Shoemaker, and the horse won in spite of him." I was really mad. I told everybody I met around the track that Turner had to be a fool to say that. I rode

Tomy Lee the best way I knew how in the Derby. The way it turned out, I thought we got a break.

Turner said he wouldn't let Tomy Lee go in the Preakness or the Belmont. Harry liked that. "Hey, Shoe," he said, "now you get your wish. You ride Sword Dancer for Burch." I was happy. Sword Dancer was owned by Mrs. Isabel Dodge Sloane. She was a sportswoman who never would have acted the way Turner did.

In the Preakness, Sword Dancer didn't run up to his ability. He finished second in the mile and three-sixteenths race, four lengths behind Royal Orbit. In the Belmont, he would have to go a mile and a half. Everybody wondered whether he could get the distance.

When it was announced that I would ride Sword Dancer in the Belmont, Fred Turner blew his top again. He said he thought Harry had given him his word that I would be on Tomy Lee in the Cinema Handicap at Hollywood Park the same day as the Belmont. He went around saying he would sell out his racing stable because he no longer believed the game was a sport. Besides, he said the Triple Crown was a joke and that if I had any idea of what racing was about, I'd ride his horse in the Cinema Handicap instead of Sword Dancer in the classic Belmont. I never did get the whole picture.

The next thing Turner did was to say that when he sold Tomy Lee, the buyer would have to guarantee him that I would not be allowed to ride the horse in the Hollywood Derby if Harry was still my agent. The reporters called me. "What about this?" one asked. I always liked the press. The reporters are good for the

Sitting on my first winner in the Preakness Stakes in 1963, Candy Spots. We had lost the Derby to Chateaugay a few weeks earlier, but we beat him at the Preakness.

game and I am for anybody or anything that helps the sport of racing. All I could say was something like "horseshit." Funny thing about that. When I read one column, the writer had changed what I said to: "This is not worthy of comment by me."

We went to New York for the Belmont. I felt at home. Belmont Park was Elliott Burch's base. He knew his way around and I found it a comfortable place. Arcaro was around, too, and that was fun. He was scheduled to ride Black Hills in the Belmont. I always liked Belmont Park, going all the way back to my first visit in 1951, when the mile-and-a-half track looked huge to me. Then I was a boy. Now, as a man, I was approaching my 4,000th winner. Only three other jockeys had ridden 4,000 winners at the time. Johnny Longden, Eddie Arcaro, and Sir Gordon Richards, the Englishman.

The track came up sloppy for the 1959 Belmont. I remember the mud not because of the way the race was run, but because of what happened to Arcaro. Going around the far turn toward the five-sixteenths pole, Black Hills broke down. Eddie went off the horse head down. He was knocked out and lay in the mud with his mouth and nose down. He couldn't breathe and was almost suffocating. A track hand rushed out and picked up Eddie's head out of the mud. It saved his life.

I didn't know anything about Arcaro's close call until the race was over, because I had been running in front when he went off Black Hills. I won on Sword Dancer that day, beating Bagdad by three quarters of a length. I was happy on two accounts. Winning

was nice, but it would have been a dark day for me if Arcaro had been seriously hurt.

People think my darkest day was when I blew the Derby on Gallant Man. I have to tell them they're wrong. One of the really dark times happened up at Bay Meadows when I was young. Some guy brought me a horse to ride and Harry said it was all right with him. Before the race the owner said he had bet $50 on the horse for me. I said that was all right, and he told me the best thing to do with his horse was to lay about third and then to let him go in the stretch. I did just what he said and I brought the horse home. He was something like 50–1, paid $115. I thought, Man, this will be more money than I've ever seen. I told Harry to go see the owner. The owner was gone. He had put his horse in a van, shipped him right out of the track and scrammed. I've never seen him since.

If you've never been a raggedy kid, the way I was, you might get a laugh out of what happened to me that time at Bay Meadows, but I felt terrible. Later, when I got up in the money, I got a laugh out of it, too, but when it happened, it wasn't very funny to me.

When I started getting up in the big money, I didn't forget the old days. Harry grew up poor, too, and he knew the value of a dollar. He made some good deals for me. By this time a lot of owners and trainers paid me bonuses to ride their horses. One time Harry told me that the great trainer Max Hirsch wanted me to go to Rockingham Park in New Hampshire to ride a horse for him. Harry told him he would have to give up a lot of mounts to

go to Rockingham. Harry said to Max Hirsch, "I'll have to charge you $2,500 and 10 percent across the board." Max Hirsch couldn't believe what he was hearing. He said, "Eddie Arcaro never charged me nothing extra." Harry told him, "Oh, I forgot. We'll need expense money, too." Max said to Harry, "When can you go?"

We went, but I don't remember how the race came out. If you ask me, I can't even remember the name of the horse I rode. After almost forty thousand rides, you kind of start to forget some of them. But that Belmont, the one I won on Sword Dancer, was sure one I can remember. I also remember that Tomy Lee did run in the Cinema Handicap at Hollywood Park on the same day. My good friend Don Pierce was on Tomy Lee and found the horse hard to handle. He bore out again and finished out of the money. I felt sorry for the jockey, and I felt sorry for the trainer, Frank Childs. They were both good guys.

The year had been a good one for me. I won the Derby on Tomy Lee and the Belmont Stakes on Sword Dancer and I ended 1959 with 347 winners, the most in the country. My mounts had earnings of $2,843,133. It was the fifth time I was the leading rider in America. I was in love with Babbs Bayer. We were talking about getting married. I said if she married me I would get her everything she wanted—cars, houses, clothes. We were married two years later.

8

I was thirty years old when I married Babbs. She insisted on calling me William. That's how the papers started calling me William. She even asked the bible of the game, *Daily Racing Form*, to list me as William instead of Bill in the records. It never bothered me. She knew I was baptized Billie Lee, but I guess William sounded fancier. She liked fancy things. We lived high on the highest hog in those days. I went to live at first in her apartment in Beverly Hills. Her adopted son, Mitchell, lived with us. We got along for openers, but I can't say that was always the case.

When we were at Del Mar during the summer, I'd spend a lot of time with Mitchell, trying to keep his nose on straight. We'd take long walks on the beach and talk about a lot of things. But when he got older, he started hanging out with hippies and that bothered me. We were living in the Sierra Tower, on the edge of Beverly Hills, on the thirty-first floor. We paid $1,000 or so in rent and that was a lot of money then. It was a beautiful apartment and I remember a writer visiting us and saying the apartment "glistened with trophies." I don't know why I remember that, but I do.

One night, when my stepson was old enough to drive, I let him borrow my car. The next day the engine was burned out. He had left it running all night and to say I was mad is selling it short. I tried to take a tough hand to him, but it wasn't easy. I liked him a lot.

Babbs was a social whirlwind. We were always either going to parties, or throwing our own parties. That way of life after a while really started bothering me. Babbs insisted on living near Beverly Hills. She posed a lot. She was a beautiful woman and knew it, and she wanted more than anything else to be recognized as a great hostess. Her friends were all fancy people and I wasn't very comfortable around them. I've never forgotten that I was just a little guy who got lucky and found my niche, and I liked racetrack people more than the crowd we started running around with. The problem was that we lived across town from the racing people. They liked to stay nearer to Santa Anita, which is a long way from Beverly Hills. I'm telling you all this because it kind of explains why I liked Del Mar so much. Del Mar was the only place during my married days with Babbs where I was close to the racing crowd. At Del Mar the racing crowd was always there, and I was comfortable.

People sometimes ask me if I remember all the races I rode. I tell them I remember 90 percent of them, and that is why I can tell you twenty-five years later about the San Juan Capistrano

Handicap of 1962. I rode Olden Times for Mesch Tenney and Rex Ellsworth. They were the people who put me on Swaps and gave me my first win in the Kentucky Derby. They were good to me, and I was good to Olden Times. He was carrying 119 pounds, going about a mile and three quarters on the grass at Santa Anita, and I put him in the lead right out of the gate. I had to fight off challenge after challenge, while saving ground, and when people say, "What's the best ride you ever had?" I say, "On Olden Times, in the San Juan Capistrano." Olden Times beat off a horse called Juanro by a nose, while giving away ten pounds.

I went to New York that same year in June to ride Jaipur in the Belmont Stakes. Jaipur was a son of the great sire Nasrullah and was owned by George D. Widener. Mr. Widener was a pillar of the racing community. They had named the Widener Course at Belmont Park for him. The Widener Course was a mile-long chute that cut across beautiful Belmont diagonally on a straight line. Because of the slash it made, it was difficult to see the horses coming on in the Widener Chute. Joe Palmer used to write about it, "If the Russians ever invade New York, they'll come up the Widener Chute."

The old chute is gone now, but I remember it. When I went up on Mr. Widener's Jaipur in the Belmont Stakes of 1962, I felt good. I knew all about Jaipur. He wasn't an easy horse to ride because he liked to have his own way and he needed to be informed who the boss was right out of the gate. I have never fought a horse. By this I mean I can let them know right off who's running the show. You can make a horse understand this if you've got good hands, nice, soft hands. That's important. Balance is important, too, and I have that as well. Charlie Whittingham always pays me a great compliment. He says I bother a horse less than any other rider. Maybe that's the difference, that and lots of other things that go into making a rider.

In the Belmont, Jaipur just managed to nose out Admiral's Voyage. Braulio Baeza was on Admiral's Voyage for the mile and a half race and he was one of the great ones. He just wouldn't give in to me and fought me all the way around. It was my fifteenth stakes victory that year. That was a very good year, and when it was over, I counted thirty-seven victories in stakes races.

Two months after Belmont, I was up on Jaipur again. That was in the Travers up in Saratoga. The Travers is the oldest race in America. The first time it was run was in 1864. The Civil War was still going on. Down where I come from, in Texas, they call it the War Between the States, but I'm not getting into that here. This is about racing, and in 1864, they still had corn growing in the infield at Saratoga. The course was new and the first running of the Travers Stakes was the big race on the program. It was won by a colt called Kentucky, going a mile and a half in 3:18.75. Cows run faster now.

When I went to the gate on Jaipur in the 1962 Travers, the horse Ridan was waiting for me. He was carrying Manuel Ycaza and together they made a great team. Horse and rider had one thing in common: they were both stubborn. I hooked up with

Johnny Longdon and I at the "Big A" jockey quarters in 1964. I'd just won my 5,000th race and was hot on Longdon's tail.

Ycaza in a tight race. We went the entire mile and a quarter stride for stride, but I hit Jaipur pretty good going to the wire. Jaipur just got his nostrils in front of Ridan. The people at Saratoga that day couldn't have had a better show for the money.

Babbs was enjoying my winning the big races because, you see, she loved the limelight. And she dressed the part. I have a picture of Babbs in the winner's circle at Pimlico in 1963. That was the year I finally got a winner in the Preakness. Babbs came in a white outfit, with a double strand of pearls around her neck. Her hat was some frilly stuff, as if the designer who made it couldn't make up his mind what to do with some extra silk. Geez, it was a showy thing.

Again, Tenney and Ellsworth had gotten me a big winner, and this time for the Preakness. They had Candy Spots and I rode him for them. Candy Spots was a good horse. I once told a writer, "He's a good one, but not great, not really great." He might have been the best horse in the 1963 Derby, perhaps even good enough to have won the Triple Crown that year. I won the Arlington Futurity on him in 1962 and I had a real good idea of how much he would do for me by the time the 1963 season came around. What happened to him is what happens to a lot of good horses. He got hurt. Early in 1963, I rode him when he won the Florida Derby at Gulfstream Park. He hurt a hind leg and it still bothered him when the Derby came up in May. In Louisville, Mr. Tenney worked hard to get Candy Spots in shape for the big one. Right before the race, he seemed all right, but we knew he wasn't at his best.

In the Derby, Candy Spots had all kinds of trouble. He was rank coming out of the gate and I had to check him when he almost ran up on No Robbery's heels going into the first turn. When we went into the far turn, he was trying to go wide. Again, I had to gather him in and finally got him going good inside. But then I had to check him again, and when we had a quarter of a mile to go, I straightened him out and he was flying on the outside, and beaten three lengths at the wire. I tell you this only to describe the Derby, but what actually happened was that the tough race only helped get Candy Spots into condition for the Preakness.

Candy Spots went ahead to beat Chateaugay in the Preakness. I felt very good about it. Not only was it the first time I won the Preakness, but the Derby winner, Chateaugay, was beaten by three and a quarter lengths. I got Candy Spots moving on the first turn, and at the head of the stretch, we were running in front comfortably. The winning purse was $127,500. Candy Spots went to the Jersey Derby next, but the campaign was tough. Candy Spots was losing weight. He won in New Jersey, but for the Belmont Stakes he was as dry as a prune. That year, the Belmont Stakes wasn't run at Belmont Park because the old stands at Belmont Park were being rebuilt. The officials had condemned them. They said the stands were unsafe. So they moved the Belmont Stakes to Aqueduct. They could have moved it to China as far as Candy Spots was concerned. The long campaign had robbed him of zip, and he was beaten by Chateaugay. Funny thing about that.

Chateaugay's sire was Swaps, my first Derby winner. People said Chateaugay was the best among Swaps' offspring. Swaps gave me my first Derby and gave Chateaugay to racing, and then Chateaugay gave me a pain in the neck. Well, that's racing for you.

9

In 1964 I had all sorts of good things happen to me. Early in the year, at Santa Anita, I got on another horse owned by Mr. Ellsworth and trained by Mr. Tenney. The Texas kid with the bad teeth was approaching another record. I had started in racing as a $75 stablehand and now I was going after a record held by Eddie Arcaro. If I won that race, it would put me over the top. Only Arcaro had ridden horses that had won at least $30,000,000 in purses. Now it was my turn and I turned the trick.

Later that year, at Belmont Park I passed another milestone and rode my 5,000th winner. The horse I won on that day in New York was called Slapstick. Now only two riders in the world had ever had more than 5,000 winners. The other guy was Johnny Longden. Imagine, he had pushed me around a little bit in my first race at Golden Gate Fields back in 1949. In fifteen years, I had proved I wasn't a flash in the pan. Even then, when I was still only thirty-three, people began asking me how long I was going to ride. I said I was having too much fun to quit and I meant it.

Now, of course, people always ask me when I'm going to hang up my tack. I say, "Look, I'm not as good as I was at twenty-five, but I'm a lot better than a lot of twenty-five-year-old riders."

Back then, in 1964, giving up riding was not in the cards either. Babbs and I were spending money freely. She liked the good life and so did I, and the world for us was a shining place. Man, it was great; it was real great. In 1964, I was the leading rider in total purses for the year. That was the tenth time in a fifteen-year career. This had happened seven years in a row.

I think maybe I was getting too smart. That year disappointed Mr. Tenney and Mr. Ellsworth. I had a chance to ride Mr. E. P. Taylor's Northern Dancer. Mr. Taylor was a very rich Canadian who was big in racing. His horses were trained by Horatio Luro, a handsome dude from Argentina. I've got to interrupt now to tell a story about Mr. Luro. For a while he trained for Mrs. Elizabeth Arden Graham. She hired and fired more trainers than anybody in racing. She changed them as quick as it took a lady to powder her nose—with Elizabeth Arden's powder. One Sunday, before they ran races on Sundays, she phoned her trainer, Horatio Luro. He was very upset and with his slight accent told her, "Look, Mrs. Graham, on Monday, Tuesday, Wednesday, Thursday, Friday, and Saturday I train for you. On Sunday I make love. Goodbye." She did not fire Luro.

Everybody used to call him Señor Luro and everybody around racing respected him as a trainer. He wanted me to ride Northern Dancer in the 1964 Derby. I made a terrible bonehead call. Harry and I had already agreed to ride Hill Rise instead. I had won the

Florida Derby on Northern Dancer and the Santa Anita Derby on Hill Rise. I picked Hill Rise. Maybe I haven't told it right. The real reason I picked Hill Rise was that Mr. Tenney and Mr. Ellsworth had a horse called The Scoundrel that had finished second to Northern Dancer in the Florida Derby. They thought The Scoundrel could beat Northern Dancer the next time they met. Mesch Tenney kept telling this to Harry when Harry would come around the barn in the mornings, and Harry was putting pressure on me to make up my mind.

What I kind of knew was that Mr. Tenney and Mr. Ellsworth really didn't want to see me ride Northern Dancer, so they built an escape hatch for me. Mr. Tenney said, "Look, Bill, if you can get Hill Rise, go ahead. We think he's the best of the lot. But if you can't get Hill Rise, we'd rather have you ride The Scoundrel than Northern Dancer." So I rode Hill Rise. Going into the 1964 Derby, I thought Hill Rise was almost the best around. He might have been, too, but he didn't prove it in that Derby. Hartack beat me. He was riding Northern Dancer and he gave him a good ride. I came in second on Hill Rise. We got bumped going into the first turn and then went wide leaving the backstretch. But Hill Rise did beat The Scoundrel, with Manuel Ycaza up, by a good margin.

The Derby always produces problems, and a lot of Derby winners have not always been the best horse on that first Saturday in May. In 1965, I won my third Derby. I rode Lucky Debonair. He was a horse who took a long time developing. When the meeting at Santa Anita began after Christmas of 1964, he was still a

maiden. A maiden is a horse who has never won a race. But when that meeting at Santa Anita was over, Lucky Debonair had won the Santa Anita Derby. He had shin problems, and maybe that's why he didn't develop as quickly as he should have. When he got to the Derby, he was my ride. That year, Tom Rolfe was, in my opinion, the best horse at Churchill Downs.

Ron Turcotte rode Tom Rolfe. He was a Canadian jockey who got banged up in a race in New York years later and has been in a wheelchair ever since. He was an outstanding rider and a good guy to have around. The last time I was at Saratoga, for the 1987 Travers, I saw Ron in his wheelchair. He was smiling and you would never know that he had been in a wheelchair for that many years. Jockeys have guts. When I saw Turcotte, I couldn't help thinking of the 1965 Derby and his ride on Tom Rolfe.

In that Derby, Bobby Ussery, on Flag Raiser, got bumped early, but later on he took a clear lead. I was running second. We were a little off the rail, ready to drop into the turn, and suddenly we saw Turcotte on Tom Rolfe, trying to get in there fast to keep from getting cut off. I remember Ussery shouting over to me, "This sap's trying to get by on the inside. He's never going to make it." Ussery closed the hole on him. Tom Rolfe was running fast by then and Turcotte had to check him and move around. That didn't do Tom Rolfe any good. If Turcotte stayed in there and moved around on a smooth run, he might have won it himself. I thought a lot of Tom Rolfe. Later, Turcotte won the Derby twice, on Riva Ridge in 1972 and Secretariat the next year. It couldn't have happened to a nicer guy and a spunkier rider.

Three weeks later, just to prove that he might have been the best horse in the Derby, Tom Rolfe won the Preakness.

After the Belmont that year, I took Tom Rolfe to all those races in Chicago. He won them all. He was a pretty shifty little horse, small but with a lot of heart. He could beat almost everybody except the real top horses. He had his chance that fall when I rode him in Paris in the Arc de Triomphe at Longchamps. In France the horses run the wrong way. They go clockwise. In the United States, they run counterclockwise. Considering this, Tom Rolfe gave the Arc a good performance. Longchamp's up-and-down grass course was also tough for Tom Rolfe. What made it worse, they made him wear those flat French shoes. The shoes ended up making him slip all over the place.

I remember the Arc very well. It was the first time I had ridden over there and I laughed when we weighed in. The scale was like an old grocery scoop, the kind they used to weigh loose beans and stuff like that back in the old days. The jocks sat in it with their tack and got weighed. It was like being in a cradle, or almost like that. When I remember back to that now, I laugh. I remember Arcaro, when he was having problems making weight, standing on a scale with his tack cradled in his arms. He would reach up on the old scales and put a finger on the balancing bar, with the tack hiding his finger. That way he beat the scale a few times. But in France there was no way he could do it. Me, I never had a problem making weight. I weighed about 97. I think the heaviest I ever got was the time I told you about, when I was at the Suzy Q Ranch in La Puente, a kid eating three square meals a day. Then I

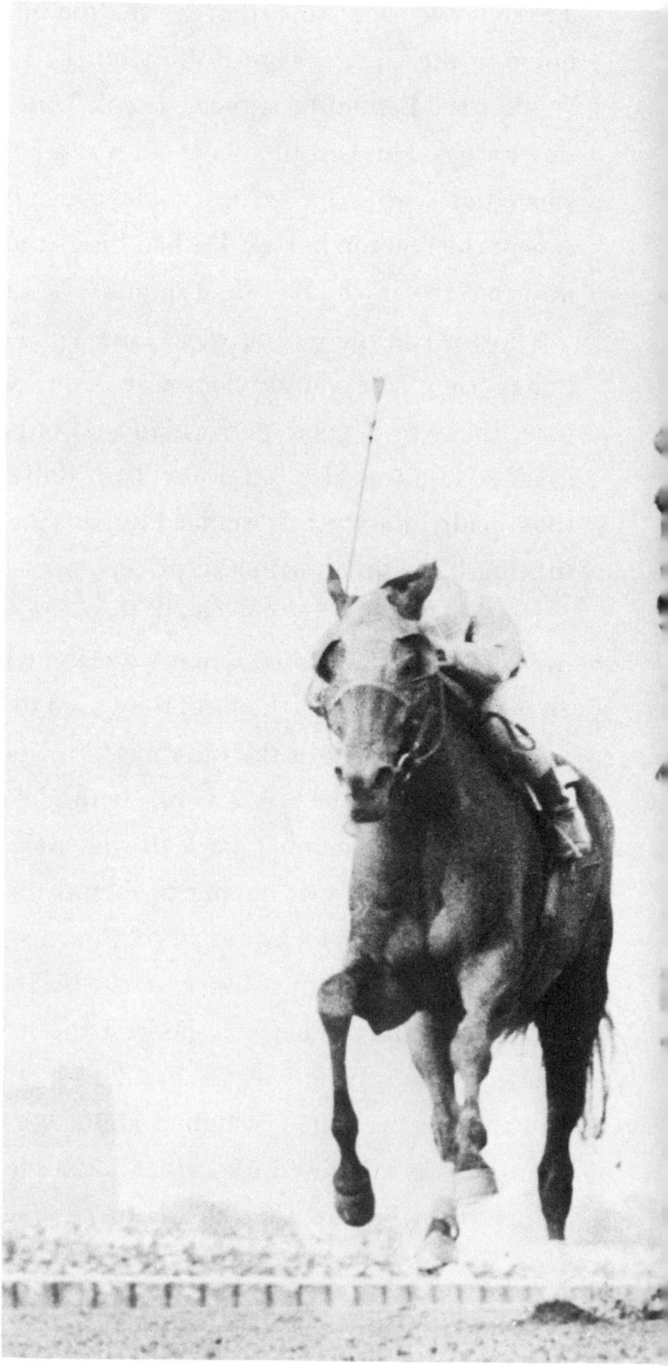

Aboard Damascus, winning the 1966 Aqueduct Stakes.

hit 100 or so. (Once when I was in Acapulco I decided to stay a couple of extra weeks and I think I got up to 103 that time.)

Tom Rolfe ran sixth in the Arc de Triomphe. Maybe he should have gotten third or fourth. He was going all right in the mile and a half race, going uphill after the start, but near the top something spooked him. He got rank with me. He took the bit in his mouth and he didn't want to make the right turn down the hill. I fought him hard and kept him maybe a dozen feet off the rail. This didn't help him. It was a tiring thing for him and yet, turning for home, after losing all that ground, he was right with the leaders. He was a game dude.

I liked that French experience with Tom Rolfe. I remember posing with Bing Crosby coming out of the riders' room. I knew Bing from Del Mar. He put money into it when they started the track. In Paris, Bing came only as a horse owner. He had a horse called Meadow Court in the Arc. The race was won by Sea Bird II. It was nice seeing Bing over there, but what I remember most about the Arc is that I learned a lot about how those French jockeys rode.

In French racing, they tend to bunch up their horses a lot closer than we do in America. What the French jockeys do is tuck their mounts in behind the horses as near to the rail as they can get, and they almost press right against each other all the way around. It's when they hit the stretch that they begin to fan out. The horses know this, and when they are moved out of the bunch heading into the stretch, the horses know that then they are expected to make a run for it.

I rode Lucky Debonair in the 1966 Santa Anita Handicap. I liked the colt and I liked his trainer. Frank Catrone was a little guy, maybe three or four inches taller than me, but there was a difference. He was as round as he was tall, a regular Mr. Five-by-Five. But he sure could train his horses. Lucky Debonair won the Santa Anita Derby, the Kentucky Derby, and the Santa Anita Handicap. Only a good horse in the right hands could do that.

Nineteen sixty-six wasn't a good one for me in total races won. I had only 221 winners, the lowest total since my first year as a rider back in 1949. But I did win some very big races. I did a lot of riding in New York that year, and while I was there, I started getting up mornings to work a colt named Damascus for Frank Whitely. You had to know Whitely to appreciate him. Some people said he was sour. Not me. I liked him, and I liked him mostly because he was a real horseman. When he said a horse was a good one, that horse had to be good or Mr. Whitely wouldn't talk about him. Damascus was owned by Mrs. Edith W. Bancroft. She was an important lady in racing. I won ten stakes races on Mrs. Bancroft's bay colt in 1967, and seven of them were hundred-granders. That was some year for Damascus. He won $817,941 and that was a money record for the time. He didn't win the Kentucky Derby, though.

In the 1967 Derby, we ran third to Proud Clarion, with Ussery in the irons. Damascus was more rank than he had ever been. Even in the saddling area, or going to the post, he just wasn't himself. And in the race, he took a great deal out of himself in the first half mile or so. By the time we turned for home, he had no finishing kick left. Ussery, on Proud Clarion, clearly had the best horse and beat Barbs Delight by a length. The race was a shocker. Damascus was a big favorite and never gave his backers a run for their money. But that was the last bad race he turned in for me.

After the Derby, he took everything that wasn't nailed down. He won the Preakness, the Belmont, and beat such great runners as Dr. Fager and Buckpasser in the Woodward by ten lengths. Those feats easily gave him horse-of-the-year honors.

The next year was a sad one for me. I was badly hurt in a fall at Santa Anita and didn't get to ride Damascus again. Later, he bowed a tendon and was retired from racing. He's still around, that wonderful old horse, doing stud duty. He deserves every bit of fun he can get.

10

Up to this point I have been lucky in my career. A few falls, some sprains and scraped shins, but nothing much more than that. It's not much to pay, because people say I'm the most successful rider in the 200-year history of thoroughbred racing. It's 1968 and I'm thirty-seven years of age and I've been riding for nineteen years. In those years I've racked up a lot of victories. I don't count how many. I leave that to other people, and if I looked in the records, I would see that by January 1968, I have had 5,785 wins. The record also shows that by this time I have won the Kentucky Derby three times. Horses I've ridden have won more than $40,000,000 in purses. Each year I make money in the six figures, and I'm living in luxury with my second wife, Babbs, and my adopted son, Mitchell, in Beverly Hills. All the rich dudes live there.

Going down off a horse is bad news. You go down and you try to roll into a tight ball, and for nineteen years my luck's held. I still remember riding Dutch Wife. She was trained by Buster Millerick and I'm on her in a seven-furlong race. I'm in the post

nearest the fence and I get to the lead quickly. We get to the gap the horses come through when they come on the track and Dutch Wife kind of goes left. I'm looking the other way, clocking the field to the outside, and I'm not paying attention to Dutch Wife. It's right then when I go flying, hit the dirt, and roll underneath the rail. Dutch Wife goes down and hits a support post, and we wind up together on the other side of the fence in the infield. I'm right on the horse's belly, in between her legs. She's already dead. I think, What the hell's going on? I'm sore, but I don't have any broken bones. I'm safe, I'm okay.

I think, when they come to get me, that all jockeys are crazy. But jockeys, well, they are the luckiest athletes of all. How can I think anything else? The next day I'm back in the saddle.

I'm riding Candy Spots in the 1963 Santa Anita Derby and we're going around the first turn. I'm tucked in behind the first flight of horses. Maybe five are in front of me and I'm not too far behind. The jockey on Tourlourou is Hank Moreno and as he begins to move up, his horse bolts and hits me. The force knocks me to the outside. Milo Valenzuela's mount, Win-Em-All, clips the heels of his stablemate, Sky Gem. Down he goes. Three other horses wind up in a tangle. I am lucky. When Moreno's horse knocks me out of the way, he saves me. Otherwise, I might have gone right over the top of the tangle of horses and riders. I win the race on Candy Spots, you bet. I win a race that I could have been killed in.

On the twenty-third day of January, 1968, I'm not even thinking of a spill. After a spill, a jockey tries to put it far back in his

mind. I talk to Harry a little bit about it. It isn't going to happen to me again. I'm the lucky one. The other jocks have something to worry about. One day, I get lucky three times. I'm riding three horses that day at Santa Anita and all three go down with broken legs. Each time I pull up without going off my horse. I think, What's next?

Danger is always there on the racetrack, even in the mornings. In the old days, I used to gallop an old mare named Gallahue. It was so far back in my career, George Reeves had Gallahue. Every morning, at one spot, she'd stop on her own and go the other way. That was her danger spot and she knew it. I always thought she'd look at me when she propped and say something like, "You silly bastard, I got you again." Jockeys also have spots like that. When a jockey has an accident at a certain spot, he thinks about it every time he comes to that spot. Maybe he even prays when he's going by the spot, hoping that he gets by without an accident.

With this Gallahue that I've mentioned, it isn't funny. I'm galloping her at the old Tanforan track one morning and she runs off with me. She's running out toward the rail and I'm trying to shake the bit in her mouth, figuring that way she might change her mind. It doesn't work. I am off balance and I go down off Gallahue and land on my back in the middle of the track at old Tanforan.

I am down for a long time. It seems like hours, but it probably was minutes. It just seems long. I feel paralyzed from the waist down. I have a real pain in the back, but pretty soon that is gone and I am able to get up. Nobody comes to help me, so I just walk back to the barn.

The year I rode Swaps in the Derby, I fell off a horse leaving the gate in a race. I went to the hospital for X rays and the doctor said, "Do you know you once had a broken vertebra?" I said, "Who, me?" Then I remember old Gallahue and that day at old Tanforan. Gallahue was a temperamental old bitch, I remember, but I smile. After all, I won a lot of races on her.

Early in 1968 I win two big stakes races on Damascus. I'm thinking he is a cinch for the Strub Stakes two weeks later. But then, on January 26, it happens. I'm riding a horse called Bel Bush at Santa Anita. My pal Don Pierce is on the right, just outside me, on a horse called Top Floor. I am looking ahead. There's an apprentice, Juan Gonzalez, on Kodiak Kid. He thinks he sees an opening, but it's just not there. He's inexperienced and he heads for the hole he thinks he sees. I yell, "Hey, don't do that. Don't go in there, don't go in there." Pierce happens to be looking to the outside. He hears me and he turns around. By this time, Gonzalez is down.

If Pierce had been looking toward me, he might have had a chance to go outside and maybe I could have gone outside after him. By the time Pierce comes back in my direction, Kodiak Kid has clipped the heels of the horse running in front of him and is down. That's when Pierce really sees what is happening. He wheels out, but I am in a trap. Gonzalez has caused all this by trying to go where he shouldn't have gone. He is only a bug rider and lots of kids do things like that sometimes. This time it causes

a lot of trouble. I am caught in the middle. I go right off my horse and he goes down, and while he is trying to get up, he hits my right thigh and breaks my right femur. I am out for a few seconds. All the other times I've been down, I've gotten up on my own. But not this time.

The ambulance comes up to get me and they take me to Arcadia Methodist Hospital. That's just down the road from Santa Anita, across Huntington Drive. Pretty soon they move me to Daniel Freeman Hospital in Inglewood, clear across town near Hollywood Park. I'm a lucky man, but not as lucky as Gonzalez, the bug boy. He got away in that race without a scratch. His luck doesn't hold. Seven years later he was killed in a spill at a track in Pleasanton, California.

Dr. Robert Kerlan is my friend. He's one of the best orthopedic doctors in the country. He brings Dr. Frank Jobe in on my case. Dr. Jobe handles a lot of the pro teams around Los Angeles. They look at the X rays and decide that the only thing to do to repair my broken right thigh is to insert a metal pin into the marrow of the femur. That's what they call my broken bone in medical lingo. There is one problem, though, and they don't tell me about it. I hear about it later. Dr. Kerlan has to search high and low in the hospital supply room for a metal pin that is the right size for my thigh. He finally finds one in the children's department.

They insert the pin into the marrow of my broken thigh and wait for it to heal. Harry comes around every day to see me. Babbs does, too, and when the reporters from the papers and TV come around, they interview her, too. She is busy doing needle-

Getting back into shape after my 1968 spill. I couldn't ride for a year after that.

point most of the time. That gives her the domestic look. For a sophisticated lady, that's something different. I'm going crazy in the hospital. It's no fun, and it's no fun either when they tell me that because the femur is the longest and strongest bone in the body, it takes longer to heal.

It's three weeks before they wheel me out of the hospital. I go back to my apartment in the Sierra Towers. I make a promise to myself. I'm not going to be a sour ball. When people are around, I keep smiling. I have a lot of time to think and I realize that I might never ride another horse. My right leg is knitting, but the inactivity has done something to it. The muscles have deteriorated and the leg has withered. The thigh is about as big around as a Coke bottle. I think to myself, I'll never ride again. Look at this leg. But I never lose hope, not deep inside. I don't ever tell Babbs or Harry what I am thinking.

Dr. Kerlan is a big help. He keeps encouraging me, telling me I'll get back to normal and that I'll be as good as new. I have my doubts, but nature has a way of making people forget after a while. I hobble around on crutches. I lift weights. Mornings, before the town gets up, I walk on Sunset Boulevard. The exercise is good for me. I begin riding a stationary bike. Later, I begin running. It is thirteen months before I return to the scene of the crime, the track. On February 11, 1969, I am back riding at Santa Anita.

Harry gets three rides for me on that day. Two of the horses are owned by Liz Whitney Tippett. She owns Llangollen Farm and is a grand lady of the turf. The two horses I ride for her my

first day back are a filly named Princess Endeavor in the seven-furlong sixth race and a bay horse named Racing Room, in the eighth race. Charlie Whittingham trained both horses for Liz. I feel I am among friends. For my third ride Harry has booked Jay's Double.

Babbs is with me this day and so is Mitchell. It is Tuesday and they have a good crowd at Santa Anita. The fans give me a good hand when I come into the saddling area to mount Princess Endeavor. I feel great. Then I hear a fan yell, "She's going to bump you off!" I think, They never change.

Now I'm in the gate and I'm thinking only of the race, fillies and mares, four-year-olds and upward, going seven furlongs out of the chute. I'm back in action. Princess Endeavor gets off alertly. I feel comfortable on her. We settle down behind the leaders, save ground in the stretch, and my mount responds when I call for her to go into her drive. We wear down the leaders and win by two-and-a-quarter lengths. The Shoe is fit again, I think. I go back to the winner's circle, and Liz is there with Charlie, and so is Babbs, and we all pose for pictures.

For the eighth race, I'm on Racing Room. He's a son of Restless Wind. I remember the sire because I rode him a lot. He was as fast as his name and he gave me some very good rides. Now I'm riding his five-year-old son. Racing Room runs a good race, but I have to whack him left-handed while moving toward the rail at the furlong pole. We win going away. That's two in a row. I think to myself, I'm really back.

Now it's the ninth race, the last one on the program. I'm on Jay's Double. We have a nice ride. It is close all the way, but we win. I am tired and tense. When I get home to the apartment, I cry just a little, but I'm back.

11

I want to tell you something right now about trainers, and I've worked for the best. Harry always went for the top horses, and the top horses are usually in the hands of the best trainers. I always got along with trainers. They deserve a lot of credit for the shape of all the horses I've been on over the years. Don't get me wrong, all trainers are not great. Some of them send horses out when they're not fit and I've been on a few of those. I've gone to the gate with a horse and then reported to the stewards that the horse wasn't right. When that happened, the horse was scratched from the race. That's only fair to the horse and the fans betting on him.

When I think of all the trainers I've worked for, I think of some great men. I'm going to get in trouble here. Sure as hell, I'm going to leave a lot of guys out and they're going to say, "Hey, Shoe, you forgot me." I can't mention them all. The list would fill a book.

I've got to tell you about Charlie Whittingham first. I like Charlie outside racing too. He's a big old bear, but he knows how to laugh at himself. And he knows all about life. When I talk about retiring, he says, "Hey, Shoe, you know what a jockey is when he's retired? He's just another little man." He says that and he laughs, and he gets that sly little look that puts creases around his eyes and mouth. If you ask him, he'll tell you a toast he always associates with a horseman life. It goes, "Fast horses and beautiful women are the two things I love best, and when I die, I hope from my hide they make a side saddle so I'll always rest next to the two things I love best—fast horses and beautiful women."

Charlie always gives you the toast with a smile. Every time he does, I think about it. It's not a bad idea. Reporters and television people are always asking Charlie about me. He makes believe he is amazed. He says, "What can you say about Shoe that hasn't been said before?" Then he says, "Shoe has the disposition of a great athlete. He can ride every type of horse, on grass or dirt. And when he's got the lead, forget it. He'll trick you with that pace and will always have a little left at the finish."

No wonder I'm crazy about Charlie. You've got to like a guy when he goes all out for you. I don't remember when I first met Charlie. Maybe it was when I went back to New York in 1951 for my first ride there. Charlie's a Californian, but he spent a few years training in New York. He says he remembers me, but I don't remember him from back in those days. I remember a lot of other trainers. John Nerud was around then. He was one of the great trainers. So was Preston Burch. He helped me prove that

dead weight isn't a handicap to a rider who has perfect control over his balance.

Mr. Burch's son, Elliott, called me after my thirteen-month layoff. He had a horse called Arts and Letters going in the 1969 Florida Derby and said he wanted me to ride the colt. Harry said, "Shoe, let's go. I like that Ribot colt, and we like Elliott, so we'll ride him." We figured Arts and Letters would win in Florida. But a real good horse called Top Knight, with Ycaza riding, beat us by five lengths.

Arts and Letters wasn't easy to ride. He had a mind of his own and ran the way he wanted to. He had the idea the jockey was just along for the ride. So we got beat, but I thought a lot of the horse.

I thought I knew how to get the most out of him. I went to Keeneland for the Blue Grass. The Blue Grass is really a test for the Kentucky Derby. I remembered how Arts and Letters ran in the Florida Derby. Around the first turn, I had him in a strong hold, but when we got into the backstretch, I gave him his head. He could accelerate in a flash and proved it right there. He went to the lead by five lengths and was the best at the wire by fifteen lengths. I thought, This dude can't miss winning the Derby.

The 1969 Derby was scheduled for May 3. On the Wednesday before the Derby, Harry got me a ride on a filly named Poona's Day at Hollywood Park.

Nothing exciting about that. It's just another ride. The filly's trainer is Lou Glauberg, a friend of Harry's. It's the fourth race on the card, six furlongs for three-year-old filly maidens. When a rider climbs into the saddle, it is the trainer who gives him a leg

With Chuck Whittingham and Liz Whitney Tippett, just before my comeback aboard Princess Endeavor on February 11, 1969.

up. Suddenly Poona's Day starts flipping over backward. Instead of letting me go, so I can jump off, Glauberg tries to help me by hanging on to me. I'm trapped under the horse. I wind up in the shrubs against the cement wall circling the saddling area. I'm knocked out. I'm hurt. I'm hurt real bad.

They move me to the dispensary at the track. Harry is with me and he puts in a call to Babbs. She takes it hard. Harry tells her it's not the leg with the metal pin in it but that it's something worse. They take me to Centinela Hospital and Harry rides in the ambulance with me. At the hospital, they strip away my pants, which are soaked in blood. They call Dr. Kerlan and he tells them to move me to Daniel Freeman Hospital. I'm back where I was fifteen months ago. They x-ray my entire body. The X rays show that my pelvis is broken and that I have a dislocation of the left sacroiliac joint. My pelvis is splintered in five places, my bladder is ruptured, and my left leg is paralyzed. The pain is the worst I've ever felt.

They put me on the operating table and they operate. It takes Dr. Kerlan two and a half hours. I didn't even know that Poona's Day, the horse that had hurt me, runs in her race anyway. They put a new boy on her. Danny Velazquez tries his best but Poona's Day finishes twelfth and last. When the people around the barns hear about my accident, they shake their heads and say, "Hey, poor Shoe, he's finished. He'll never make it out of the hospital to the jockeys' room again."

They put a catheter in my penis. It helps me to urinate. The damage is pretty bad. I feel nothing but pain. I think, Hey, my days as a lover are over. In the jocks' room, my pals pray for a miracle because they are saying that only a miracle will let me ever ride again. If I ever get back, it'll take six months, maybe a year. They don't know Shoe and they don't know anything about medicine. Dr. Kerlan comes to my room in the hospital and talks to me a lot. He talks to me about guts. He says when they handed out courage, I got a lot of it.

What I really worry about is my ability to ever ride again. At first I think I am through, that the grooms and the hotwalkers are right when they say I'll never make it back. Dr. Kerlan tells me I'll have to do a lot of therapy before I ride again. He says running is important. He knows what I have to do to get fit again. I listen carefully. I never become mean or sour.

The first Saturday I'm in the hospital, Arts and Letters runs in the Derby. He gets beat by Majestic Prince. The difference is a neck. Braulio Baeza rides Arts and Letters for Elliott Burch. He gives the colt a good ride, but in the stretch Arts and Letters tires. Majestic Prince comes on to win in a game race.

As soon as I get out of the hospital, I start thinking about getting back to racing again. I work hard. In the morning, I go out to Hollywood Park and jog around the empty track. It gives me time to think. I think that two bad accidents in fifteen months might make some guys take the hint. Not me. I'm going to ride again and I know it. The odds are against me, but I'm not walking away. The next time the ambulance might be too late. What am I going to prove by getting on a horse again? I've had maybe

twenty-five thousand mounts by then. When is it enough? When does a jock's time come?

After a while, my muscles seem stronger to me. Nature is working for me and I feel better. Marje Lindheimer Everett convinces me I'd be better off in Chicago. I go out there and begin exercising horses in the morning—six, seven horses every morning. I start getting my timing back. On the day I finally get back into action, I don't win on three mounts like I did the first day back after I broke my right leg. But I'm not worried. I am thirty-eight years old now and time is still on my side.

12

The 1970 meeting at Santa Anita is important to me. The San Gabriel Mountains in the background have snow on their peaks, but the weather is great. I'm not so great. I am not getting winners the way they used to come. My back is hurting me and the people watching me ride say I've lost something. My seat is different. Charlie says to me, "Hey, Shoe, what's wrong?" I say there's nothing wrong, I feel as good as I've ever felt. But maybe I'm lying a little. I'm not as graceful as I used to be, and that winter, at Santa Anita, I can't seem to ever find the wire.

Then, out of nowhere, it all comes back to me. I feel myself riding closer to the inside rail. I see holes when the speed goes wide, and I go through them. Now the other jockeys aren't winning those close finishes I used to win. I really feel good again.

The whispers stop. Maybe Harry is right. He used to say in our early days, "What are you worrying about, Shoe? We're still moving up. It's when you're sliding down that you have to worry." That winter is the first time in seventeen years that I don't win

the riding championship at Santa Anita. That doesn't bother me. I mean, heck, I've got plenty of records. What's another one? Well, one other one is very important to me. It's the one Johnny Longden owns. Most lifetime victories. The number is 6,032. Longden isn't riding anymore. He's training now, and when Majestic Prince wins the Derby, Johnny is taking bows in the winner's circle.

Longden got his 6,032d win on George Royal in the San Juan Capistrano Handicap back in 1967. It was his last ride. Many of his early victories came on the old bush tracks of Canada. His record for the most winning rides was his proudest. We used to talk about that a lot in the jocks' room. But at Santa Anita Park, in 1969, I'm not thinking of Longden and his record. All I was concerned with is getting back my timing and healing my back. Pretty soon, they both improve. Then, I know that I'm really back. Now the papers are full of stories about my going after Longden's record of 6,032 wins. People ask which horse will I be on when I break the record. I shrug my shoulders. I think, Who knows?

On June 24, 1970—how can I forget the date—I'm really back at the top of my game. I'm riding at Hollywood Park and I boot home six winners, the first time I've turned the trick in seventeen years. When Hollywood's season is over, the horsemen move down the coast to Del Mar. We take a house on the ocean front and I take long morning walks with Babbs. Sometimes Mitchell joins us. It's been twenty years since the first time I came to Del Mar. That's a lot of lead in my saddlebag.

In the afternoons, there is work to be done. The adding machines are working overtime. There is a lot of noise being made about my going after Longden's record. On Saturday afternoon, September 5, 1970, I tie Longden's record. I get my 6,032d win on a horse called Esquimal in the ninth race. The excitement is really beginning to build. It's like Joe DiMaggio's fifty-six-game hitting streak. It's all a lot of nonsense, but it's history. The sportswriters are all over the place. TV people bring their gear down to Del Mar. The press gang gets so big, they have to put a guard rail on top of the roof to make sure the TV cameras don't fall off.

On Labor Day, Harry gets me seven rides. He wants to make sure I'll ride at least one winner to break Longden's record. I ride the filly Dares J. in the fourth race, an allowance at six furlongs for two-year-old fillies. She goes off at even money. The track is fast and there's a field of seven going after a purse of $5,500. Dares J. breaks on top and she wins by two-and-a-half lengths. She pays $4.20.

Afterward in the winner's circle, they drape a blanket of white carnations over my shoulder. THE CHAMP, it says. It's my 6,033d win. Johnny Longden is there and we shake hands. The winner's circle is jammed with photographers, jockeys, track officials, friends. Babbs is there, and so is Harry, and Longden is asked to speak. He says, "Well, it's a great day for Bill. I held it for fourteen years and I know it is going to be a hell of a lot longer before they break it again." He's still a feisty little guy. He doesn't let it rest there. Longden says, "I think it took a good man to make this record and it took a damn good guy to break it." The TV cameras and press photographers are there. When they are around, can Babbs be far behind? I wonder what I'm going to say. They give me a gold cup for setting the record. I say something about how much I owe to Longden. Everybody knows that if he hadn't set the record, there'd be no record to break. "I'm glad," I say, "that I could win today's race in Longden's style, in front all the way."

What I didn't say was something that everyone knew that day at Del Mar. It took Longden forty years to set his record. I broke it in my twenty-second year as a jockey. That sounds like more than it is. He rode in another time, on little country tracks, and they didn't run nine races a day then, the way they have during most of my career. So don't let the time difference fool you.

I will never be able to get Longden out of my shadow. If you go to Santa Anita any hour of the day, you can see both of us there cast in bronze. In April 1971, they unveiled a bust of me close to a bronze bust of Longden. When Bob Strub, who runs Santa Anita, was finished speaking, they asked me to say something. I said, "I think it's appropriate that John and I should be looking at each other, because in the past we've looked at each other in a lot of different ways." Just think of it. Johnny Longden tried to take advantage of me in my very first race as a jockey and now we were together in bronze, forever.

That year of the dedication of the bronze busts, I broke Bill Hartack's record for the most stakes wins in one year. In 1957, Hartack rode forty-three stakes winners. I set my record with forty-six stakes wins. I was lucky. I had great horses to ride and

Charlie had helped me. Horses he trained gave me twenty-nine of those stakes victories. He trained Ack Ack, the horse of the year, and Turkish Trousers, the champion three-year-old filly that season. He also had Cougar II in his barn. I want to tell you more about Cougar II later on.

Right now, I want to get into the business of records. I didn't think much about breaking records. I didn't aim for them. They just came along. In 1972, I rode enough stakes winners to raise my career total to 577. Along the way, that broke Eddie Arcaro's career record of 554.

But I must go back to Charlie Whittingham for a moment. Talking about stakes victories, Charlie has trained more stakes-winning horses than anybody in the world. But that's not why he is my man. We just make racetrack music together. We agree on horses and how they should be run, and it makes a neat and tidy package.

In the early days, owners always wanted The Shoe to handle their horses. Harry knew that, and he never let the trainers forget it. If there was no job in one barn, then Harry would go to another and get a job for me. Later on, some owners didn't even want me on their horses. If a man's been around a quarter of a century, it figures that somebody is going to say, "Hey, don't you think this guy is getting a little long in the tooth? Can't we get a younger rider?"

In 1973, Mary F. Jones had Cougar II in Charlie's barn. I rode him to several stakes victories and we fit each other, but when the Hollywood Gold Cup came up in 1973, Mary Jones said she didn't

want me to ride him. She asked Charlie to go get Laffit Pincay. It didn't bother me. She thought Pincay was a better rider and, hey, he could have been. He's a great rider, right up there with the best there ever was. Charlie was upset. He was so nervous about it, he couldn't find the words to tell me and Harry about Mary Jones' request for Pincay.

When Charlie finally told us, I said, "Hey, that's her privilege. She doesn't want me, fine. I'll get another ride. I'll go on anything else you have in the race. If there's nothing for me here, I'll go look in another barn." Harry put on his sad face. Nobody could look sadder than Harry if things weren't going the way he thought they should be going. He was with me 1,000 percent. In a minute, Harry was smiling again. Charlie said, "You'll ride Kennedy Road for me." Kennedy Road was a good horse owned by Mrs. A. W. Stollery, a Canadian lady.

Going into the race I thought that my pal Don Pierce, on Quack, had the best shot. Not that Kennedy Road didn't have the ability. He did, but he was an in-and-outer. Temperamental, they called him, but when he was right, he could run like a scared hare. He was right for the Hollywood Gold Cup.

I had a great ride on Kennedy Road. He shook off Quack's bid and then went on to win. Cougar II ran third. I got a big kick out of Kennedy Road's win. On the wall over the commode in the den powder room in our house in San Marino is a blowup of the chart of the 1973 Hollywood Gold Cup. Anybody standing at the john can read it. It shows clearly that Kennedy Road, with Bill Shoemaker up, caught up with Quack and won the Gold Cup. I had

the last laugh, but I didn't laugh in public. Every time I go into the den powder room at home now, I look at the blow-up of the chart from *Daily Racing Form* and laugh. There, nobody is around to laugh with me.

In my book, things that happen always happen for the best. I don't believe in predestination, but I do know I'm a fatalist. Not that I have a what-the-hell attitude. Some things happen and there's nothing that I can do about them. I think Charlie's the same way. He owned a half interest in Cougar II. When he had the argument with Mary Jones, he told her to take Cougar II out of his barn. When they made up, Mrs. Bradley bought back Charlie's half interest in the horse. Cougar II went on to earn $1,151,476 under Charlie's training. Somebody asked Charlie about that during the week before Ferdinand's Derby. Charlie set his felt hat back on his head, looked at the one who had asked him the question, and said, "Pretty expensive mad, wasn't it?"

Around the time of Cougar II's differences, I was having real differences with Babbs too. She was deep into the social grind. There were parties to go to and people I didn't know and didn't really care about hanging around. I didn't like it a bit and I started to rebel. Mitchell was into his hippie bit and that wasn't easy to take either. The handwriting was on the bedroom wall. I knew Babbs and I weren't going to last much longer.

Funny thing about that. The trouble at home sure didn't affect my riding. In 1973, my mounts helped me get past $50,000,000 in earnings. That doesn't mean I earned that much. The horses I rode won that. The best I could get out of it was around

$5,000,000, but that ain't too bad. I only get 10 percent off the winning rides and a straight riding fee for the others, so I can't be real sure of this figure. A lot of it was gone. Taxes, alimony, and being good to people took most of what was left. Don't get me wrong. I wasn't broke, but I wasn't as rich as some people thought.

The number of rides I had in 1973 was way down. I rode only 639 times and won only 139. That was my lowest number since the year after I broke my leg. I wasn't worried because I knew the rides would come. And I knew something else.

For years I had been playing tennis down at La Costa, near Del Mar. A very pretty girl named Cynthia Barnes was one of the other players down there. When I first met her, she was eighteen. That was twenty years ago. She was tall, five-ten, and she had ash-blond hair and blue-green eyes. I always look at the eyes. It tells a lot about a person. My eyes are blue-gray. I'm farsighted in one, nearsighted in the other, but let me tell you, both of my eyes were on that girl.

Everybody called her Cindy. She lived in Cardiff-by-the-Sea, down by Del Mar, and all that I knew about her was that she was a real good tennis player and that her father had graduated from West Point. He had been a brigadier general in the Army. She was just one of the gang that played around La Costa and sometimes I'd play tennis with her. She had a lot of friends and was into horses. Her father had been in the cavalry and she jumped horses, and that's something I liked about her.

I think maybe that was what was wrong with my marriage to

Setting a new record of 6,033 wins at the Del Mar Thoroughbred Club in 1970.

Babbs. That and a lot of other things, but one of the worst things about our marriage was that Babbs really didn't like horses. She liked the idea of socializing around the racetrack, but when it came to horses, she could either take them or leave them. No, that's not right. As a matter of fact, she was allergic to horses. I mean real allergic. When I'd come home from a day's work at the track, she would make me take my clothes off immediately and take a shower. She just couldn't stand the odor of horses.

I was in a riding slump about then, and looking back, I have to think that was one time when I really thought about quitting. That wasn't surprising. In 1973, I was forty-two years old. That age may be great for a guy practicing law, but for a jockey it's beyond middle age, especially after twenty-four years of riding. A lot of people who used to greet me with a smile now walked the other way when I came around. The only one I discussed it with was myself. I'd stand in front of the mirror naked and look at myself, and think, Hey, how about that little belly you've got? That doesn't mean you're not in the best shape of your career. What it means is you're not fit, not really fit. And you're not riding at your best. Maybe it's time to hang it up, but the argument always went against quitting. I stayed with my tack. I began to take better care of myself and I cut down on the whiskey and on parties, and I went on a diet.

Pretty soon the little belly got flatter. This made me feel better about myself, and better about the way things were working out. I went to see Dr. Kerlan and he put me into something called the National Athletic Health Institute. In the testing there, I landed

in the top 10th percentile of mature athletes in power, endurance, and muscle strength. I tested twenty-five years younger than I was. You know who else was tested at the same time? There was Wilt Chamberlain, my old friend from the Los Angeles Lakers, Ron Cey, who was with the Dodgers, Dennis Harrah, who was with the Los Angeles Rams, and John Walker, a great mile runner. I felt I had a lot of years of riding left in me. My family was full of people who lived a long time. That was also on my side. I started feeling better about a lot of things.

While things weren't going any better at home, they began going a lot better on the track. And I thought, Hell, Longden rode until he was fifty-nine and I'm a lot younger. I had no beef. When I was winning 485 races a year, which I did back in 1953, I was riding a lot more than I rode twenty years later. I'd win three or four a day, and no matter who you are or how you think you are, that gets kind of monotonous. You start thinking, Hey, another race, another victory. Boring, isn't it? But when you are older and the mounts and the victories are few and far between, you start wondering about that.

Besides, I wasn't the big shot I once was. The long layoffs when I was hurt didn't help. Other riders came along and made a name for themselves. Now, Harry was finding that trainers didn't want Shoe the way they used to. They wanted younger riders because they thought younger riders had more get-up-and-go. They didn't reckon with the fact that experience keeps a dear school and boy did I have the experience. I could think a lot better and a lot faster than a lot of the other riders. That's what pulled me out of my slump. That, and Charlie. He never lost his faith in me.

In 1974 I won three races worth $100,000 or more with a horse called Agitate. It was a good year for stakes victories. Out of Charlie's barn I got Miss Musket and she won three for me, including the $100,000 Fantasy Stakes. Charlie also let me ride Tree of Knowledge. The Hollywood Gold Cup that year carried $150,000 in added money. That year, Charlie put Miss Musket into a three-year-old match race with Chris Everet, the three-year-old filly champion, but we didn't win. My luck wasn't up, though.

13

At this point you must think that I haven't got much fun out of life. That's not the truth. I know how to laugh and I know how to laugh at myself. That's the real good thing about me. I like to be funny and to make people laugh, and it doesn't bother me if they're laughing at me.

I remember the 1965 Kentucky Derby, the one I won with Lucky Debonair. The night before the Derby, I went out to a party where I had to wear a tuxedo. After the party, while we were going back to the hotel, a friend who had a horse at Churchill Downs said, "Let's go to the track and you work my horse."

It was four-thirty in the morning, just before Churchill Downs lights up with horses coming to work out on the track. I was nuts, but a dare is a dare, and I accepted my friend's invitation. I was still in my tuxedo. What bothered me was the cold; it must have been forty degrees out there. So, with my tux still on, I went to the track and worked my friend's horse, only hours before I had to ride Lucky Debonair. I didn't know how fast my friend's horse worked, with me on him in a tuxedo, but that afternoon Lucky Debonair went 2:01.2 to win the ninety-first Derby.

When I was in the hospital after my bad accidents, Dr. Kerlan used to find me in pretty good humor whenever he came around. Later, he told people that I was fun to be around. "His word is absolute and dependable," Dr. Kerlan said. That's nice. It's nice to hear, even if it might not be true. What Dr. Kerlan said was that I was of "a school that says, 'If you lose your head, your butt goes, too.' "

I didn't lose my head over the way things were going at home. Babbs and I were together, but I wasn't happy. We were still going to all the parties and I was going along with the gag. But I had my best times when I was out on the golf course or playing tennis with people like Don Klosterman, who ran things for the Los Angeles Rams, and Ricardo Montalban. I played a lot of tennis, especially down at La Costa, when they were running at Del Mar.

Cindy Barnes showed me a lot about that area of California that I didn't know before. She grew up there, in Cardiff-by-the-Sea. She used to talk about it a lot, how the area was changing from what it had been in her younger days. She loved the outdoors. She liked to ride, and she jumped horses, but what she liked about growing up near Del Mar, in Cardiff, was the freedom it gave the kids. There were trails on which to ride and they led down to the sea.

Riding can be a lot of fun, even for a jockey. I've never considered riding hard work. When I was a kid, I used to laugh at guys

who said it was a tough game and hard to do. I thought it was the easiest game I ever got into in my life. I often think about the first big week I ever had, when I won seven races. That week was fun, real fun, and it wasn't the money that made it so great. It was just riding and winning. What a thrill it was for me, just seventeen years old at the time.

I once met a man who had that same feeling about riding. He was Ronald Reagan and he was the governor of California then. We met at Hollywood Park and we talked, and I think we talked about how much fun riding was. He had some horses. I don't remember much about them, because I never rode them. Then he became the President and we lost touch.

I also once met a king. When Gerald Ford was the President, he invited me to a formal White House dinner. I went with Babbs. King Hussein of Jordan was the guest of honor and he liked horses so he had asked that I get an invitation to the dinner. He said he knew about me as a rider and we hit it off pretty good. I don't meddle in politics. Sometimes I vote Democrat, sometimes Republican. I vote for the man, not the party, and I don't want anybody thinking I liked Hussein because he was the King of Jordan. I found him a nice guy and we talked, and that's about all there was to that.

That dinner at the White House might have been the last big party I went to with Babbs. By then, our party was pretty much over though. I kept riding right through a difficult divorce. Babbs made it tough on me. When the divorce was finally settled, she asked for a lot of money from me, and she got it. Cindy said she

Coming off another victory aboard Damascus. I'm in a muddy infield here with Frank Whitely.

admired me more for working the way I always did through that tough divorce period.

Those were difficult days. I wasn't getting the classic horses I used to get. Still, in 1975, my mounts earned $3,514,213. I had 215 winners that year, and right in the middle of all my difficult time with Babbs, I got a big thrill riding a colt called Avatar. He was a California horse owned by Arthur A. Seeligson, a Texan. In the Derby, he should have had a real shot, but he was bumped by Diablo, another California colt. Right while this was happening, Foolish Pleasure went by us in the stretch to win it. In the Preakness, Avatar couldn't handle the track at Pimlico and finished fifth. Off we went to New York and the Belmont Stakes. I had won it four times before, on Gallant Man, Sword Dancer, Jaipur, and Damascus. I wanted to win another. The way it turned out, it was one great day for Avatar and for me. Avatar had good position all the way around. In the upper stretch, he got in front and then held off Foolish Pleasure by a neck. I had my fifth Belmont Stakes and Avatar had beaten the Derby winner to get it for me.

I was seeing Cindy Barnes regularly by 1977. My romance with her hadn't started out that way. Tennis brought us together and for many years I just saw her on the tennis court at La Costa. We weren't dating, or anything like that, but I always thought she was nice.

It was just a friendship thing in the beginning. We played tennis and we knew a lot of people in common. Our first fifteen dates, maybe more, it would be Cindy and eight or nine of my pals. We'd all go out and do something together. I was never alone

with her. I was sitting at one end of the table and she was down at the other end.

I doubt that I charmed her, but we had one thing in common—horses. She had won more blue ribbons than I had won big races. For this alone, I liked her. We used to laugh a lot. Cindy was smart and we talked a lot, and I was in love.

She told me about her father, Brig.-Gen. Wallace Hayden Barnes. He was born in St. Joseph, Missouri, in 1903, but his family moved to Idaho, where he attended high school in Boise and prep school in Moscow. He was appointed to West Point from Idaho in 1926, and when he graduated four years later, he ranked high in his class. He had been in the 10th Cavalry at Fort Huachuca, Arizona, and later, in World War II, served with the 10th Armored Division in England, France, and Germany. After the war, he met Elisabeth M. Annyas. She was Dutch and beautiful, and the first time I saw her I couldn't take my eyes off her. Cindy's mother and father were married in The Hague, Holland, on October 25, 1947. Almost three years later, Cynthia Elisabeth was born.

Cindy was as beautiful as her mother. I was head over heels in love. I was paying Babbs a bundle each month in alimony. She had made a big score in court. That lasted ten years until December 1987. I asked Cindy to come live with me. She said it was a tempting offer.

When Cindy told her mother about us, Elisabeth Barnes almost went berserk. She was really mad and said to Cindy, "You're not allowed to do that." Cindy said, "I'm not allowed?" Her mother

answered, "No, you're not allowed." Cindy said, "I don't have to ask you, Mummy, I'm not living under your roof anymore. You can't tell me what I'm allowed to do and what I'm not allowed to do. I'm in love with this man and I'm going to see him."

Cindy flew out of her parents' house. She thought about it on the way out, she told me later, and she said she realized she was being a bit unfair. Before she left, she said to her mother, "And I want you and Daddy to meet Bill, too." Her mother said, "Absolutely not, no, no, no." Next, Cindy went to plead with her father. She loved him a lot and respected him very much. Cindy's father copped a plea. He told Cindy, "Listen, why don't you discuss it with your mother?" Mrs. Barnes wouldn't have anything to do with it. Her English still has edges of Dutch in it, but she has a way that makes everything plain to anybody who's ever listened to her. She said, "First of all, your ages." I was forty-five, Cindy was twenty-six, going on twenty-seven. "That's only one thing to be reckoned with, but what about the height, you two will look like you are right out of the freak show, the circus."

To this day, Elisabeth Barnes denies she ever said that. Edie Arnaz, one of Cindy's friends, heard her say the same thing later. When Edie died, Cindy lost one of her best friends. She still misses her a lot. Another of Cindy's friends, Marge Durante, is still around and anybody who asks her is told that my mother-in-law said that very thing. I laughed when I heard about it.

Cindy laughs about it now, but she remembers how horrified her mother was. Mrs. Barnes said, "I am so mortified, I don't want anybody to know about this." When Cindy left the house,

Mrs. Barnes got on the phone and called three or four of Cindy's friends to tell them the terrible news.

In 1978 I made a promotional poster for Santa Anita Park. I've been very lucky in California and I have always gotten along good with the people who run the tracks. Hollywood Park and Santa Anita are home to me. I've found a lot of success and fun in both places. At both Hollywood Park and Santa Anita, the people running the places think of me as the hometown jockey who made good. So when Santa Anita dressed me up in red, white, and blue silks, with stars all over the cap, I posed for the poster.

It was based on an old World War One poster put out in Washington. The poster showed Uncle Sam all duded up in a pipestove hat and red, white, and blue coat, and pointing his right index finger. UNCLE SAM WANTS YOU! the recruiting poster said.

The one I made for Santa Anita had me pointing, in the style of Uncle Sam. Above me, it said, THE SHOE WANTS YOU. Below me, Santa Anita was identified as THE GREAT RACE PLACE. When the Barneses once went to a restaurant in Eden Gardens one night, the poster was on a wall. The Barneses went into the bar. Pretty soon Cindy's mother said, "Wally, I can't sit here. I cannot because that man is pointing straight at me."

Cindy's father got a chuckle out of it. Her mother didn't like that at all. She was in a rage. "I want to move," she said, and so they moved clear around the bar to the other side. Mrs. Barnes looked again up at just the right height and there I was still pointing straight at her. She said, "Wally, I want to go in and eat dinner. I will not sit in here. He's still pointing at me."

The next day, Mrs. Barnes called Edie Arnaz and told Edie she was terribly upset. Edie cooled her out. She said, "Elisabeth, you are being stupid. I've seen Cindy and Bill together. They're terrific. They're obviously quite in love with each other. You're the fool, because you will be the one left behind."

Cindy's mother liked Edie Arnaz. Edie was Desi Arnaz' wife. She finally gave in because of Edie. She called and said, "Well, you win. I want you to come and have dinner at home and bring Bill."

I was calm going to meet the Barneses. When we sat down for dinner at the nice house in Cardiff-by-the-Sea, I remembered all my table manners. So did Cindy. It was the same table she'd had dinner at thousands of times. General Barnes couldn't have been nicer. He was at the head of the table. Cindy's mother was at the other end. She watched every move I made.

After dinner, General Barnes asked me if I would like to go upstairs with him to his living room. I followed him up the stairs. He was warm and gracious, and he broke out a bottle of brandy. This was an enjoyed ritual for him, a snifter of brandy after dinner. We got along real well. We talked about horses and that's always one subject I can listen to and get into. But, this old cavalry officer mostly asked me questions about riding. Cindy kept running up the stairs with pots of coffee to go with the brandy. At one point, Cindy said, "You know, honey, we really ought to get going. You've had enough brandy and you've got to ride a lot of horses tomorrow." Cindy's mother flew across the room and said, "You leave him alone!" She pointed at me and she said to

In the winner's circle at Santa Anita, 1976, on Royal Derby II, after my 7,000th victory.

Cindy, "This is a wonderful man. In fact, I don't know. You may not be good enough for him."

I talked to Cindy soon after that about getting married. She agreed and we told Cindy's parents about it. They were happy. Cindy's mother said, "I want the wedding right here in this house." I remember the day we went to get our marriage license in Santa Monica. We were wearing identical raincoats and carrying umbrellas, and the press photographers were out in front of the courthouse. We posed, Cindy smiling and me trying to break my face into a grin.

It was March 7, 1978, and Cindy and I were getting married, and it was a wonderful wedding. I had Harry and Temmie there, and some friends from Arizona, and maybe twenty other racetrackers. Cindy had a lot of her friends there too.

Judge Louis Welsh came up from San Diego to marry us. He was a member of the California Supreme Court. We knew him from around Del Mar. We used to see him walking on the beach every day. It was like a ritual. For three hours a day, he'd walk on the beach. It was great to have him perform the ceremony.

Cindy was the third Mrs. Billie Lee Shoemaker. I told her right from the start that she had taken on a tough job. I said it wasn't easy being Bill Shoemaker's third wife, not if you were sensitive. I told her she had to relax, to stop being thin-skinned, and to stop worrying about what other people said. They were going to say she'd married me for my money and for my popularity. So what? Cindy said she'd try. One morning she found a note on her car when it was parked in the driveway. It was from Babbs and what

it said wasn't a big deal to either of us. We both knew Babbs was still angry.

Babbs still tries to get to Cindy. When Babbs goes to the racetrack, she gets a table right in view of Cindy's table, and she glares at Cindy all day long. It's ten years now since I married Cindy and I think that Babbs should stop bothering her.

Two years before Cindy and I were married, I got the 7,000th win of my career. It was on Royal Derby II on the grass. Royal Derby II was an old horse and I liked him. He ran kindly for me that March day in 1976 at Santa Anita. He was an eight-year-old, kind of ancient in the world of horses. After we came out of the pack, it was easy going from there. Charlie was Royal Derby's trainer and when I got to the winner's circle there he was with Harry and Greer Garson and Buddy Fogelson, her husband. They had me hold up a sign that said in big letters: 7,000TH VICTORY. SANTA ANITA PARK. March was a very good month for me.

14

Cindy and I moved into a split-level ranch house in the Coldwater Canyon Drive area off Beverly Hills. Cindy liked the place and at night, if you listened, you could hear coyotes out in the hills. We were very happy there. When I had a day off and wasn't playing tennis or golf, I'd just lie around reading the papers. I used to kid Cindy. She would tell me what a good rider she was, and I would say it was a big deal. I was only fooling, because I really had a lot of respect for Cindy's ability on a horse. I promised myself that one day I would go out and watch her jump horses.

In 1978, I went to England to ride in the English Derby at Epsom Downs. My mount was Hawaiian Sound. When I got there, people kept saying that I looked too small to be a good jockey. Cindy was with me, and the English writers said I looked like a doll next to her. In Europe, people thought that a jockey had to weigh something like 114 pounds or more. It was the same old story, the weight thing again.

Maybe that was true in Europe, where the tracks are all differ-

ent and a jockey has to have power to get a tight hold on horses in the early parts of races.

My first ride in England was in the Derby. Like the Belmont Stakes, the Derby is run over the classic distance of a mile and a half. I put Hawaiian Sound into the lead. It was my first ride at tricky Epsom, but I was happy with the pace. The reason the course at Epsom is called "tricky" is that after your horse climbs a hill, you come to the downhill slope called Tattenham Corner, which leads into the rising homestretch.

Tattenham Corner is a real trap. Year after year horses in the English Derby sprawl and lose their balance at this point. When this happens, you should see the expressions on the jockeys' faces change. It's almost like they become unnerved. Even the people watching on television can see this. What happens is that the pace is fast and the field large and closely bunched, and if you're not in control of your horse at this point and your horse is not fully balanced, you are in trouble.

But as I came down toward Tattenham Corner and into the turn, I thought, Hey, this is fun. In the stretch I asked Hawaiian Sound for something extra and he responded. But in the end we were beaten a head by Shirley Heights. I made one mistake, I think. I gave the rail away to Greville Starkey, the rider on Shirley Heights. Some English racing correspondents wrote that my failure to go to the rail was a sporting thing to do. I just thought it was stupid.

After England, I went over to Ireland for the mile and a half Irish Derby and I rode Hawaiian Sound again. This time the race

was at the Curragh. That's Gaelic for a marshy ground. You've never seen a pasture like this one. The sheep graze right in the infield. The race course at the Curragh—the Curragh is the headquarters of the army of the Irish Republic—has the longest straight whiskey bar in the world. It's a sight to see a hundred or more elbows bent right down the line.

Hawaiian Sound made his own pace early in the race. It was too fast, but I struggled to get him to relax and settle down. A colt named Exdirectory took over the lead. When we got into the stretch, Hawaiian Sound was going easier and I had high hopes, but in the last few yards Hawaiian Sound tired. He was beaten a head and a neck by Shirley Heights and Exdirectory. I think Hawaiian Sound was a good mile-and-a-quarter horse. I told a TV reporter, "We lost because we went too fast early on, and we went too fast because I couldn't hold Hawaiian Sound." This straight talk made a hit with the Irish and the English, but it wasn't a new thing for me. I have always been like that.

I came home from England, and Charlie put me on a horse called Exceller. He was a five-year-old son of Vaguely Noble and Too Bald, and was owned by Nelson Bunker Hunt, the Texas millionaire. In October, we went to New York for the Jockey Club Gold Cup at Belmont Park. I was back at my lucky track. The race was worth $321,800, with a purse of $193,080 to the winning owner. The Jockey Club Gold Cup is one of the most prestigious races in the sport. It is called "Racing's Crowning Event." Owners like to win it because it represents a major achievement, and when Charlie put me on Exceller in the 1978

Jockey Club Gold Cup, he knew he was putting me in with one of the best. Two Triple Crown winners were in the race. Not only had Seattle Slew and Affirmed won the Derby, the Preakness, and the Belmont, but each was at the top of his career. Angel Cordero was on Seattle Slew and Steve Cauthen rode Affirmed. It rained that October 14, and the track was very sloppy. Cordero, on Seattle Slew, was a strong rider. His determination to win reminded me a lot of Longden and Hartack.

Nobody was letting anybody "steal" the Gold Cup. I knew I had to keep my eyes on Seattle Slew and Affirmed. Right from the start, they got into a speed duel. Going around the first turn, Cordero's right foot slipped out of the stirrup for a second or two, but he was making the pace into the backstretch, outrunning Affirmed. They went a fast half mile in 45.1 and measured three quarters in 1:09.4, a terribly tiring pace for a race over a mile and a half.

I was at least twenty-five lengths behind the leader at one point. I was sitting chilly. Cordero was pulling his old trick. He kept looking back over his shoulder, the way he always does, but he couldn't see me. He didn't know where I was. He was off the rail, and when he looked to the right, looking for anybody he could spot, I moved in on his left and he couldn't shut me off. I shot past him and got a small lead with a furlong to go. Exceller had just enough left to win the race by a nose.

Everything was starting to come up roses. I was happily married and I was doing all right for an old guy. We went home to Santa Anita and I won the Oak Tree Invitational on Exceller.

(l–r) Harry Silbert and his wife, Tammie; Vernon O. Underwood, Chairman of the Board of Hollywood Park; Cindy with our daughter, Amanda; me; Jim Murray, L.A. Times *columnist, presenting a bronzed pair of my riding boots.*

In June 1979, I got a call from Harry Meyerhoff. Harry owned Spectacular Bid with his wife, Teresa, and his son, Tom. He lived at Hawksworth Farm on the eastern shore of Maryland, near the town of Easton. He had bought Spectacular Bid at auction in Kentucky for $37,000, and Spectacular Bid had proven to be a great two-year-old. He was trained by a Marylander named Bud Delp. Bud had trained all of Harry's and Teresa's and Tom's horses, and he had done a fine job with Spectacular Bid. He was one of the best trainers in the East.

When Harry phoned me, he asked if I'd be interested in riding Spectacular Bid. The big gray colt had already won the Kentucky Derby and the Preakness, but hadn't done well in the Belmont Stakes. Delp said the Bid had been wounded by a safety pin used to hold a bandage in place. The public and the press laughed. People said it was a lame excuse and they didn't believe him.

Even before the Triple Crown races, Ron Franklin was knocked in the papers for a ride he gave Spectacular Bid in the Florida Derby. He took the gray colt all over the track, but the colt overcame the bad ride and won. Only great horses can do that. Reporters asked me if I would like to ride Spectacular Bid. I said, "Sure, who wouldn't?"

The Meyerhoffs decided not to ask Bud Delp to get a new rider for Spectacular Bid. The trainer felt like Franklin's father, and so he kept Ron on the horse. Spectacular Bid won the 1979 Derby by two and three-quarters lengths. Then came the Preakness in Baltimore, the Meyerhoff's home base. Only four horses took on the job of trying to beat Spectacular Bid. The gray colt won again,

beating Golden Act by five and one-half lengths. The horse's ability again overcame the ride he got from Franklin.

Spectacular Bid had gotten bumped by Flying Paster at the start and was outrun. Franklin angled him out after three furlongs and went very wide. With almost half a mile to go, the gray colt got in front. The jockey whacked him pretty good and he had an easy run to the wire.

Then came the Belmont, and before the race there was a big stew about a safety pin stuck into Spectacular Bid's foot. Delp had said there was an infection in one hoof. In the race, Franklin used the horse early. With a half mile to go, he asked Spectacular Bid for more, but the colt just couldn't respond. He had nothing left and finished third. Coastal was the winner. The Meyerhoffs were crushed. Their horse had missed taking the Triple Crown. They talked the situation over with Delp and they agreed that Spectacular Bid needed a new rider.

Franklin, they felt, needed more experience, and some cooling off. Franklin was also in all sorts of trouble. In New York he had called Angel Cordero a racial name and gotten into a fistfight. Then a woman in Baltimore charged him with being the father of her child. In California he was hit with a drug charge. He just plain needed a rest. That's when they came looking for me. Here I was, a forty-eight-year-old jockey and they were asking me to take over from a nineteen-year-old kid.

I thought to myself, Hey, maybe Spectacular Bid would have lost the Belmont under any rider. But a lot of people for whom I had respect in matters like these told me that Franklin helped get Spectacular Bid beat.

Anybody can make a mistake riding a race. Remember, I misjudged the finish line and threw away a Derby once. Arcaro, about as great a rider as any in the twentieth century, eased a horse a mile too soon and was disqualified in a race at Pimlico. It happens. It just happens. The kid was getting a lot of knocks. That's not my game. I don't knock other riders.

Bud Delp got Harry on the phone. He said he wanted me to ride Spectacular Bid. That was in the summer of 1979. Harry said, "Sure, I'll ride Spectacular Bid. It'll be my pleasure."

I got lucky with Spectacular Bid. At my age, I got to ride a great horse. Swaps, Gallant Man, Round Table, Jaipur, Forego, Damascus, Sword Dancer, Ack Ack, John Henry, Ferdinand. When I start thinking about all the great horses I have ever ridden, sometimes I put them all in, sometimes I forget a few. But I never leave Bid out. He was the best. He went off at 1–20 eight times in his career and broke seven track records at six different tracks. He ran everywhere under all conditions and won.

I rode Spectacular Bid for the first time five days after my forty-eighth birthday, on August 26, 1979. When I got on the horse down in Delaware, I thought, Hey, what's this? This horse can't move. He's muscle-bound. His muscles were something to feel. They were long and deep. The race at Delaware Park was an allowance at a mile and one sixteenth. Spectacular Bid covered the distance in 1:43.3 for a track record. He won by seventeen lengths.

It wasn't too long after that race that I had to come back from California to ride Spectacular Bid again. Back on the red-eye, the long flight from home, and I was at Belmont Park for the Marlboro Cup. Spectacular Bid won that one, too, but before the Woodward Stakes a few weeks later, he came up with a fever. He was laid off and couldn't get a race in before the Jockey Club Gold Cup. Affirmed beat him by three quarters of a length. But he came right back in the Meadowlands Cup in New Jersey and the race was another win for him.

At about the same time, Cindy and I were trying to have a baby, and the doctor had just told us she was pregnant. We were very happy. I had adopted three kids before, but now I was going to have my very own. I was as proud as a rooster.

Delp and the Meyerhoffs decided to campaign in California. I liked that. I would be close to home and riding the big horse. Spectacular Bid won the San Fernando Stakes and the Strub Stakes at Santa Anita, and in the Strub he set an American record of 1:57.4 for a mile and a quarter.

By this time, we had become very friendly with the Meyerhoffs. They were fun and we got along good. They went to Acapulco that winter and rented a house from Frank McMahon. He was a Canadian who owned Majestic Prince, the colt that beat Arts and Letters the year I got racked up pretty good and didn't get to Louisville. The Meyerhoffs invited us to Acapulco. We spent a week there and we had a ball. I got back just in time to ride Spectacular Bid in the Santa Anita Handicap on March 2, 1980. He won. He went on to win the Mervyn LeRoy Handicap

With Sonny Werblin and Jorge Velasquez, Meadowlands, October 1, 1977.

at Hollywood Park, and on June 8, he took the Californian at Hollywood Park.

The next Fall I thought about that house in Acapulco so much that I rented it for myself. Cindy and I thought we'd stay a week, but one night, after a party, I slipped on a tile floor and cracked my face open on the edge of the pool. My upper lip was split open. It took about eleven stitches to close my wounds. When I looked at myself in the mirror the next morning, I looked as if Joe Louis hit me.

Cindy's time was getting close. Her due date was June 15, but she didn't get out of the gate. On Saturday, June 21, she got the feeling that the baby was on the way and we called her obstetrician. Dr. Joseph Marmet told her to get to the hospital. I drove her to Cedars-Sinai in Beverly Hills and Cindy spent the night at the hospital. The next day I was scheduled to ride Bold Tropic in the Hollywood Gold Cup. To me, it was an important race. I had won it six times, but that day I just couldn't concentrate on it. Early that morning, I went to the hospital to see Cindy. About two o'clock in the afternoon, Cindy's labor pains were coming closer together. She said, "Hey, don't you have a race to ride? Go on, go ride your horse." I stayed long enough to see the baby's head come out. I didn't want to leave, but I had to report to the jocks' room at Hollywood Park. I still didn't know the baby's sex.

The baby was delivered at 3:01 in the afternoon of June 22, 1980. I was on a horse just going up to the gate and somebody yelled, "Hey, Shoe, it's a girl." That's how I learned that I was a father of a little girl. Later, they made an announcement on the public address system. The baby got a big hand. All I could get with Bold Tropic was fourth. The race was won by Go West Young Man. I couldn't wait until I could go to the hospital. I rushed in, kissed Cindy, and asked about the baby. Cindy said, "Go see her, she's in the nursery."

I went looking for the nursery. Down the hall I saw a large window and I walked toward it. Two guys were standing at the window, looking in at the babies in their cribs. On each crib there was the baby's last name.

One guy says to the other, "Hey, look at all them babies." The other guy says, "Hey, look at that one over there. That's the biggest one in the room." The guy sees the name "Shoemaker" on our baby's crib. He says, "Hey, that can't be the famous jockey's baby, can it?" The other guy says, "Hell, no, that baby's bigger than the jockey is already." He turns and sees me standing just in back of him. He says to his friend, "Hey, let's go, it's getting late."

I look through the window and see my new baby girl. She is beautiful. She weighs nine pounds, ten ounces, and she looks about two months old. This is the greatest thing that ever happened to me, having that baby. We name her Amanda Elisabeth. We just like the name Amanda and Elisabeth is for my mother-in-law. When the time comes to take Amanda home, Cindy and I take her to our new house in San Marino. I can't remember ever being happier.

15

I hadn't really appreciated the three children I'd adopted—two with Ginny and one with Babbs. I was just too young then, and I was building a career and doing everything but being a family man. I was forty-nine years old when Amanda was born and that made a difference. I was settled in my ways and I spent a lot more of my time at home. For the first two months, Cindy didn't leave Amanda alone once. But in August, I got word that the Meyerhoffs were going to run Spectacular Bid in the Haskell Handicap at Monmouth Park in New Jersey. Cindy and I talked it over and we decided that Cindy should make the trip with me. We left Amanda at home with jockey Fernando Toro and his wife, Lola, probably the two best parents on earth. I liked Monmouth Park a lot. It's a suburban track with big-city style. If I had to use a word for it, I would say it was "lovely." And I knew Cindy would like it.

So we went to Monmouth Park and stayed at the Reading Room. That's a nice house on a hill overlooking the racetrack.

The people at Monmouth Park keep it to accommodate horse owners and other guests. It has six bedrooms and a bright sun porch where they serve breakfast. A guy can get a shooter when he wants it because the service is good. Harry and Teresa Meyerhoff were there and so was Tom Meyerhoff. Tom is Harry's son, and a very nice guy, too. Teresa's mom and pop stayed over at the Reading Room.

The Haskell wasn't an easy race. The handicapper put 132 pounds on Spectacular Bid. I weighed 96 pounds. That meant that there was 36 pounds of lead in my saddle bag. The valet who had to carry the load was in danger of getting a hernia. But it was nothing new for Spectacular Bid. That year he carried 130 pounds five times and he set track records twice under that load.

The problem wasn't how much weight Spectacular Bid carried, but how much of a weight difference there was between the Bid and a filly called Glorious Song. She was a good gal and could beat the boys under the right conditions, and she was in under 117 pounds. That meant she had a 15-pound pull in the weights.

Teresa Meyerhoff loved Spectacular Bid. Later Cindy said Teresa was so nervous watching the gray colt in the Haskell, she cried. Spectacular Bid beat Glorious Song by a length and three quarters. That night we ate and drank, and we had a great time. I like to joke around, and I kept planting ice cubes in everybody's pockets. Everybody laughed, even those who got wet. It was a perfect weekend and Cindy had a hell of a good time.

Five weeks after the Haskell, the Woodward was scheduled for Belmont Park. That's one of the major New York races for three-

year-olds and older horses. I first won it back in 1958 on Clem. Then I won it on Damascus' three-year-old season. Eight years later, I won it on Forego. He owned the Woodward. He won it three years in a row. In 1980, the Woodward Stakes was a hollow victory for Spectacular Bid. Not a single horse came out to give him a race. They ducked him and he won it in a walkover. All he had to do was to cross the wire to pick up the purse. Even with no horses running against him, Spectacular Bid ran the mile and one eighth in 2:02.4. That's pretty good time against the clock. The Meyerhoffs were very disappointed. So was the crowd of 72,000 at Belmont Park. There was a sour taste in a lot of mouths after that race.

Three weeks after the Woodward I had a bad spill at Belmont Park. I was riding a horse called Happy Edwardo in the first race. The horse in front of me broke a leg and I went right off my mount. I landed on my back and rolled under the rail. That's what saved me from getting hit by trailing horses. The ambulance picked me up and they rushed me to Long Island Jewish Hospital a few miles from the track. Somebody said I might have a punctured lung and a few fractured ribs. X rays were taken and the doctors said I was all right. Before I even got out of the hospital, the Meyerhoffs were on the phone. They wanted us to come down to Maryland and rest and recuperate. I was stiff and sore, and Cindy knew I needed the rest so we went to the Meyerhoff farm, Hawksworth, for a few days.

The farm is a great place, maybe four hundred acres on the Miles River not far from Easton, Maryland. Canadian geese stop

there to feed when they fly south in the fall. The Meyerhoffs have several boats tied up at their dock. From a rolling lawn, you can see the town of St. Michaels across the river. There is a main house and a pool house with guest rooms. A guy can have a lot of fun there. When you drive into the place, there is a sign: BEWARE OF THE PEACOCKS. You drive a little way up the winding road and you see a sign that says: 6,667 KILOMETERS TO LONDON. The sign I like best is the one that warns: BEWARE OF THE OWNER!

We went for a couple of days and stayed more than a week. We'd go into Easton to shop or sit around and have a few shooters. Harry and Teresa Meyerhoff were great hosts. Everybody in the house was on his own. One day Harry put some tapes of Spectacular Bid's races on the VCR. I sat there with Amanda on my knee, doing a blow-by-blow of the races. She loved it. I said something like, "See the nice horsey. That's some kind of horsey. That's Daddy up there riding him."

Right after dinner one evening, Cindy and Teresa decided to go into town to shop. We went with them and wound up in the local bar. In the bar there were a couple or three guys who came up on motorcycles. One was big, I mean very big. He wore a ten-gallon white hat, cowboy boots, leather jacket, and in his mouth there was a cigar maybe a furlong long. He kept staring at me. He said, "Ah know you, boy. You're that jockey feller. It's Shoe something or other."

I said to the big guy, "Hey, I like your hat. I'm from Texas myself, pardner." He let me try his ten-gallon hat on. It went right down over my eyes. Everybody was laughing, and the big

With Lester Piggott of England and Yves Saint-Martin of France, 1981.

guy said, "You can't see down there like that, Shoe." He lifted me up and sat me on the divider between the dining room and the bar, and he gave me one of his big cigars. I went along with the gag. Harry was laughing his eyes out. When I got down from the divider, I shook hands with the big guy. Then we went out into the nice cool air. I felt about as good as I've ever felt.

I finished 1980 with 159 wins in 1,052 races. That was the lowest winning percentage in my career. I wasn't worried, but Harry Silbert was. He was worried because the rides weren't coming as easy as they did in the old days. He knew that a lot of trainers in the mediocre races, the $25,000 races and down, they want a hungry rider on their horses. They began to feel that I was used to only riding the big horses and why would I want to ride in ordinary races? They were wrong, but Harry couldn't convince them. That's the way they felt.

So Harry had to go after the top allowance horses or the horses in stakes. And those races were tougher to win on. In the cheaper races, you can get a horse and win four, five in a row with him.

I was happy if I got three, four mounts a day. Harry could sense how I felt. He used me like a trainer uses a good horse. He knew how many I could ride in a day. If I got a chance to ride five or six ordinary mounts in a day, I'd knock out two or three. I didn't want just any horse. I wanted something that could run. I sure didn't need the money that bad.

Right smack in the middle of 1981, I got some good news. Harry told me that Ron McAnally wanted me to ride John Henry in the Sword Dancer Stakes in New York. McAnally trained the

six-year-old gelding for Dotsam Stable. Actually, Dotsam Stable was Sam Rubin, a bicycle importer in New York, and his wife, Dorothy. Rubin was an interesting guy. He got into racing because he liked to bet, and when he could afford it, he bought John Henry for about $25,000.

From the start John Henry was a tough horse to handle and had been gelded. What they do if a colt shows early signs of orneriness is they castrate him. They do this because it quiets the horse down. He's no good for breeding after that, but he can be used as a pure racehorse. John Henry was a gelding. He wasn't much in his early racing years, but when he was five, he was elected the best grass horse in America. The Thoroughbred Racing Association gave him an Eclipse Award and about this time he was the talk of the racing world.

At six, he was a sensation. That was 1981 and the talk around racing was the first Arlington Million to be run in Chicago. The race was the first one in racing history with a million-dollar purse. Gulf and Western owned Arlington Park then, and Sonny Werblin worked for the big conglomerate. He was the one that came up with the idea for the Arlington Million.

McAnally and Rubin had been pointing John Henry for the million-dollar race. John Henry won five of his six races before the big race in Chicago. The race he didn't win, he had been carried wide. He was a grass horse, but now he was running on the dirt and winning races and everybody was amazed that he was so versatile. Even before the Arlington Million, the John Henry people decided to change jockeys. That's when they called

Harry Silbert to get me. The Sword Dancer Stakes was coming up in New York. That was an important race named for the horse I didn't ride in the Derby in 1969 because I was hurt.

I flew back to New York and rode John Henry in the Sword Dancer for the first time. It was an easy win for the old horse, and the trainer and the owner liked the ride I gave him. So now we were all set in Chicago and getting ready for the Arlington Million. The race was on the grass at a mile and a quarter. I was feeling good. I was back at the track where I had won a lot of big races. I was fifty years old and there were riders in the race I had a lot of years on. Steve Cauthen was on Fingal's Cave and he was only twenty-one. Lester Piggott was on Madam Gay. Piggott was the greatest rider in England. He was five years younger than me. There were a dozen horses in the race.

Going into the gate, I looked over and saw Pincay on Kilijaro. Fernando Toro was on Super Moment. I knew Toro from back in the jocks' rooms in California. Super Moment was trained by McAnally and was coupled with John Henry in the betting. That meant that if you bet on Super Moment, you won your bet even if John Henry won. We went off the favorite in the race.

This was no easy thing. There were some very good horses in the first Arlington Million, and the turf was soft. If the race had been run on the dirt, the track would have been called muddy. It had rained all week in Chicago and the grass was like a bog. Could John Henry handle the situation? I was cautious. I left the outside post all right, and took John Henry back while three or four horses up front were fighting for the lead.

After the first mile, Key to Content and The Bart were dueling up front. On the soft course, the pace was very slow, 1:42.4 for the first mile. Going into the backstretch, John Henry was about six lengths behind the leaders and apparently out of it. He wasn't grabbing the soft turf and had to use up too much of his energy just to keep going. Now there was an eighth of a mile to go and Eddie Delahoussaye on a 40–1 shot called The Bart was in the lead and maybe on his way to a major upset. I was about a length and a half behind him. I didn't go to the whip. I spared my old mount the lash. Instead, I hand-rode him only, urging him to keep going, battling the heavy going. Going to the wire, John Henry stuck his nose in front of The Bart. It was so close that the people doing a national telecast called the wrong horse. It took a long time for the placing judge to come up with the winner. After they studied the pictures, they decided that John Henry was the winner by a nose. The time was 2:07.6, five seconds slower than the track record. In racing everything is translated into lengths. The experts said John Henry's pace was twenty-five lengths slower than the course record.

Nobody mentioned records or times when we went to the winner's circle. Sam Rubin and his army of followers were there, and they filled the circle. When Sam got the winner's trophy, he looked like the happiest guy in the world. He was a lot happier when he got the winner's share of the purse. It came to $600,000. My end was $60,000.

Six weeks later, I rode John Henry again. He gave me my third win in the Jockey Club Gold Cup at Belmont Park. He beat an outsider named Peat Moss, 50–1, by a head. John Henry tired in the end and tried to run out, but I held him together. The trouble was, the horse had gone a little faster than I had expected in the early going.

We went back across the country. I was giving the red-eye more business than anybody I knew, but I didn't mind. What I thought about was John Henry. What a great old guy he was. He had raced in Chicago, then in New York, and now he was coming back to California for the Oak Tree Invitational on November 8 at Santa Anita. We had a tough ride in the Oak Tree, but we won it in the final yards to beat Spence Bay a neck. There were 47,710 fans at Santa Anita that day, and after the race, they stood and cheered John Henry for five minutes. It was a close but great victory. I told Rubin, "It wasn't as close as it looked." Rubin had a great sense of humor. He said, "The next time that happens, wave your whip at me in the stands so that I can relax, too. I almost had a heart attack this time."

John Henry got an invitation to go to Japan for the first Japan Cup at the Tokyo Race Course, but Rubin decided against the long trip and I was glad he had. It was near the end of the year and I wanted to stay home. Amanda was almost a year old and she was beginning to walk and say "Daddy" and if that wasn't the biggest thrill in the world for me, I'm not Billie Lee Shoemaker.

I had traveled a lot that year. I had gone to England for the Chivas Regal trophy competition. The way that worked, we had an American team going against an English team of jockeys. Cordero was on our team, and so was Steve Cauthen, Laffit Pincay,

and Jorge Velasquez. We beat the English riders, but it really didn't matter. I enjoyed myself over there. I said before that English racing is a lot different than American racing, but it is fun.

Once, I was riding at a track in England and I heard a lot of talk about Swindley Bottom. I asked them what Swindley Bottom was. I thought it was a new drink. Some English guys laughed and told me it was a part of the track called Swindley Bottom because when you came down the hill at this figure-eight race course and started around the turn, there was a dip of about five feet where the horse goes up and then comes down. It's a big dip, maybe fifteen feet across. The way I remember it, some horses could handle it and some couldn't. The reason it was there is that English race courses follow the terrain where they are built. They just laid down a course to follow the lay of the land and that was that.

When John Henry's owner turned down the invitation to race his horse in Japan, he and McAnally decided to enter him in the first running of the Hollywood Turf Cup. It was late in the season, but some good runners were in the field of ten horses. John Henry went off a 2–5 favorite. My good old friend Charlie Whittingham had a horse in the race. Providential II had a French jockey named Alain Lequeux in the saddle. He was the third choice in the betting and won it all. The best John Henry could do was fourth. He just ran out of steam, but at the end of the year he was voted the Horse of the Year for 1981. And for the first time, I was voted the Jockey of the Year. My association with Sam Rubin and his wonderful old horse John Henry had helped me. I

went to Miami to get the award and Cindy went with me. I was all duded up in a tuxedo and Cindy wore a gown in which she looked more beautiful than ever. I took the trophy from Mike Sandler, the publisher of *Daily Racing Form,* and made a little thank-you speech. It was a great year, 1981 was, anyway you look at it.

During the year I won my 8,000th race. Everybody was waiting for the day and Cindy brought Amanda out to Hollywood Park to see if her daddy could get his 8,000th winning ride. They both looked beautiful. Cindy put a white bonnet on Amanda's round little head and held her in her arms. They watched me come out on War Allied for the first race. I was one shy of 8,000 victories. I had seven other mounts that day. Harry was making sure that I would get the big one along the way. I nursed War Allied behind the pace-setting Royal Trinity for the first half mile of the six-furlong race. Then going into the stretch, I moved War Allied to the front. I won by two lengths. The crowd of some twenty thousand fans stood and cheered, and I went to the winner's circle and posed with Cindy and Amanda and Harry and Temmie Silbert. Somebody asked if I thought I could make it 10,000 winners in my career. I said that was an impossible dream. Then I went out and won three more races that day. I had 8,003 winners. I said, "Amanda means more to me than any of them 8,000 winners ever did." You bet.

16

When I married Cindy, we had a long talk about money. My financial situation wasn't as good as you'd think. I had earned more than $10,000,000 in my riding career, maybe closer to $12,000,000, but if I was pressed, I could say my net worth was less than $500,000. I had no pension plan and no retirement plan, and I was forty-seven years of age. I had few assets. What I had were some oil and natural gas stocks, and a little real estate that wasn't producing very much. We moved into a big house in Coldwater Canyon on the rim of Beverly Hills and it proved too much to carry. Where had all my money gone?

My marriages had cost me a lot. Babbs was no piker when it came to spending. She hit me pretty good. I always helped out my mother, Ruby Call. She was living over in Riverside, not far from us. Whenever she wanted to visit, I would send a car to bring her out. We saw a lot of her. I'm not telling you this now to make it seem my family was a drain. Whatever they got, they deserved. Uncle Sam didn't help either. He had his hand out for a lot of income taxes. I don't begrudge him that either. Hell, no. I'm just talking about how my money was drained away. Bad investments took some.

Cindy and I agreed we had to do something. I was still earning a lot of money and we wanted to make sure that what I got from then on wasn't squandered. What we did was to hire a business manager. I don't know that that's the right way of telling you what Vincent Andrews does for us because he's more of a financial consultant. The way we got to him was through other jockeys. Laffit Pincay was one of his clients. Pincay told me he was happy with the job Vinnie did. So we talked to Vincent Andrews and we liked him. He had his main office in Connecticut, but he had offices in New York and California, too. We hit it off.

He was easy to talk to and wasn't a smart-ass. Maybe he was even a little too conservative, but he read the riot act to us. He said from now on he was running our money drawer. He set up William Shoemaker, Inc., and the corporation started paying me a salary. He set up two plans for me. One is a retirement fund. The other one is a pension plan. When I think of my corporation, I laugh. I think it's the littlest corporation in the world.

Now when I have a business decision to make, I call Vinnie. He gives me straight answers. The way he gets paid is through a percentage of the corporations' gross income. If I do good, he does good. When things go bad, he's working for nothing. We get along. Cindy likes Vinnie. She's very smart. She runs the whole thing. We've got accountants, but she knows about everything that's going on.

The house we live in now, in San Marino, cost us about $400,000. It was small to begin with, but we've added a lot to it. We have nine rooms and a swimming pool. It's really not a big house. Charlie always says it's a small house. He says big houses aren't nice, they're not comfortable to live in. I agree with him. Charlie is a down-to-earth guy. He puts on no airs. That's why I like him. He doesn't even like to dress up. He wears that old battered hat around the barn and that's good enough for him.

I'm not mad about clothes either. I dress up when we go out, but I like to wear leisure clothes more. I have to have my suits custom made. A tailor over in Arcadia makes them for me. He's called Rocco Crupi and he charges me $600 a suit. I wear size one and a half shoes. I have them made at Gucci's. They're pretty expensive—$150, $200, $250—depending on what I want. I have my shirts made over in Beverly Hills and they come in at $85 a shot.

The reason I'm telling you this is that I want to show how I don't try to live beyond what I can afford. Vincent Andrews keeps me down. We have two cars in the garage, a Mercedes and a BMW. One we own, the other is leased by our corporation. There's nothing really fancy about either one. Don't get me wrong about that. I know how it is to live poor and how it is to live rich. Rich is better. And I'm not being a smart-ass about it. When I see poor people around, I don't like it. I don't understand why it has to be like that.

Cindy never was rich. Comfortable, but not rich. She was an Army brat, moving around with her father and mother. When he

With Cindy and Amanda on my fifty-fourth birthday.

retired from the Army in 1956, he went to work for some corporation. He was a wonderful guy and when he died—when Amanda was two years old—I thought, Hell, I'll miss him. He was an all-around guy. Smart, too, and I learned a lot just from talking to him.

He had Amanda around for two years, and I like to think my little girl brought General Barnes more joy than even his daughter. I know Cindy made him very happy. He used to give her advice. He'd say, "Cindy, test the water before you jump. Don't just leap in." When we finally got married, in a large tent on the lawn at Cindy's old home, she said she always remembered what her father had told her about testing the water. She said that's how she knew she was making the right decision when she agreed to marry me.

I rode only 717 races the year General Barnes died. His death took the edge off a lot of things. I had only 113 winners, about 16 percent of my mounts. The horses I rode earned $4,691,342, if you add in the horses I rode out of the country.

I started off the year by winning the San Carlos Cup at Santa Anita on a horse called Solo Guy. Then John Henry brought me another victory in the Santa Anita Handicap. That made it ten in that race, more than any other rider. The day before the Kentucky Derby that year, I rode a good filly named Blush With Pride in the Kentucky Oaks. That's a major race for fillies. Blush With Pride won the Oaks. She was a great gal and I felt I knew her well. Back in California, she won two stakes with me aboard and I wasn't surprised when we won in Kentucky. I rode Star

Gallant in the 108th Derby the next day. The best I got was eighth.

In September, I flew to England to face Lester Piggott in a match race at Ascot. The race was for the Multiple Sclerosis Society in Great Britain. Both Piggott and I donated our services to the charity. I was fifty-one, Piggott forty-six. The English papers made a big deal out of the race. We rode at natural weights. I threw my 100 pounds up on a horse called Prince's Gate. Piggott's natural weight was 117. It was advantage Mr. Shoemaker. They were betting all over the United Kingdom on the race. Piggott's horse was the 8–11 favorite.

I always had one great psychological advantage over Piggott. He had to diet hard to make weight. I had to eat to make 100 pounds. The race was run over the old mile course at Ascot. I won easy. Piggott made a run at me once, but I shook up Prince's Gate and we had a length and a half edge when we got to the wire. Prince's Gate was owned by the Sheik Maktoum al-Maktoum. When the race was over, he doubled the $17,000 grant to the Multiple Sclerosis Society. I rushed back to Heathrow Airport and took the Concorde back to New York. I had a date the next day to ride in the $500,000 Super Derby at Louisiana Downs. My horse didn't win.

Not everything went well in 1982. John Henry didn't get back to the races until March 7 that year. The long, hard campaign of 1981 had been rough on the great old horse. He was seven years old. For a horse, that's old age. Still he was campaigning, and on March 7, he went into the Santa Anita Handicap. The year be-

After winning the 1965 Kentucky Derby.

fore, he had won that race with Pincay up. Now I was riding him and we were carrying top weight of 130 pounds. The crowd loved John Henry. They made him the 13–10 choice.

John Henry was back in the pack in the first part of the race, but at the head of the stretch we were fighting Perrault for the lead. Perrault, on the rail, was drifting out, and at the sixteenth pole he forced John Henry wide. Perrault went under the wire first. His margin was a nose. The inquiry sign flashed on the board. Perrault's number came down. John Henry was declared the winner. Perrault was placed second. Fourteen days later, John Henry ran on the grass at Santa Anita. He was hurt and didn't run again until October 17. He got fourth in the Carleton F. Burke Handicap.

McAnally was pleased and so was Sam Rubin. They thought the race had tightened John Henry for the Oak Tree Invitational, one mile and a half on the turf. They were right. John Henry won that one by two and a half lengths.

An invitation came again from Tokyo. Would Sam Rubin bring the old horse across the Pacific to Tokyo for the 1982 Japan Cup? Sam Rubin thought it would be a nice trip, but there was other business to do first. He wanted to show John Henry to his friends in the East and he decided to do this at the Meadowlands in New Jersey in the Meadowlands Cup. The purse was $400,000 and the date was November 14. Rubin thought this would give John Henry some spending money and set him up right for the trip to Japan. The gelding was assigned top weight of 129 pounds. He

went off the 11–10 favorite, but couldn't handle the track. He finished fourth.

We went to Japan anyway and got a great reception. The Japanese racing people really rolled out the red carpet. We were wined and dined. I was surprised that the Japanese remembered me so well from the year before. John Henry trained well. He figured in the mile-and-a-half race through nine furlongs, but then tired. The best we could get was thirteenth in a fifteen-horse field. It was a long flight home.

17

Our lives changed completely when Amanda came. We spend more time at home. We're in bed by nine o'clock. I like that. I read the papers and get a good night's sleep. We get up early. I go out to work horses at Santa Anita, usually for Charlie, and Cindy takes care of our little girl. Later, in the morning, Cindy goes to San Pascual Stable where she keeps her two horses, Left Alone and Springfield. That isn't easy. When she gets home, I'm back from the track. We discuss how the morning went.

I ask her, "How'd you ride?" She says, "It was a tough morning. They gave me a lot of trouble. One was jumping fine, but the other one was so fresh, I was lucky to get out of there in time."

In some ways, I think Cindy is a better rider than I am. We have lots of her blue ribbons around the house. My trophies are there—the silver cups, the silver plates, the crystal vases—but in the middle, all over the place, are Cindy's blue ribbons. When I say she is a better rider than I am, she gets hot. She says, "No. No. How can you say that? We ride differently. I couldn't begin to do what you do, and yet you can ride in the jock's class and ride one of our show horses in the show ring." I say, "Cindy, you're a better rider by far in what you do." She says, "I am a better rider in what I do? Well, yes. My kind of riding, yes."

She is modest about her riding ability. I think she's great, but what I like best is that she is in love with horses. She knows how hard it is to ride them in competition. That is why, when I get home from a hard day of riding, she knows I need rest, and she lets me get it. Social events are not the way we live, not the way it was when I was younger and I'd stay out late with Babbs, and the papers would print that it was hard for me to ride because I was seen at three o'clock in the morning in some joint or other.

Cindy says I'm an animal person. The first thing I do when I get home from the track is check on the dogs. We have a few dogs around the house. One is a Welsh corgi, one is an Australian shepherd puppy, and the third one, she's just a teacup poodle. I used to have five poodles. I had a mother and a father and a daughter and a son and an aunt. That's the way it works. This one is named Miss E., named after Marje Everett. We often called Marje "Miss E." How the poodle was named Miss E. was because I had a little female poodle in foal, and Marje went with me when I took her to the vet. The bitch had to have a cesarean because the twins were almost bigger than her. One of them died, and the one over there lived, and I named her Miss E. because Marje Everett came to the vet's with me.

The Welsh corgi, we call Crystal. She was a gift from Miss E. also. The way it happened, she really gave her to Amanda for

Christmas because her Labrador had just been killed. We also have singing birds in the house. They sing and the house lights up. Cindy is good at that. She knows how to give the house a lift. It always seems bright. In the den off the guest powder room, Cindy's put together a lot of our trophies. The wall is covered with pictures of some of my best days—the great days at tracks all over the world. We have a kind of family room that I like. That's where the television set is and I'm a television person. I watch sports a lot, and talk shows and the news.

In 1983, I had a good year. I wasn't getting a lot of mounts, but the horses I was riding were winning a lot of money for their owners. I wound up winning 125 races and $4,277,930 in purses. I rode eleven stakes winners that year, which wasn't bad for a fifty-two-year-old guy. I played a lot of golf with Don Pierce, my pal, and I spent a lot of time with Amanda. She was becoming a real little lady. Sometimes she'd be at the races with Cindy and she'd come into the saddling area and get a big kick from seeing me dressed in silks. The day I won the Rancho Santa Fe Stakes on Cardell, she came to Del Mar dressed up in a little blue dress with a square collar. She wore a little necklace and Cindy had combed her ash-blond hair upward and had tied it in a ribbon on the top of her head. When they gave me the silver cup for winning the race, Amanda posed with me. She smiled and played coy. She was the hit of the show.

Harry wasn't booking my mounts anymore. He had gone to the doctor one day and underwent a lot of tests. They showed that he had an enlarged prostate gland. He was seventy-one years old. He

My fourth Kentucky Derby win aboard Mrs. Elizabeth Keck's Ferdinand.

told me it was nothing, he was going to have surgery. They did the operation and it worked pretty good. Harry was in Cedars-Sinai, the hospital where Amanda had been born. They had all kinds of catheters in Harry and one day, he was half asleep when he saw Temmie standing with two doctors at the foot of the bed. They were whispering.

Harry thought, Hey, I must have the Big C, that was what Temmie and the doctors were whispering about. He said to Temmie, "What's happening? What's happening?" Temmie didn't know what to say. The doctors were tongue-tied, too. Temmie said, "Harry, I've got bad news for you."

Harry said, "Tell me, tell me, I can take it." Temmie said, "Harry, our son, Bert, is dead." Harry didn't hear it clearly. He said, "Who's Bert?" Temmie repeated it, "Bert's dead. Bert, our son." She told him that their son, a forty-seven-year-old lawyer, had been out jogging and had had a heart attack. It killed him. Because he was wearing a jogging suit, he was carrying no identification. The body was taken to the morgue. When Bert Silbert didn't come home, his wife notified the police. She was sent to the morgue and identified her dead husband.

Harry got out of bed and pulled the catheters out of him. He walked past the doctors. One doctor said, "Where do you think you're going?" Harry said, "Take me home." One of his sons-in-law came into the room. He said, "Dad, Dad, where are you going?" Harry said again, "Take me home." When they got Harry home, he went berserk. He tried to break up the house. He thought of his dead son and the two children he had left behind.

Then he had a stroke, and when he got out of the hospital again, Harry didn't want to do anything. He didn't want to work. He didn't want to see anybody.

I got Vince DeGregory to handle my book. He knew Harry, and they were friends. Vince was a good agent, but I sure missed Harry. I needed him and I knew he needed me. One day I got in touch with Temmie. I said, "Tell, me, Temmie, is Harry all right to go to work?" She said, "He's still brooding, but there's nothing wrong with him. Going back to work might do him some good."

I went to Harry's house. It was near Beverly Hills, in the Cheviot Hills section of Los Angeles. I planned to stay only a few minutes, but I ended up staying four hours. Temmie served supper and I ate with Harry and Temmie and one of their sons-in-law. Before I left, I had Harry's word that he would come back to work. It had been six or seven months since his son's death. I told Vince DeGregory that Harry was coming back. Vince knew that he was only handling my book until Harry took it back. I felt better.

Harry and I had never been apart before. Once, years before, when we were in New York, Harry said he had heard that I was going to fire him and give my book to Arcaro's old agent, Bones LeBoyne. He was going back to California for the Jewish holidays and he just had to tell me about the rumor.

I said, "Hey, Harry, when I'm through with you, I'll tell you myself. I haven't told you, have I?" He felt good. I found out what had happened. Babbs was with me in New York. She was sitting around in a box with some of the other women whose husbands

were in the racing business. John Nerud said he had overheard her saying that Harry's days with me were numbered, that Bones LeBoyne was taking my book. Nerud was Harry's friend. He told him what he had heard and that it was a lie.

I said to Harry, "Hey, Harry, you go home and come back after the holidays. Nothing's going to separate us." And nothing ever did. Until he died on March 11, 1987, Harry was my agent.

18

Amanda rode at Santa Anita when she was three. Cindy's friend, Barbie McCoy, owned a lovely hunter called Clipse, and Amanda got on her in the Santa Anita Horse Show. That was 1984, the year they held the Olympic Games in Los Angeles. The equestrian events took place at Santa Anita Park, and in connection with it they held a horse show. Cindy put Amanda on Clipse and led her into the show ring. It was her first ride. She was dressed in regular riding togs and looked like a doll. Later Cindy jumped her old mare, Crystal Bowl, in the competition. She won six of the nine blue ribbons up for grabs. I liked that. Horses run in the family.

I was fifty-three and still riding. In the jockeys' room, I felt like a grandfather. In fact, I was a grandfather. My adopted son, John, had children of his own by then. When he'd visit us in San Marino, his daughter, Courtney, would play on the floor with Amanda. There was only a few years' difference in their ages.

That was funny. I never thought of it, but there was my daughter playing with my granddaughter.

In the jockeys' room nobody dared call me "the old man." I wasn't. I had a lot of years on the kids in the room, but I could still ride with the best of them. The big difference was that the young jocks were hungry riders. I wasn't. Some owners wanted the "hungry riders," and I couldn't blame them.

Most of the guys I started with were gone. When I first went into the room in 1949, I found a pretty good bunch of guys. I got friendly with a lot of them. Jackie Westrope was one. He was the guy who sent me to that dentist in Beverly Hills who finally capped my teeth the way they should have been capped in the first place.

That was in 1958. Only a few months after Westrope put me in touch with Dr. Thomas, he was riding the filly Well Away at Hollywood Park. He was moving into the lead when Well Away tossed him. The filly hit the fence and Westrope bounced off the top of the rail. I was trailing him and I saw him go. His horse had been lugging in through the stretch and I watched Westrope trying to keep her from going into the rail. When they picked him up, most of the bones in his body were smashed. He died in the hospital two hours later. He was forty years old.

That was tough to take, and why I bring it up now is that when a jockey gets older, he thinks about such things. He's got to. He's smarter and he should pick his spots. He doesn't go where he doesn't think he's safe. If you've got enough horse under you to go into a hole, you do. The other jockeys in the room know I'm

My thirteenth Sunset Handicap win aboard Nelson Bunker Hunt's Swink, July 27, 1987.

not what I was when I was younger, but they know I can still ride. Experience is the difference.

In 1984, I had only 830 mounts. That was about two thirds of the number I used to ride. But I still won on 13 percent of my horses. My mounts won $4,324,667, including some in foreign countries. I was nearing the $100,000,000 mark. No jockey had ever earned that much money for his owners.

The next March, I got into another fix with Mrs. Mary F. Jones. She was now Mrs. Mary Jones Bradley, but nothing had changed since she got Charlie to take me off Cougar II in the 1973 Hollywood Gold Cup. Charlie put me on Kennedy Road and Laffit Pincay rode Cougar II. I overtook Quack in the stretch and won by a nose. Cougar II and Pincay were a distant third. I never held a grudge against the owner because I simply don't hold grudges. I forgive people.

In 1985, Mrs. Bradley was up to her same old tricks. Charlie wanted me to ride her colt Greinton. She said she wanted a stronger rider. People have always said I wasn't strong enough to ride certain horses. Maybe Greinton was one, but I don't think so.

I went to Charlie's barn one day with Harry Silbert. Charlie said, "She don't want you, Bill." Harry blew his top. He was making a lot of noise. I told Whittingham, "Charlie, if you don't want me, that's okay."

Charlie had a one-third interest in Greinton. He told Mrs. Bradley he didn't care if she took the colt out of the barn. He was burning up. She said she wanted Chris McCarron on the horse.

That was all right with me. It wasn't the first time I had been taken off a mount. It is a part of racing, a jockey losing a mount.

Charlie said to Harry, "How about you riding Lord at War?" Harry said, "That's fine with me." I liked the idea, and I'll tell you why. In a jockey's switch, you get lucky sometimes. I got lucky getting Spectacular Bid from Ron Franklin. Hey, in racing, strange things happen. Besides, I like the people who owned Lord at War. In racing, people show their colors, even owners. A lot of them are one-way-street people. If you're loyal to them, that's great. When you take off one of their horses, they get angry with you. But if they take you off one of their horses, that's a whole different ball game.

Diane and Peter Perkins owned Lord at War. They had a couple of horse farms, one in Kentucky and the other in Argentina. They bred Lord at War at the Haras San Francisco del Pilar, their farm in Argentina.

I actually thought Greinton was going to beat Lord at War. So did Charlie. At first he said, "Shoe, ride Greinton. He's got the best of it." When Charlie had two horses in a race, he always let me take my pick. But this time he came right out with it and said I should ride Greinton. I had ridden Lord at War before. He had won two or three hundred-granders and I was on him. So when Charlie told me he had to put Chris McCarron on Greinton, I didn't feel bad. I didn't think Mrs. Bradley was looking to get even with me about that Kennedy Road thing in the Santa Anita Handicap twelve years ago. I never even gave that a thought. She

just wanted a younger and stronger rider and, hell, I can't ride every horse.

Charlie said Greinton was getting five pounds from Lord at War. He said Greinton was coming up to the race really good, and it's a mile and a quarter and he can get the distance better than Lord at War. I said to Charlie, "Hey, Charlie, these people have been nice to me, the horse has been good to me, I'm going to stick with Lord at War, win, lose, or draw." Besides, when in my confusion I had asked Amanda who she wanted me to ride, she had said, "Lord at War, Daddy."

So on March 3, 1985, I was on the Perkins' chestnut colt when we went to the gate for the Santa Anita Handicap. I didn't think of the ten horses that had won the same race for me—Rejected, Poona II, Round Table, Prove It, Lucky Debonair, Pretense, Ack Ack, Stardust Mel, Spectacular Bid, John Henry. I had enough on my plate right there. When you're riding, only the race in which you're riding is important. History never moved a colt up an inch.

I held Lord at War back early, with the rank outsider, Ayman, taking the lead under Gary Stevens. McCarron, on Greinton, kept his eyes on me, going right behind me. At the far turn, I moved Lord at War. He was full of run, so I let him go. We took over with a quarter of a mile to go and beat Greinton to the wire by a length and three quarters.

The Perkins' part of the $560,000 purse came to $275,600. That put me over the $100 million mark. Santa Anita printed thousands of phony handbills in the shape of a dollar bill, only it said

"$100,000,000" on them. They gave them away to the customers. That was in 1985. After that, Laffit Pincay raised the ante. He has accounted for more than $100 million in purses. Records, like the "$100,000,000 bills," are made to be broken.

19

I can't say enough about Charlie Whittingham. He is the best trainer this country ever saw. Once a guy on a paper asked me if I knew any trainer of Charlie's stature who would be out at the barn at four-thirty in the morning watering the shed row. I thought about it and I said, "I don't know any other trainer of Charlie's stature."

I love big Charlie. He's seventy-four, going on seventy-five, and he's trained almost 500 stakes winners. I've ridden half of his stakes winners. He trains 'em, I ride 'em. He's got patience. He takes his time with the horses in his barn. He's got a little temper. He gets mad, but he gets over it fast. Charlie's been around for more than fifty years. He started as a stable hand and became a jockeys' agent. In 1934, he became a trainer of claiming horses. He was doing good, but things went sour and he blew everything. He became an assistant to Señor Luro, and when Pearl Harbor happened, his racing career was put aside for a while. When peace came, he went back with Luro and worked as an assistant for five years. He paid his dues.

In the summer of 1985, one morning at Del Mar, I was at Charlie's barn. That was the first stop I'd make every morning. I asked Charlie if he wanted me to work any horse. I like working horses mornings. The air is clean and the day is just starting, and everybody's alert. That morning at Del Mar, Charlie said, "Hey, Shoe, look at this one." He had his sloppy hat on, the pepper-and-salt one with the brim going every which way, and he was full of pride. He pointed to a big, gangly colt. "He's by Nijinsky II," Charlie said. Everybody in racing remembers Nijinsky II. His sire was Northern Dancer. In 1964, I rode Hill Rise in the Kentucky Derby and got beat a neck by Northern Dancer. It's like I said, racing is a very small world.

I looked at the colt in Charlie's barn, Ferdinand. He was big. His chestnut coat was caught by the sun. It looked like gold. Charlie said, "Here's one I've been saving for you." I wasn't thinking of the Derby, but Charlie was. The Kentucky Derby had never been Charlie's favorite race. He always thought it came too early in the season. He said a three-year-old needed to develop more before going in a tough race the first week in May.

Nineteen eighty-five was a tough one for me. I was president of the Jockeys' Guild. In April, the guild sued the New Jersey Racing Commission over the commission's policy of testing riders for drugs. I wasn't against drug testing, but I was only one guy. The guild has 1,700 members.

In New Jersey, the tracks began giving breath tests to every

jockey before a race. At the end of each day of racing, three jockeys were asked to give urine samples. In California, an informal system was used. If the California Racing Board believed there was a reason to test a rider, he would be tested. We had one young jockey who started falling asleep in the jocks' room. He was tested for drugs and had his license revoked. He got it back when he tested negative, but when he was on the stuff, he was endangering many of the other riders on the track.

So I got into the drug thing because it was my job as the president of the guild. The case went as high as the U.S. Third Circuit Court of Appeals. That federal court said testing was all right. Then the Supreme Court refused to hear the case. We lost, but it was all right with me. So long as they don't go out in the parking lot and grab jocks and ask for urine samples, I'm for it.

I'm for anything that's good for racing. When there is talk about crooked riders, I get mad as hell. I don't think there's anything wrong on the big racetracks, because the money is there. There's enough money for everybody. I don't know anything about the smaller racetracks. I remember in the old days, whenever Hollywood made a picture about horse racing, they always had a crooked race. Some people got together in 1970 and made a television film about me. They called it *6,033—Nice Guys Finish First.* I have a tape of it. It shows me winning races and what happened in my two bad accidents.

Amanda loves to watch the tape. Walter Matthau is the commentator. At one spot in the tape, he says about me, "He's the best there is," and Amanda says, "Of course he's the best. He's my daddy." When she sees me get hurt, she cries. I mean she cries real tears. She just can't stand seeing her daddy get hurt.

Amanda goes to a Catholic school on Palomar Road in San Marino. It's about a mile from the house and when I'm home I either take her to school or pick her up after school. I like that. I can talk to Amanda and find out what she's thinking about. It's good for her and it's good for me. The kids at school talk to her about "her little father." She says, "He has to be little, because he's a jockey."

I take her to the movies sometimes. One day I took her to see *Top Gun.* I didn't know what the picture was about. The language was pretty rough, something like the language around the jocks' room. I was embarrassed. I talked fast to Amanda, trying to cover up the dirty words. I don't know if I did, but I tried.

When the Kentucky Derby came around in 1986, Charlie decided to run Ferdinand in Louisville. Ferdinand had run five times as a two-year-old. After breaking his maiden, he was third in the Hollywood Futurity, behind Snow Chief and Electric Blue. As a three-year-old, he was beaten a head by Badger Land in the Los Feliz Stakes at Santa Anita. In that season Ferdinand won the Santa Catalina, ran second in the San Rafael, and then finished third, behind Snow Chief and Icy Groom in the Santa Anita Derby. By the time we got to Louisville, I knew him well. Charlie used to say, "Hey, Shoe, that Ferdinand is so big, you'll get lost on him." I'd laugh. I knew how Charlie felt about me. I never let him forget how I feel about him. He's my friend.

We went to Louisville and stayed at the Executive Inn West

near the airport. At the airport, people were pointing me out. I remembered once how it was a few years before that when I flew into Detroit Metropolitan Airport to ride Recusant in the 1982 Michigan Mile and One-Eighth Handicap at Detroit Race Course. A guy saw me and just stood there with his mouth open. He was carrying a suitcase in each hand. Suddenly, he put the valises down, turned to his wife, and said, "Shoe! That's Shoe!" I'm not bragging, but it happens to me often. Hell, they can't miss me, can they?

Cindy came to Louisville with me for the race and so did Elizabeth and Howard Keck. They owned Ferdinand. Only Amanda wasn't with us; she was back in San Marino. We worked hard in Louisville. The Derby is always a tough grind. Charlie was out at the barn with the first light of day. I worked Ferdinand. The guys from the papers came around to our barn in Derby Row and I felt good.

Jack Nicklaus had just won the Masters at forty-six. Billy Reed of the Louisville *Courier-Journal* told me, "Bill, you've got a shot. Look at Nicklaus. And Vladimir Horowitz just returned to Russia, for a triumphant tour." I said, "Who'd Horowitz ever ride?" The great pianist was eighty-six years old.

I was going to be fifty-five and Charlie was seventy-three, and we were the old guys, the oldest jockey and the oldest trainer. They were all saying I couldn't win another Derby. They said I wouldn't take the chance if I saw the opening I needed to win. They said Ferdinand was just another California horse, not even the best out there.

I am going after the 8,537th victory of my career. That includes 941 stakes victories. Of all my stakes victories, 216 of them are worth $100,000 or more. I am in the twilight of my career, well past my prime, and the crowd of 123,819 is singing "My Old Kentucky Home" and mostly ignoring Ferdinand. The weather is great, sunny and mild. The Kecks are getting a big kick out of the scene. They're good folks, and you'd never know he sold his oil business for $5.7 billion to Mobil two years earlier.

Well, we win it. We win the 112th Kentucky Derby. I make all the right moves and get into the winner's circle, and the crowd is going mad. I have a few tears in my eyes coming back to the winner's circle. To tell you the truth, I think, Well, old Jack Nicklaus did it, and I did it, too. It is certainly emotional.

Then I see Cindy and she's crying. Like I told you, Charlie is so nervous he can't speak. In the press box, the reporters ask me about moving Ferdinand into the hole when I saw it at the head of the stretch. How much time did I have? I say, "One, two, three, boom. When you have enough horse, you can go through those holes." Three seconds. I have been riding thirty-seven years and only three seconds of time gives me my greatest victory. How sweet it is. You bet.

SHOEMAKER'S RECORD OF VICTORIES IN $100,000 STAKES

RACETRACK ABBREVIATIONS

(AP)	Arlington Park, Illinois	(Hia)	Hialeah Park, Florida
(Aqu)	Aqueduct Race Track, New York	(Hol)	Hollywood Park, California
(Atl)	Atlantic City Race Course, New Jersey	(Jam)	Jamaica Race Track, New York
(BM)	Bay Meadows Race Track, California	(Kee)	Keeneland Race Course, Kentucky
(Bel)	Belmont Park, New York	(LaD)	Louisiana Downs, Louisiana
(CD)	Churchill Downs, Kentucky	(Mth)	Monmouth Park, New Jersey
(Dmr)	Del Mar Race Track, California	(OP)	Oaklawn Park, Arkansas
(GG)	Golden Gate Fields, California	(Pim)	Pimlico Race Course, Maryland
(GP)	Gulf Stream Park, Florida	(SA)	Santa Anita Park, California
(GS)	Garden State Park, New Jersey	(Sar)	Saratoga Race Track, New York
		(Was)	Washington Park, Illinois

DATE	STAKE (TRACK)	WINNER
Feb. 3, 1951	Santa Anita Maturity	Great Circle
Feb. 27, 1954	Santa Anita Handicap	Rejected
Mar. 20, 1954	Florida Derby (GP)	Correlation
Apr. 24, 1954	Wood Memorial (Jam)	Correlation
Feb. 26, 1955	Santa Anita Handicap	Poona II
May 7, 1955	Kentucky Derby (CD)	Swaps
Aug. 20, 1955	American Derby (Was)	Swaps
Sep. 5, 1955	Washington Park 'Cap	Jet Action
Mar. 3, 1956	Santa Anita Derby	Tarrang
Jly. 4, 1956	American 'Cap (Hol)	Swaps
Jly. 14, 1956	Hollywood Gold Cup	Swaps
Jly. 25, 1956	Sunset Handicap (Hol)	Swaps
Sep. 3, 1956	Washington Park 'Cap	Swaps
May 25, 1957	California S. (Hol)	Social Climber
Jun. 15, 1957	Belmont Stakes	Gallant Man
Jly. 13, 1957	Hollywood Gold Cup	Round Table

DATE	STAKE (TRACK)	WINNER
Jly. 20, 1957	Westerner Stakes (Hol)	Round Table
Aug. 31, 1957	American Derby (Was)	Round Table
Sep. 2, 1957	Washington Park 'Cap	Pucker Up
Sep. 14, 1957	U. N. 'Cap (Atl)	Round Table
Oct. 12, 1957	Champagne S. (Bel)	Jewel's Reward
Nov. 23, 1957	Pimlico Futurity	Jewel's Reward
Mar. 1, 1958	Santa Anita Handicap	Round Table
Mar. 8, 1958	Santa Anita Derby	Silky Sullivan
Mar. 22, 1958	Gulfstream Park 'Cap	Round Table
Jly. 12, 1958	Hollywood Gold Cup	Gallant Man
Jly. 22, 1958	Sunset Handicap (Hol)	Gallant Man
Aug. 2, 1958	Arlington Futurity	Restless Wind
Aug. 30, 1958	Washington Park Fut'y	Restless Wind
Sep. 13, 1958	U. N. 'Cap (Atl)	Clem
Sep. 20, 1958	Futurity Stakes (Bel)	Intentionally
Sep. 27, 1958	Woodward S. (Bel)	Clem
Oct. 11, 1958	Hawthorne Gold Cup	Round Table
Nov. 22, 1958	Pimlico Futurity	Intentionally
May 2, 1959	Kentucky Derby (CD)	Tomy Lee
May 30, 1959	Metropolitan 'Cap (Bel)	Sword Dancer
Jun. 13, 1959	Belmont Stakes	Sword Dancer
Jun. 27, 1959[1]	Hollywood Derby	Bagdad
Jly. 25, 1959	Monmouth Handicap	Sword Dancer
Aug. 22, 1959	Arlington Handicap	Round Table
Aug. 29, 1959	Hopeful Stakes (Sar)	Tompion
Sep. 7, 1959	Wash. Pk. 'Cap (AP)	Round Table
Sep. 19, 1959	U. N. 'Cap (Atl)	Round Table
Mar. 5, 1960	Santa Anita Derby	Tompion
Oct. 22, 1960	Gardenia Stakes (GS)	Bowl of Flowers

[1] Run as the Westerner Stakes prior to 1959.

DATE	STAKE (TRACK)	WINNER
Jan. 28, 1961	Santa Anita Maturity	Prove It
Feb. 25, 1961	Santa Anita Handicap	Prove It
Mar. 11, 1961	Capistrano 'Cap (SA)	Don't Alibi
Oct. 7, 1961	Frizette Stakes (Aqu)	Cicada
Oct. 21, 1961	Gardenia Stakes (GS)	Cicada
Nov. 4, 1961	Garden State S. (GS)	Crimson Satan
Nov. 18, 1961	Pimlico Futurity	Crimson Satan
Mar. 10, 1962	Sn. Jn. Cap. 'Cap (SA)	Olden Times
Jun. 9, 1962	Belmont Stakes	Jaipur
Sep. 3, 1962	Wash. Pk. 'Cap (AP)	Prove It
Sep. 8, 1962[2]	Arl.-Wash. Fut'y (AP)	Candy Spots
Sep. 15, 1962	Futurity Stakes (Aqu)	Never Bend
Nov. 10, 1962	Garden State Stakes	Crewman
Mar. 2, 1963	Santa Anita Derby	Candy Spots
Mar. 30, 1963	Florida Derby (GP)	Candy Spots
May 18, 1963	Preakness S. (Pim)	Candy Spots
May 30, 1963	Jersey Derby (GS)	Candy Spots
Jly. 13, 1963	American Derby (AP)	Candy Spots
Aug. 3, 1963	Arlington Classic	Candy Spots
Aug. 31, 1963[2]	Arl.-Wash. Las. S. (AP)	Sari's Song
Jan. 25, 1964[4]	Strub Stakes (SA)	Gun Bow
Mar. 3, 1964	Flamingo Stakes (Hia)	Northern Dancer
Mar. 21, 1964	Gulfstream Park 'Cap	Gun Bow
Apr. 4, 1964	Florida Derby (GP)	Northern Dancer
Jun. 20, 1964	Illinois Handicap (AP)	Olden Times
Sep. 12, 1964[2]	Arl.-Wash. Fut'y (AP)	Sadair
Oct. 10, 1964	Frizette Stakes (Aqu)	Queen Empress
Nov. 7, 1964	Gardenia Stakes (GS)	Queen Empress

[2] Arlington and Washington Park Futurities combined into one race, beginning in 1962.
[4] Run as Santa Anita Maturity prior to 1963.

SHOEMAKER

DATE	STAKE (TRACK)	WINNER
Mar. 6, 1965	Santa Anita Derby	Lucky Debonair
May 1, 1965	Kentucky Derby (CD)	Lucky Debonair
Jly. 24, 1965	H'wood Juv. Ch.	Port Wine
Aug. 7, 1965	Chicagoan Stakes (AP)	Tom Rolfe
Aug. 28, 1965	Arlington Classic	Tom Rolfe
Sep. 13, 1965	American Derby (AP)	Tom Rolfe
Jan. 29, 1966[4]	Strub Stakes (SA)	Bold Bidder
Feb. 26, 1966	Santa Anita Handicap	Lucky Debonair
Mar. 3, 1966	Flamingo Stakes (Hia)	Buckpasser
Aug. 6, 1966	Sapling Stakes (Mth)	Great Power
Sep. 5, 1966	Aqueduct Handicap	Tom Rolfe
Sep. 10, 1966[2]	Arl.-Wash. Fut'y (AP)	Diplomat Way
Feb. 25, 1967	Santa Anita Handicap	Pretense
Apr. 22, 1967	Wood Memorial (Aqu)	Damascus
May 20, 1967	Preakness S. (Pim)	Damascus
Jun. 3, 1967	Belmont Stakes (Aqu)	Damascus
Jly. 24, 1967	Sunset Handicap (Hol)	Hill Clown
Aug. 5, 1967	American Derby (AP)	Damascus
Sep. 4, 1967[5]	Aqueduct Stakes	Damascus
Sep. 9, 1967[2]	Arl.-Wash. Fut'y, 2nd Div. (AP)	Vitriolic
Sep. 23, 1967	Futurity Stakes (Aqu)	Captain's Gig
Sep. 30, 1967	Woodward S. (Aqu)	Damascus
Oct. 28, 1967	Jky. Club G. C. S. (Aqu)	Damascus
Sep. 1, 1969[3]	Arl.-Wash. Las. S. (AP)	Clover Lane
Mar. 28, 1970	Santa Anita Derby	Terlago
Apr. 4, 1970	Capistrano 'Cap (SA)	Fiddle Isle DH
Jun. 20, 1970	H'wood Pk. Inv. T. 'Cap	Fiddle Isle

[2] Arlington and Washington Park Futurities combined into one race, beginning in 1962.
[5] Changed from handicap to allowance conditions in 1967; renamed the Governor Nicolis Stakes in 1969.
[3] Run as Arlington Lassie prior to 1963.
DH Dead Heat

DATE	STAKE (TRACK)	WINNER
Mar. 13, 1971	Santa Anita Handicap	Ack Ack
Apr. 10, 1971	Capistrano 'Cap (SA)	Cougar II
May 22, 1971	California Derby (Hol)	Cougar II
Jun. 26, 1971[6]	Ford Pinto Inv. 'Cap (Hol)	Cougar II
Jly. 17, 1971	H'wood Gold Cup 'Cap	Ack Ack
Jly. 24, 1971	H'wood Juv. Ch. S.	Royal Owl
Oct. 30, 1971	Oak Tree Inv. S. (SA)	Cougar II
Dec. 18, 1971	California Juv. S. (BM)	Royal Owl
Feb. 12, 1972[4]	Strub Stakes (SA)	Unconscious
Mar. 4, 1972	Margarita 'Cap (SA)	Turkish Trousers
Apr. 22, 1972	California Derby (Hol)	Quack
Apr. 29, 1972	Century 'Cap (Hol)	Cougar II
May 20, 1972	California S. (Hol)	Cougar II
Sep. 13, 1972	Del Mar Futurity	Groshawk
Nov. 1, 1972	Oak Tree Inv. S. (SA)	Cougar II
May 5, 1973	Century 'Cap (Hol)	Cougar II
Jun. 24, 1973	H'wood G. C. Inv. 'Cap	Kennedy Road
Jly. 23, 1973	Sunset Handicap (Hol)	Cougar II
Sep. 12, 1973	Del Mar Futurity	Such a Rush
Mar. 30, 1974	Fantasy Stakes (OP)	Miss Musket
Apr. 23, 1974	California Derby (GG)	Agitate
Jun. 23, 1974	H'wood G. C. Inv. 'Cap	Tree of Knowledge
Jun. 30, 1974	Swaps Stakes (Hol)	Agitate
Jly. 14, 1974	H'wood Inv. Derby	Agitate
Jly. 22, 1974	Sunset Handicap (Hol)	Greco II
Sep. 11, 1974	Del Mar Futurity	Diabolo
Feb. 9, 1975	Strub Stakes (SA)	Stardust Mel
Mar. 9, 1975	Santa Anita Handicap	Stardust Mel

[6] Run as Hollywood Park Invitational Turf Handicap prior to and after 1971.
[4] Run as Santa Anita Maturity prior to 1963.

DATE	STAKE (TRACK)	WINNER
Jun. 7, 1975	Belmont Stakes	Avatar
Jly. 6, 1975	Vanity Handicap (Hol)	Dulcia
Oct. 19, 1975	Oak Tree Invit'l. S. (SA)	Top Command
Nov. 1, 1975	Nat. Thoro. Ch. Inv. S. (SA)	Dulcia
Apr. 17, 1976	Hollywood Derby	Crystal Water
May 31, 1976	Hollywood Pk. Inv. T. 'Cap	Dahlia
Sep. 6, 1976	Del Mar Handicap	Riot in Paris
Sep. 18, 1976	Woodward 'Cap (Bel)	Forego
Oct. 2, 1976	Marlboro Cup 'Cap (Bel)	Forego
Oct. 24, 1976	Oak Tree Inv. S. (SA)	King Pellinore
Nov. 6, 1976	Chpn. Invit'l. 'Cap (SA)	King Pellinore
Nov. 7, 1976	Norfolk Stakes (SA)	Habitony
Feb. 13, 1977	La Canada S. (SA)	Lucie Manet
Mar. 27, 1977	Santa Anita Derby	Habitony
May 30, 1977	Metropolitan 'Cap (Bel)	Forego
Jun. 26, 1977	Hollywood Oaks	Glenaris
Jly. 3, 1977	Swaps Stakes (Hol)	J. O. Tobin
Jly. 25, 1977	Sunset Handicap (Hol)	Today 'n Tomorrow
Sep. 17, 1977	Woodward 'Cap (Bel)	Forego
Oct. 23, 1977	Oak Tree Invit'l. S. (SA)	Crystal Water
Nov. 6, 1977	Norfolk Stakes (SA)	Balzac
Apr. 9, 1978	Capistrano 'Cap (SA)	Exceller
May 29, 1978	H'wood Invit'l. Turf 'Cap	Exceller
Jun. 25, 1978	H'wood Gold Cup 'Cap	Exceller
Jly. 16, 1978	Vanity Handicap (Hol)	Afifa
Jly. 24, 1978	Sunset Handicap (Hol)	Exceller
Aug. 27, 1978	Longacres Mile 'Cap	Bad 'n Big
Oct. 14, 1978	Jky. Club G. C. S. (Bel)	Exceller
Nov. 4, 1978	Yellow Ribbon S. (SA)	Amazer
Nov. 5, 1978	Oak Tree Invit'l. S. (SA)	Exceller

DATE	STAKE (TRACK)	WINNER
Feb. 25, 1979	St. Marg. Inv. 'Cap (SA)	Sanedtki
Mar. 11, 1979	Santa Susana (SA)	Caline
Jly. 8, 1979	Citation Handicap (Hol)	Text
Jly. 15, 1979	Vanity Handicap (Hol)	It's in the Air
Jly. 21, 1979	H'wood Juv. Ch.	Parsec
Aug. 25, 1979	Haskell Handicap (Mth)	Text
Sep. 1, 1979	Flower Bowl 'Cap (Bel)	Pearl Necklace
Sep. 8, 1979	Marlboro Cup 'Cap (Bel)	Spectacular Bid
Sep. 9, 1979	Del Mar Debutante	Table Hands
Oct. 18, 1979	Meadowlands Cup 'Cap	Spectacular Bid
Jan. 19, 1980	San Fernando S. (SA)	Spectacular Bid
Feb. 2, 1980[4]	Strub Stakes (SA)	Spectacular Bid
Feb. 18, 1980	San Luis Obispo 'Cap (SA)	Silver Eagle
Mar. 2, 1980	Santa Anita Handicap	Spectacular Bid
Mar. 15, 1980	San Felipe 'Cap (SA)	Raise a Man
Apr. 20, 1980	Native Diver 'Cap (Hol)	Replant
Apr. 27, 1980	Century 'Cap (Hol)	Go West Young Man
May 18, 1980	LeRoy 'Cap (Hol)	Spectacular Bid
May 24, 1980	Golden St. Brdrs. Sire S.	Rumbo
Jun. 8, 1980	California S. (Hol)	Spectacular Bid
Jly. 4, 1980	American 'Cap (AP)	Bold Tropic
Jly. 19, 1980	Wash. Pk. S. (AP)	Spectacular Bid
Jly. 21, 1980	Sunset Handicap (Hol)	Inkerman
Aug. 16, 1980	Haskell 'Cap (Mth)	Spectacular Bid
Aug. 31, 1980	Roman 'Cap (Dmr)	Queen to Conquer
Sep. 13, 1980	Arl.-Wash. Lassie S.	Truly Bound
Sep. 20, 1980	Woodward Stakes (Bel)	Spectacular Bid
Mar. 21, 1981	Santa Susana (SA)	Nell's Briquette
Mar. 28, 1981	Fair Grounds Oaks	Truly Bound
Apr. 5, 1981	S. Bernardino 'Cap (SA)	Borzoi
Jly. 4, 1981	American 'Cap (Hol)	Bold Tropic
Jly. 11, 1981	Sword Dancer (Bel)	John Henry

DATE	STAKE (TRACK)	WINNER
Jly. 20, 1981	Sunset 'Cap (Hol)	Galaxy Libra
Aug. 30, 1981	Arlington Million	John Henry
Oct. 3, 1981	Man o' War (Bel)	Galaxy Libra
Oct. 10, 1981	Jky. Club G. C. (Bel)	John Henry
Oct. 11, 1981	Beldame Stakes (Bel)	Love Sign
Oct. 17, 1981	Alcibiades Stakes (Kee)	Apalachee Honey
Nov. 8, 1981	Oak Tree Inv. 'Cap (SA)	John Henry
Dec. 13, 1981	Silver Bells 'Cap (Hol)	Happy Guess
Dec. 20, 1981	Citation 'Cap (Hol)	Tahitian King
Jan. 9, 1982	San Carlos 'Cap (SA)	Solo Guy
Mar. 7, 1982	Santa Anita Handicap	John Henry
Mar. 14, 1982	Santa Susana (SA)	Blush With Pride
Apr. 17, 1982	Ashland Stakes (Kee)	Blush With Pride
Apr. 22, 1982	Blue Grass Stakes (Kee)	Linkage
Apr. 30, 1982	Kentucky Oaks (CD)	Blush With Pride
Jly. 11, 1982	Vanity Handicap (Hol)	Sangue
Sep. 6, 1982	Del Mar Invitational (Dmr)	Muttering
Sep. 12, 1982[7]	Golden Harvest 'Cap. (LaD)	Blush With Pride
Sep. 12, 1982[7]	Golden Harvest 'Cap. (LaD)	Miss Huntington
Oct. 31, 1982	Oak Tree Inv. (SA)	John Henry
Dec. 4, 1982	Cal. Jockey Club (BM)	Buchanette
Feb. 21, 1983	San Luis Obispo (SA)	Pelerin
Apr. 17, 1983	San Bernardino (SA)	The Wonder
May 7, 1983	Century Handicap (Hol)	The Wonder
May 15, 1983	Mervyn LeRoy (Hol)	Fighting Fit
Jun. 12, 1983	California Stakes (Hol)	The Wonder
Sep. 5, 1983	Del Mar Handicap (Dmr)	Bel Bolide
Sep. 11, 1983	Ramona Handicap (Dmr)	Sangue
Sep. 18, 1983	Arlington Handicap (AP)	Palikaraki
Oct. 2, 1983	Golden Harvest Handicap (LaD)	Sangue

[7] Golden Harvest Handicap run in two divisions.

DATE	STAKE (TRACK)	WINNER
Nov. 6, 1983	Yellow Ribbon (SA)	Sangue
Dec. 4, 1983	The Matriarch (Hol)	Sangue
Mar. 18, 1984	Santa Ana Handicap (SA)	Avigaition
Oct. 6, 1984	Fall Festival Juvenile (BM)	Michadilla
Nov. 4, 1984	Goodwood Handicap (SA)	Lord at War
Nov. 24, 1984	Citation (Hol)	Lord at War
Dec. 1, 1984	National Sprint Championship (Hol)	Lovlier Linda
Dec. 5, 1984	Hollywood Prevue (Hol)	First Norman
Dec. 22, 1984	Native Diver Handicap (Hol)	Lord at War
Feb. 17, 1985	San Antonio 'Cap (SA)	Lord at War
Mar. 3, 1985	Santa Anita 'Cap (SA)	Lord at War
Mar. 10, 1985	Arcadia 'Cap (SA)	Fatih
Apr. 1, 1985	Genesis 'Cap (GS)	Hail Bold King
May 7, 1985	Valkyr 'Cap (Hol)	Shywing
Aug. 31, 1985	Del Mar Oaks (Dmr)	Savannah Dancer
Sep. 8, 1985	Ramona 'Cap (Dmr)	Daily Busy
Oct. 17, 1985	Goodwood 'Cap (SA)	Lord at War
Oct. 19, 1985	Las Palmas 'Cap (SA)	Estrapade
Nov. 3, 1985	Linda Vista 'Cap (SA)	Savannah Slew
Nov. 10, 1985	Yellow Ribbon 'Cap (SA)	Estrapade
Mar. 23, 1986	Santa Anita Oaks (SA)	Hidden Lights
May 3, 1986	Kentucky Derby (CD)	Ferdinand
May 4, 1986	John Henry 'Cap (Hol)	Palace Music
Jun. 6, 1986	Nassau County 'Cap (Bel)	Roo Art
Jly. 6, 1986	Hollywood Oaks (Hol)	Hidden Light
Jly. 19, 1986	Majorette (LaD)	Eloquack
Aug. 16, 1986	James Iselin 'Cap (Mth)	Roo Art
Aug. 23, 1986	Chula Vista 'Cap (Dmr)	Fran's Valentine
Aug. 24, 1986	Del Mar Oaks (Dmr)	Hidden Lights

DATE	STAKE (TRACK)	WINNER
Sep. 13, 1986	Flower Bowl 'Cap (Bel)	Scoot
Nov. 3, 1986	C. F. Burke 'Cap (SA)	Louis La Grand
Nov. 16, 1986	Hollywood Derby (Hol)	Thrill Show
Nov. 29, 1986	Bay Meadows Derby (BM)	Le Belvedere
Dec. 7, 1986	Hollywood Cup Turf (Hol)	Alphabatim
Dec. 14, 1986	Hollywood Futurity (Hol)	Temperate Sil
Dec. 26, 1986	Malibu (SA)	Ferdinand

HIGHLIGHTS OF SHOEMAKER'S CAREER, YEAR BY YEAR

1949

Mounts	*1st*	*2nd*	*3rd*	*Win Percentage*	*Rank (in races won)*	*Amount Won (in total purses)*	*Rank (in total purses)*
1,089	219	195	147	20%	2	$458,010	14

On March 19, in the fifth race at Golden Gate Fields, Shoemaker rides his first race, finishing fifth on a filly named Waxahachie.

On April 20, on his third mount, he rides his first winner, in the second race at Golden Gate Fields, aboard Shafter V. (See chart.)

On October 26, he wins his first stake race at Bay Meadows, aboard a horse named Al.

1950

Mounts	*1st*	*2nd*	*3rd*	*Win Percentage*	*Rank (in races won)*	*Amount Won (in total purses)*	*Rank (in total purses)*
1,640	388	266	230	24%	1	$844,040	5

Shoemaker wins the first of his many riding championships when he ties Joe Culmone with a record of 388 winners, which broke a record that had stood for forty-four years, having been established in 1906 by Walter Miller.

On October 12, at Bay Meadows, he wins five races. The next day he wins six races, for a total of eleven winners in two days.

For the year, he wins seven stake races with purses totaling $51,095.

1951

Mounts	1st	2nd	3rd	Win Percentage	Rank (in races won)	Amount Won (in total purses)	Rank (in total purses)
1,161	257	197	161	22%	2	$1,329,890	1

Shoemaker wins his first $100,000 stake race, the Santa Anita Maturity, on February 3, on Great Circle. Value to winner: $144,325.

He is the leading rider in the nation for first time in purses won. The earnings of his mounts, $1,329,890, marks the first time his mounts have gone over the $1 million mark.

With sixteen winners in stake races and a total of $497,050 money earned in stake races, he is the third-leading rider in the category of money earned in stake races and he ranks fourth in the number of stake winners.

1952

Mounts	1st	2nd	3rd	Win Percentage	Rank (in races won)	Amount Won (in total purses)	Rank (in total purses)
1,322	315	224	174	24%	2	$1,049,304	4

With 315 winners, Shoemaker is one of two jockeys in the nation whose mounts won more than 300 races. Tony DeSpirito won the title with 390 winners. With $1,049,304 in purse earnings, Shoemaker is one of four jockeys whose mounts earned more than $1 million. He finished behind Eddie Arcaro, Ted Atkinson, and Eric Guerin.

1953

Mounts	*1st*	*2nd*	*3rd*	*Win Percentage*	*Rank (in races won)*	*Amount Won (in total purses)*	*Rank (in total purses)*
1,683	485	302	210	29%	1	$1,784,187	1

In his fourth year as jockey, Shoemaker ranks first in both number of races won and in amount of purses won.

His total of winning mounts, 485, is the first time in the history of racing that a jockey ever rode more than 400 winners.

He rode six winners in a single day on three occasions, on April 4 at Tanforan, on June 20 at Hollywood Park, and on October 10 at Golden Gate.

On thirty days, he rides four or more winners on a single card.

From May 6–8 at Tanforan, Shoemaker posts fourteen winners in twenty-two chances, for an average of 64% in three days.

On seventy-seven days, he rides three or more winners.

1954

Mounts	*1st*	*2nd*	*3rd*	*Win Percentage*	*Rank (in races won)*	*Amount Won (in total purses)*	*Rank (in total purses)*
1,251	380	221	142	30%	1	$1,876,760	1

Shoemaker ranks first in jockey standings both for number of races won and in amount of purses won. His win percentage, 30%, is the highest of any American rider in the twentieth century.

He wins three stake races worth $100,000: Santa Anita Handicap on February 27 on Rejected, Florida Derby on March 20, and Wood Memorial on April 24, both on Correlation.

On October 20, five and a half years after winning his first race, Shoemaker rides 2,000th winner of his career at Tanforan aboard Florence House, a five-year-old Irish-bred horse.

On September 4, at Del Mar, he wins with six of his eight mounts. On October 26–28, at Tanforan, he rides twelve winners. Twenty times he rides four or more winners in a single day.

1955

Mounts	*1st*	*2nd*	*3rd*	*Win Percentage*	*Rank (in races won)*	*Amount Won (in total purses)*	*Rank (in total purses)*
1,149	307	178	138	27%	2	$1,846,884	2

Shoemaker wins his first Kentucky Derby on Swaps. (See chart.)

Wins three other $100,000 races: February 26, Santa Anita Handicap on Poona II. On August 20, American Derby on Swaps. On September 5, Washington Park Handicap on Jet Action.

On August 16, at Washington Park in Chicago, Shoemaker rides six winners in seven chances. Fifteen times during the year he has four winners on a single card.

On August 31, at Washington Park, in a $100,000 winner-take-all match race at a mile and a quarter, he rides Rex Ellsworth's Swaps and is beaten by one and a half lengths by Eddie Arcaro riding William Woodward's Nashua.

By the end of the year, his sixth year in racing, he moves into seventh place in lifetime records of races won with a total of 2,351 winners.

1956

Mounts	*1st*	*2nd*	*3rd*	*Win Percentage*	*Rank (in races won)*	*Amount Won (in total purses)*	*Rank (in total purses)*
1,229	328	187	165	27%	2	$2,113,335	2

Shoemaker wins five stake races worth $100,000: Santa Anita Derby on March 3 on Terrang, American Handicap on July 4, Hollywood Gold

Cup on July 14, Sunset Handicap on July 25, and Washington Park Handicap on September 1, all on Swaps.

Receives the George Woolf Memorial Trophy from the California Turf Writers for his sportsmanlike conduct and professional excellence.

With 328 winners, Shoemaker is one of three riders with over 300 winners. Bill Hartack, 347, and Johnny Longden, 320, are the others. With $2,113,335 in purse earnings, Shoemaker is one of three jockeys whose mounts earned—for the first time in racing history—more than $2 million in a single year. Bill Hartack, $2,343,955, and Eddie Arcaro, $2,043,001, are the others. Shoemaker's winning percentage, 27%, ranks above other leading jockeys, Hartack and Longden, each 25%, and Arcaro, 20%.

Eight times during the year, he rides four winners on a single card.

At Hollywood Park, in a sequence of five winning races, he rides Swaps as that horse ties one and breaks three world records.

At year's end, Shoemaker's career totals—2,679 winners out of 10,524 mounts and $11,302,410 in amount of money won—make him the fifth all-time leading jockey in amount won, and rank him seventh in the all-time category of races won.

1957

Mounts	*1st*	*2nd*	*3rd*	*Win Percentage*	*Rank (in races won)*	*Amount Won (in total purses)*	*Rank (in total purses)*
1,191	295	183	134	25%	3	$2,544,782	2

Shoemaker wins nine $100,000 stakes: California Stakes on May 25 on Social Climber, Belmont Stakes on June 15 on Gallant Man (see chart), Hollywood Gold Cup on July 13, Westerner Stakes on July 20, American Derby on August 31, United Nations Handicap on September 14, all on Round Table. Washington Park Handicap on September 2 on Pucker Up, Champagne Stakes on October 12 on Jewel's Reward, and Pimlico Futurity on November 23 on Jewel's Reward.

In the Kentucky Derby, the most controversial race of his career,

Shoemaker is in the saddle on Gallant Man. Gets a fifteen-day suspension for misjudging the finish line.

With $2,544,782 in earnings, he is one of two jockeys whose mounts earn over $2 million for the year. Hartack, with $3,060,501, was the leader.

On October 12, at Belmont Park, Shoemaker first rode Jewel's Reward to win the Champagne Stakes and later rode Gallant Man to victory in the Jockey Gold Cup. His personal earnings for the day were $14,000.

At the end of the year, his ninth as a jockey, Shoemaker's totals—2,974 winners and $13,847,192 in amount of money won—make him the fourth-leading rider of all time in amount of money won, the sixth of all time in number of winners.

1958

Mounts	*1st*	*2nd*	*3rd*	*Win Percentage*	*Rank (in races won)*	*Amount Won (in total purses)*	*Rank (in total purses)*
1,133	300	185	137	26%	1	$2,961,693	1

Shoemaker leads nation's jockeys for the third time in both categories of races and purses won. He wins money-winning title for the fourth time.

Wins twelve stakes of $100,000: Santa Anita Handicap, March 1, Gulfstream Park Handicap, March 22, and Hawthorne Gold Cup, October 11, all on Round Table. Hollywood Gold Cup, July 12, and Sunset Handicap, July 22, on Gallant Man. Arlington Futurity, August 2, and Washington Park Futurity, August 30, aboard Restless Wind. Futurity Stakes, September 20, and Pimlico Futurity, November 22, on Intentionally. United Nations Handicap, September 13, and Woodward Stakes, September 27, riding on Clem, and the Santa Anita Derby, March 8, aboard Silky Sullivan.

On January 31, at Santa Anita, he rides his 3,000th winner, riding Eternal Pere. At twenty-six years, four months, and fourteen days old, Shoemaker becomes the youngest rider to win 3,000 races.

Riding Round Table to victory in three major handicaps, Shoemaker

makes Round Table the biggest (at the time) money-winning Thoroughbred in history.

In August, Shoemaker is installed in the National Museum Racing Hall of Fame at Saratoga Springs, New York.

His thirty-six winners and total stakes-purse earnings of $1,600,503 earn him the title of most winning jockey for the year in amount of total stakes purses won.

1959

Mounts	*1st*	*2nd*	*3rd*	*Win Percentage*	*Rank (in races won)*	*Amount Won (in total purses)*	*Rank (in total purses)*
1,285	347	230	159	27%	1	$2,843,133	1

Wins second Kentucky Derby on Tomy Lee and wins Belmont Stakes on Sword Dancer. (See charts.)

Also wins seven other $100,000 stake races: Metropolitan Handicap, May 30, and Monmouth Handicap, July 25, on Sword Dancer. Arlington Handicap, August 22, Washington Park Handicap, September 7, United Nations Handicap, September 19, on Round Table. Hollywood Derby, June 27, riding Bagdad, and Hopeful Stakes, August 29, aboard Tompion.

For fourth time, Shoemaker ranks first among U.S. jockeys both in races and purses won. His 347 winners gives him the most-winners riding title for unprecedented fifth time. His total of $2,843,133 marks the fifth time he has led all riders in money won.

Twice during the year, on March 19 at Bowie Race Track in Maryland and on April 4 at Jamaica Race Track in New York, he rides six winners in one day. On three other occasions he wins five races on a single card, and fourteen times during the year he wins four or more races in a single day.

In 1959, the first year he is eligible (the rule being that a rider cannot be admitted until ten years after his first winner), he is elected to the National Jockeys' Hall of Fame at Pimlico Race Track in Baltimore. A group of 1,000 sports broadcasters and writers from coast to coast select one jockey a year for this honor. Shoemaker polled 436 votes. The only Hall of Fame jockeys ever to poll more were Earl Sande, 571, and Eddie Arcaro, 443.

In winning twenty-nine stake races and earning $1,034,422 in stake purses, he again leads all jockeys in this category.

1960

Mounts	*1st*	*2nd*	*3rd*	*Win Percentage*	*Rank (in races won)*	*Amount Won (in total purses)*	*Rank (in total purses)*
1,227	274	196	158	22%	2	$2,123,961	1

Shoemaker wins two $100,00 stakes: Santa Anita Derby, March 5, on Tompion and Gardenia Stakes, October 22, on Bowl of Flowers.

On six different occasions he rides four or more winners on a single card.

For the sixth time in his career, Shoemaker ranks number one in the jockey standings for the amount of money won.

1961

Mounts	*1st*	*2nd*	*3rd*	*Win Percentage*	*Rank (in races won)*	*Amount Won (in total purses)*	*Rank (in total purses)*
1,256	304	186	175	24%	2	$2,690,819	1

Shoemaker wins seven $100,000 stakes: Santa Anita Maturity, January 28, and Santa Anita Handicap, February 25, in the irons on Prove It. Frizette Stakes, October 7, and Gardenia Stakes, October 21, on Cicada. Garden Stakes, November 4, and Pimlico Futurity, November 18, riding Crimson Satan. Capistrano Handicap, March 11, aboard Don't Alibi.

On May 19, at Hollywood Park, California, Shoemaker rides his 4,000th winner, riding Guaranteeya.

His $2,690,819 total of money won is over half a million more than the second jockey in this category (John Seller's $2,141,729). His 304 winners (second to Seller's 328) make him one of two riders with over 300 winners for the year.

In reaching the 4,000-winners plateau, he joins Johnny Longden, Sir Gordon Richards, and Eddie Arcaro as the only jockeys in world history to do so. At twenty-nine years, nine months, Shoemaker becomes the youngest rider ever to do so.

With twenty-five winners in stakes races and stakes-purse earnings of $1,156,470, Shoemaker again wins the title for winningest jockey of the year in money won in stakes purses.

In winning the Capistrano Handicap at Santa Anita on March 11, he gets his eleventh stakes win of the fifty-five-day meeting, a new record. With seventy-eight winners, he becomes, for the eleventh straight year, the top rider at Santa Anita.

At the end of the year, at age thirty and after completing his thirteenth season of riding, Shoemaker has already won more national riding titles than any jockey of modern times. He has won more races with purses $100,000 and over than anyone else in history, and he has averaged more than 300 winners a year for every year he has been riding.

1962

Mounts	*1st*	*2nd*	*3rd*	*Win Percentage*	*Rank (in races won)*	*Amount Won (in total purses)*	*Rank (in total purses)*
1,126	311	156	128	28%	2	$2,916,844	1

Shoemaker ranks first in jockey standings for amount won in purses. Wins Belmont Stakes on Jaipur (see chart) and five other stakes of $100,000, as follows: San Juan Capistrano Handicap, March 10, on Olden Time, Washington Park Handicap, September 3, on Prove It, Arlington-Washington Futurity, September 8, aboard Candy Spots, Fu-

turity Stakes, September 15, riding Never Bend, and Garden State Stakes, November 10, on Crewman.

In winning 311 races with 1,126 mounts and a winning percentage of 28% (352 winners out of 1,755 mounts and a winning percentage of 20%), Shoemaker is one of two jockeys to ride more than 300 winners in 1962. His purse earnings, $2,916,844, is close to $1 million more than his closest competitor, Braulio Baeza, at $2,048,428. This makes him one of two riders with dollar earnings for the year over $2,000,000.

Shoemaker is the world's leading money-winning jockey for the fifth straight year in a row in 1962.

With thirty-eight victories in stakes events and stakes-event money totaling $1,474,516, he is again leading jockey in this category.

On February 23, at Santa Anita, he wins six races in a row, the first time anyone has ridden that many winners in a single day at that track. It is the eighth time in his career that Shoemaker has six winners on one day's program.

On March 7, he is inducted into the El Paso Athletic Hall of Fame, the first jockey to be so honored. He is presented with an elaborate plaque inscribed with his name. Present for the ceremonies are Shoemaker's eighty-four-year-old grandmother and some twenty other residents of the jockey's hometown, nearby Fabens. A few days earlier, Sunland Park Race Track outside El Paso in New Mexico had honored him with a special Bill Shoemaker Day.

The New York Turf Writers Association votes Shoemaker the top jockey of 1962. The award is presented on August 17, 1963, at the NYTWA annual dinner at Saratoga.

1963

Mounts	*1st*	*2nd*	*3rd*	*Win Percentage*	*Rank (in races won)*	*Amount Won (in total purses)*	*Rank (in total purses)*
1,203	271	193	137	23%	4	$2,526,925	1

Shoemaker ranks first in jockey standings for amount in purses won for ninth time, an all-time record. This is the sixth year in a row he leads in this category.

Wins Preakness Stakes on Candy Spots (see chart) and these other $100,000 stakes: Santa Anita Derby, March 2, Florida Derby, March 30, Jersey Derby, May 30, American Derby, July 13, Arlington Classic, August 3, all on Candy Spots. (See chart.) Arlington-Washington Lassie Stakes, August 31, on Sari's Song.

Shoemaker's mounts' earnings, $2,526,925, make him the only jockey to go over the $2,000,000 mark in this category. In amounts won he is more than half a million dollars ahead of the second-place finisher, Manuel Ycaza's $1,981,281.

Once again his thirty-two stakes winners, with stakes earnings of $996,785, wins him the title of leading jockey in this category.

1964

Mounts	*1st*	*2nd*	*3rd*	*Win Percentage*	*Rank (in races won)*	*Amount Won (in total purses)*	*Rank (in total purses)*
1,056	246	147	133	23%	6	$2,649,533	1

Shoemaker ranks first in jockey standings for amount won in purses for the tenth time.

He wins eight stake races of $100,000: Strub Stakes, January 25, and Gulfstream Park Handicap, March 21, on Gun Bow. Flamingo Stakes, March 3, and Florida Derby, April 4, on Northern Dancer. Frizette Stakes, October 10, and Gardenia Stakes, November 7, on Queen Express. Illinois Handicap, June 20, aboard Olden Times. Arlington-Washington Futurity, September 12, riding Sadair.

In the *Grand Award of Sports Show,* sponsored jointly by ABC-TV and *Sports Illustrated,* he is given an award as outstanding jockey of the year.

On January 24, Shoemaker's earnings surpassed Eddie Arcaro's all-time earnings record of $30,039,543 aboard a horse named Braganza, his fourth winner of the day at Santa Anita, California. His lifetime earnings in purses reach a total of $30,043,792, surpassing the then-retired Arcaro.

Shoemaker's record-setting totals were set at the beginning of his sixteenth year as a rider. Arcaro's totals were achieved in a thirty-one-year career span.

On May 25, in the third race at Hollywood Park, he rides Fleet Son to victory for his 4,871st career victory, moving past Sir Gordon Richards' total of 4,870 winners, to become the second-winningest jockey of all times. Johnny Longden, who was still riding then, was the leader with 5,819.

On October 22, at Aqueduct Race Track, in the 19,900th mount he had had since winning his first race aboard Shafter V in 1949, Shoemaker rides his 5,000th career winner—the second jockey in all racing history to reach that plateau.

In 1964, he is the leading money-winning jockey for the seventh consecutive year, the tenth year altogether he has won this title. With thirty-four winners and $1,243,827 won in stakes purses, he is also again the leading jockey in this category. And, by year's end, his total of 5,027 winners out of 20,001 career mounts gives him a sixteen-year average winning percentage of 25%, an unprecedented figure over such a span.

1965

Mounts	*1st*	*2nd*	*3rd*	*Win Percentage*	*Rank (in races won)*	*Amount Won (in total purses)*	*Rank (in total purses)*
1,069	247	161	120	23%	3	$2,228,977	6

Shoemaker wins third Kentucky Derby on Lucky Debonair. (See chart.)

He wins five other stake races of $100,000 and over: Chicagoan Stakes, August 7, Arlington Classic, August 28, and American Derby, September 13, on Tom Rolfe, Santa Anita Derby, March 6, on Lucky Debonair, and Hollywood Juvenile Champion, July 24, on Port Wine.

In March, he is presented with a silver plate by Santa Anita Park officials on the occasion of his having won 1,000 races at that course.

With $2,228,977 in money won for the year, Shoemaker is one of two jockeys to go over the $2 million mark. The other is Braulio Baeza's $2,582,702. In 1965, Shoemaker's mounts earn more than $2 million for the tenth year in a row, a new record. At the end of the year, his mounts have earned a grand total of $34,789,097, an all-time world record.

In October, he rides in France for the first time, finishing sixth aboard Tom Rolfe in the Arc de Triomphe at Longchamps.

1966

Mounts	*1st*	*2nd*	*3rd*	*Win Percentage*	*Rank (in races won)*	*Amount Won (in total purses)*	*Rank (in total purses)*
1,037	221	158	107	21%	13	$2,671,198	2

Shoemaker wins six $100,000 stake races: Strub Stakes, January 29, on Bold Bidder, Santa Anita Handicap, February 26, on Lucky Debonair, Flamingo Stakes, March 3, on Buckpasser, Sapling Stakes, August 6, on Great Power, Aqueduct Handicap, September 5, aboard Tom Rolfe, Arlington-Washington Futurity, September 10, riding Diplomat Way.

By year's end, after eighteen years of riding, Shoemaker has won twenty-two national riding titles: leading money-winner ten times, leading stakes winner seven times, leading race winner five times. Also at end of 1966, his total money won of $37,460,295 makes him the leading rider of all time in total money won, over $7 million more than his closest competitor, Eddie Arcaro.

For the year 1966 only he, with $2,671,198, and Braulio Baeza, with $2,951,022, are the only jockeys to go over the $2 million mark for amount of money won.

With thirty-seven winners and earnings of $1,303,787 in stakes races, Shoemaker again leads all riders in this category.

1967

Mounts	*1st*	*2nd*	*3rd*	*Win Percentage*	*Rank (in races won)*	*Amount Won (in total purses)*	*Rank (in total purses)*
1,044	244	146	113	23%	7	$3,052,108	2

Shoemaker wins Preakness Stakes and Belmont Stakes on Damascus. (See charts.)

Also wins nine other $100,000 stake races: Wood Memorial, April 22, American Derby, August 5, Aqueduct Stakes, September 4, Woodward Stakes, September 30, and Jockey Gold Cup, October 28, on Damascus, Santa Anita Handicap, February 25, on Pretense, Sunset Handicap, July 24, on Hill Clown, Arlington-Washington Futurity, September 9, on Vitriolic, Futurity Stakes, September 23, on Captain's Gig.

This year, for the first time, his mounts earn more than $3 million. For the previous eleven years, ever since 1956 his mounts had earned at least $2 million annually. By the end of the year, he goes over $40 million in career earnings, with a total of $40,512,403, more than $10 million ahead of the nearest rival Eddie Arcaro, then retired, whose total of $30,039,543 took thirty-one seasons of riding to accumulate.

Shoemaker wins thirty-eight stakes races and has stakes-purse earnings of $1,629,874, which makes him once again the leading jockey for money won in stakes races.

This was the seventeenth consecutive year that Shoemaker was the leading rider in races won at Santa Anita, California.

1968

Mounts	*1st*	*2nd*	*3rd*	*Win Percentage*	*Rank (in races won)*	*Amount Won (in total purses)*	*Rank (in total purses)*
104	19	14	11	18%	*	$175,950	*

After riding for nineteen years without a serious injury, Shoemaker suffers a broken right leg in a spectacular three-horse spill during the second race at Santa Anita while aboard a cheap claiming horse named Bel Bush. The accident on January 23 resulted in a fracture of Shoemaker's right thigh bone that would incapacitate him for thirteen months.

For the first time in seventeen years, he does not win a major ($100,000) stake race.

At the time of the accident, Shoemaker was the leading active jockey in winners, with 5,758, only 274 winners behind the all-time record. He had also been the national riding champion five times and the leading money-winner ten times.

Until the accident, which kept him out of action for the rest of the year, Shoemaker had, since he began riding in 1949, ridden an average number of 1,200 mounts a year and over that span had averaged 300 winners a year—for an astonishing winning average of 25%.

By the end of 1968, Shoemaker's mounts' earnings have reached a total of $40,688,383, an all-time high, as a result of his having won 5,758 winners in 23,355 races.

In May, unable to compete, Shoemaker is the official guest of honor of Churchill Downs at the ninety-fourth running of the Kentucky Derby.

In September and October, Shoemaker and Johnny Longden make a three-week tour of U.S. Army bases in South Vietnam for the USO to entertain the GIs. Films were shown of the two jockeys' most famous races, with both jockeys answering soldiers' questions.

* not in top 30

1969

Mounts	*1st*	*2nd*	*3rd*	*Win Percentage*	*Rank (in races won)*	*Amount Won (in total purses)*	*Rank (in total purses)*
454	97	63	58	21%	*	$1,047,949†	21

Shoemaker wins one $100,000 stake race: Arlington-Washington Lassie Stakes, September 1, on Clover Lane.

After being sidelined for thirteen months with his broken thigh bone, Shoemaker returns on February 11 and rides three winners in three attempts at Santa Anita.

Ten weeks later, on April 30, Shoemaker is injured in a freak paddock accident when, just before the fourth race at Hollywood Park, a three-year-old filly named Poona's Day suddenly rears, unseats the rider, throws him into a hedge against a stone wall, and then sits on him, causing the jockey to suffer a broken pelvis and a damaged bladder. He is sidelined for four months.

At the time of this accident, he had ridden 5,812 winners, second only to Johnny Longdon, then retired, who had 6,032.

In November, Shoemaker rides his first winner in a foreign country, scoring with two mounts at the San Isidro track in Argentina. In Argentina's richest race, the Gran Premio Internacional Carlos Pellegrini, he finishes out of the money on a horse named Snow Sporting.

At the annual meeting of the Thoroughbred Racing Association in New Orleans, he is named as 1969's Big Sport of Turfdom, an award conferred by the Turf Publicists of America, the citation emphasizing that the selection was not based on his brilliant record as a jockey, but rather on "his lifetime display of sportsmanship qualities, to include a humility at all stages of his success."

* not in top 30
† foreign earnings not included

1970

Mounts	1st	2nd	3rd	Win Percentage	Rank (in races won)	Amount Won (in total purses)	Rank (in total purses)
952	219	133	106	23%	11	$2,063,194	6

Shoemaker wins three $100,000 stakes: Santa Anita Derby, March 28, on Terlago, Capistrano Handicap (DH), April 4, and Hollywood Park Invitational Turf Handicap, June 20, aboard Fiddle Isle.

On September 7, aboard the filly Dares J., Shoemaker rides his 6,033rd winner, passing John Longden as the rider with most wins in the history of the sport.

He is appointed by Richard Nixon to become a member of the President's Advisory Conference on Physical Fitness and Sports.

He is a guest of Richard Nixon at the White House at a dinner given for President Ordaz of Mexico.

On June 24, at Hollywood Park, he wins six races and places second on his seventh mount. This feat matches his own single-day record at Hollywood Park, set seventeen years earlier on June 20, 1953. This is the ninth time in his career that Shoemaker rides six winners in one day and the third time he wins with six out of seven mounts.

At the end of the year, he has raised his total of winners to 6,072. Of these, 505 are in stake races, and he has compiled an unparalleled number of over 100 winners in stake races with purses of $100,000 and over.

On September 12, at Del Mar, he wins five races of the seven in which he has mounts.

On January 23, in New York City, the B'nai B'rith makes a special award to Shoemaker for "high principle and achievement in sports in 1970."

In September, film director Martin Ritt begins production on a one-hour television special titled *6,033—Nice Guys Finish First.* Music for this TV special on the jockey's life and career is composed by Elmer Bernstein.

And on August 13, in the one-and-a-quarter-mile Prix Gantauthiron at Deauville, France, a race worth $21,650 to the winner, a four-year-old

horse named Shoemaker, ridden by Duncan Keith, romps home, an easy winner.

1971

Mounts	*1st*	*2nd*	*3rd*	*Win Percentage*	*Rank (in races won)*	*Amount Won (in total purses)*	*Rank (in total purses)*
881	195	136	104	22%	21	$2,931,590	2

Shoemaker wins eight $100,000 stake races: Capistrano Handicap, April 10, California Derby, May 22, Ford Pinto Invitational Handicap, June 26, and Oak Tree Invitational Stakes, October 30, on Cougar II. Santa Anita Handicap, March 13, Hollywood Gold Cup Handicap, July 17, aboard Ack Ack. Hollywood Juvenile Champion Stakes, July 24, and California Juvenile Stakes, December 18, on Royal Owl.

On April 7, Santa Anita unveils a bronze statue of Shoemaker to be placed in the paddock garden alongside a similar likeness of Johnny Longden, Shoemaker being honored as the winningest rider of all time. This is how the plaque is inscribed:

WILLIAM SHOEMAKER
WORLD'S RECORD FOR
MOST RIDING VICTORIES
NO. 6,033 ON SEPTEMBER 7, 1970
DEL MAR, CALIFORNIA

FOR MOST WINNERS
IN A YEAR
NO. 485 ON DECEMBER 31, 1953
SANTA ANITA PARK

On October 30, at Santa Anita, he wins five races out of seven mounts, including the rich Oak Tree Invitational Stakes aboard Cougar II.

In January, the selection committee of the California Racing Hall of Fame names him California Jockey of the Year for 1970.

In February, at the annual dinner of the California Thoroughbred Breeders Association, an oil painting of Shoemaker by artist Lawrence Shelby is presented to be hung in the California Hall of Fame. The painting bears a plaque with this inscription: "He established the world's record of 6,033 victories, Del Mar Race Track, September 7, 1970."

In February, the United Savings Helms Athletic Foundation honors him with an award as Southern California Athlete of the Year.

In April, in Louisville, the National Turf Writers Association honors him for his long and meritorious service to racing.

On November 13, he wins the Junipero Serra Stakes at Bay Meadows Race Track on Royal Owl to record his forty-fourth stake victory of the year and surpass the record in this category established by Bill Hartack in 1957.

At the end of the year, with forty-six stakes winners and stakes-total earnings of $1,567,295, Shoemaker is the leader in this category for the ninth time.

Also, at the end of the year after twenty-three years as a jockey, his astonishing record shows: 6,267 winners out of 25,542 mounts, for a winning percentage of 24.5% and a total of $46,731,068 in amount of money won. This record compares with his two closest rivals, both retired, as follows: Longden's 6,026 winners out of 32,406 mounts, in a forty-year riding career, with a percentage of winning mounts of 18.5%, and Arcaro's money-won total of $30,039,543 in a career spanning thirty-one years, and a percentage of winning races of 19.8%.

1972

Mounts	*1st*	*2nd*	*3rd*	*Win Percentage*	*Rank (in races won)*	*Amount Won (in total purses)*	*Rank (in total purses)*
869	172	137	111	20%	*	$2,519,384	4

Shoemaker wins seven $100,000 stake races: Century Handicap, April 29, California Stakes, May 20, and Oak Tree Invitational Stakes, November 1, on Cougar II. Strub Stakes, February 12, riding Unconscious. Margarita Handicap, March 4, on Turkish Trousers. California Derby, April 22, on Quack, and Del Mar Futurity, September 13, on Groshawk.

On March 2, at Santa Anita, he wins the San Jacinto Stakes on Royal Owl for his 555th stakes win, going ahead of Eddie Arcaro's total of 554 stakes winners to set an all-time record for most stakes victories.

With 172 winning rides and a total of $2,519,384 in earnings for 1972, his totals after twenty-four years are as follows: career wins, 6,439, career money-won total, $49,250,470, making Shoemaker the all-time leader in both categories. His career winning percentage of 24.4% is higher than any other jockey riding for more than ten years.

1973

Mounts	*1st*	*2nd*	*3rd*	*Win Percentage*	*Rank (in races won)*	*Amount Won (in total purses)*	*Rank (in total purses)*
639	139	95	73	22%	*	$2,016,874	12

Shoemaker wins four $100,000 stake races: Century Handicap, May 5, and Sunset Handicap, July 24, on Cougar II, Hollywood Gold Cup Invitational Handicap, June 24, on Kennedy Road, and Del Mar Futurity, September 12, on Such a Rush.

In January, Shoemaker is injured in a spill at Santa Anita. After surgery on his right hand, he is sidelined for almost eight weeks.

* not in first 30

The year 1973 marks the quarter-century mark of Shoemaker's career, his fabulous totals showing him as the leading money-winner of all times with a total of $51,267,344, the all-time leader in races won, with a total of 6,578, the all-time leader in wins in races with purses of $100,000 and over, with 119. And, with twenty-six of his winning 1973 mounts coming in stakes races, his career total in this category is 603, also an all-time record.

1974

Mounts	*1st*	*2nd*	*3rd*	*Win Percentage*	*Rank (in races won)*	*Amount Won (in total purses)*	*Rank (in total purses)*
922	160	126	108	17%	*	$2,558,862	6

Shoemaker wins seven $100,000 stakes races: California Derby, April 23, Swaps Stakes, June 30, and Hollywood Invitational Derby, July 14, on Agitate. Fantasy Stakes, March 30, on Miss Musket. Hollywood Gold Cup Invitational Handicap, June 23, on Tree of Knowledge. Sunset Handicap, July 22, on Greco II. And Del Mar Futurity, September 11, on Diablo.

In winning the Fantasy Stakes at Oaklawn Park on March 30, on Miss Musket, Shoemaker notches his 100th victory in a race worth $100,000 or more.

The year 1975 marks the seventeenth year Shoemaker's mounts' earnings have gone over $2 million. Since 1956, the only years when his totals of amount won have fallen below the $2 million mark were 1968 and 1969, when he was out of action for a good part of those campaigns with injuries.

By year's end his totals, all records without parallel in the annals of horse racing, were: total money won, $53,826,206, total winning races, 6,738, percentage of winning rides over twenty-six years, 24.1%.

* not in top 30

1975

Mounts	*1st*	*2nd*	*3rd*	*Win Percentage*	*Rank (in races won)*	*Amount Won (in total purses)*	*Rank (in total purses)*
957	215	142	124	22%	22	$3,514,213	3

Shoemaker wins Belmont Stakes on Avatar. (See chart.)

Also wins five other $100,000 stake races: Strub Stakes, February 9, and Santa Anita Handicap, March 9, on Stardust Mel. Vanity Handicap, July 6, and National Thoroughbred Champion Invitational Stakes, November 1, on Dulcia, and Oak Tree Invitational Stakes, October 19, on Top Command.

In December, he is elected president of the Jockeys' Guild.

In April, a computer evaluation of the proficiency of professional athletes sponsored by Seagram Distillers· Corporation and called Seven Crowns of Sport competition, which rates jockeys on every aspect of their performance but does not consider amount of money won, finds Shoemaker to be the leading jockey with a rating of 79.94%. His closest competitor, Laffit Pincay, Jr., has a rating of 73.53%.

In 1975, Shoemaker wins twenty-nine stake events to finish second behind Sandy Hawley, who has thirty, and amasses stake earnings of $1,793,243 to lead all jockeys in this category.

At the end of the year, his career tally in races won is 6,953. His total money won is $57,340,419, and he has won a total of 657 stakes events, totals at this time far beyond those ever amassed by any other jockey.

1976

Mounts	1st	2nd	3rd	Win Percentage	Rank (in races won)	Amount Won (in total purses)	Rank (in total purses)
1,035	200	154	146	19%	26	$3,815,645	5

Shoemaker wins the Marlboro Cup Handicap, October 2, riding Forego, in one of the most exciting finishes of all time.

Also, he wins seven other $100,000 stake races: Oak Tree Invitational Stakes, October 24, and Champion Invitational Handicap, November 6, on King Pellinore. Hollywood Derby, April 17, on Crystal Water. Hollywood Park Invitational Turf Handicap, May 31, on Dahlia. Del Mar Handicap, September 6, on Riot in Paris. Woodward Handicap, September 18, on Forego. Norfolk Stakes, November 7, on Habitony.

On March 14, on Royal Derby II, a horse that has not won a race in three years, he rides his 7,000th winner.

On February 8, Santa Anita Park honors Shoemaker on the twenty-fifth anniversary of his first victory in a $100,000 race: his 1951 victory aboard Yolo Stable's Great Circle in the Santa Anita Maturity, a race which then had a gross purse of $205,700 with a record of $144,325 going to the winner. The occasion is honored by what the track calls Shoemaker Day Sunday.

In December, Shoemaker is re-elected president of the Jockeys' Guild.

In 1976, he wins thirty stake events and the stakes purses his mounts earns is $2,012,541, to lead all jockeys in this latter category.

By the end of the year, Shoemaker has been riding for twenty-eight years and his mounts have earned a total of $61,156,064—$25,000,000 more than that of his closest competitor, Braulio Baeza's $36,150,142.

1977

Mounts	*1st*	*2nd*	*3rd*	*Win Percentage*	*Rank (in races won)*	*Amount Won (in total purses)*	*Rank (in total purses)*
975	172	149	142	18%	*	$3,633,091	5

Shoemaker wins Metropolitan Handicap, May 30, on Forego.

He also wins eight other $100,000 stake races on eight different horses: La Canada Stakes, February 13, on Lucie Manet; Santa Anita Derby, March 27, on Habitony; Hollywood Oaks, June 26, on Glenaris; Swaps Stakes, July 3, on J. O. Tobin; Sunset Handicap, July 25, on Today 'n Tomorrow; Woodward Handicap, September 17, on Forego; Oak Tree Invitational Stakes, October 23, on Crystal Water, and Norfolk Stakes, November 6, on Balzac.

In February, he receives a special Eclipse Award, the first of three Eclipse Awards he would win, from *Daily Racing Form,* the Thoroughbred Racing Association, and the National Turf Writers Association for being top jockey of the year. Singled out as the winningest rider in the history of racing, by the end of 1976, he has ridden 7,165 winners, the most ever, and also holds the record for the most stake victories and the most victories in $100,000 stakes.

In July, Exhibition Park in Vancouver, British Columbia, stages a special Bill Shoemaker Night.

On July 6, he rides at Rockingham Park in Salem, New Hampshire, on opening day as a special opening day attraction. He had not ridden there in eleven years. The *Daily Racing Form* reported that "nearly every rider in the jockeys' room asked Shoemaker for his autograph."

With thirty stake winners and stakes-purse earnings of $1,496,920, he wins the title of jockey with most money won in stakes events for the third year in a row.

By the end of the year, his career totals show the following: 7,325 winners, $64,789,155 money won, 149 winners in races of $100,000 and up, 717 winners of stakes events, 23.7% winning percentage, four years

* not in top 30

in which his mounts have earned more than $3 million in one year—records unmatched by anyone in racing history.

At the end of 1977, he has won triple crown events ten times: five Belmont Stakes, three Kentucky Derbies, and two Preakness Stakes. He has won the prestigious Hollywood Derby six times and the Woodward Stakes four times.

1978

*Mounts**	*1st*	*2nd*	*3rd*	*Win Percentage*	*Rank (in races won)*	*Amount Won (in total purses)*	*Rank (in total purses)*
1,245	271*	194	156	22%	10	$5,231,390†	4

Shoemaker wins nine $100,000 stake races: Capistrano Handicap, April 9, Hollywood Invitational Turf Handicap, May 29, Hollywood Gold Cup Handicap, June 25, Sunset Handicap, July 24, Jockey Gold Cup Stakes, October 14, Oak Tree Invitational Stakes, November 5, all on Exceller. Vanity Handicap, July 16, on Afifa, Longacres Mile Handicap, August 27, on Bad 'n Big, and Yellow Ribbon Stakes, November 4, on Amazer.

He is one of three jockeys whose purse earnings for the year are over the $5 million mark. The others are Jorge Velasquez, $5,364,921, and Angel Cordero, Jr., $5,320,503.

On June 29, at the annual dinner at Hollywood Park of the National Jockeys Agents Benevolent Association, Shoemaker is honored as JABA Man of the Year.

In June, he rides in England for the first time, finishing second in the English Derby at Epsom Downs aboard 25–1 shot Hawaiian Sound.

In July, he rides in Ireland for the first time, bringing home Hawaiian Sound to a third-place finish in the Irish Derby at the Curragh of Kildare. He wins two other races on the Derby day card.

* includes foreign races
† includes foreign earnings

In July, Shoemaker wins the Sandringham Handicap at Ascot on Lorelene, for his first winner in England.

On September 17, at Woodbine Race Track in Etobicoke, Ontario, he is honored at a special day as the most winningest jockey in the history of the sport.

In September, he returns to France to ride Trillion in the Arc de Triomphe at Longchamps.

In November, Louisiana Downs in Bossier City, Louisiana, holds a special Bill Shoemaker Day.

In December, he is re-elected to a two-year-term as president of the Jockeys' Guild.

For the year, he has thirty-one stakes victories, finishing third behind D. McHargue and Jorge Velasquez, and wins $2,169,987 in stake earnings, finishing fourth behind D. McHargue, Angel Cordero, Jr., and Jorge Velasquez.

1979

Mounts	*1st*	*2nd*	*3rd*	*Win Percentage*	*Rank (in races won)*	*Amount Won (in total purses)*	*Rank (in total purses)*
983	168	141	118	17%	*	$4,480,825†	6

Winning the Marlboro Cup Handicap on September 8 on Spectacular Bid, Shoemaker says he is the best horse he ever rode.

He also wins nine other $100,000 stake races: St. Marg. Invitational Handicap, February 25, on Sanedtki, Santa Susana, March 11, on Caline, Citation Handicap, July 8, on Text, Vanity Handicap, July 15, on It's in the Air, Hollywood Juvenile Championship, July 21, on Parsec, Haskell Handicap, August 25, on Text; Flower Bowl Handicap, September 1, on Pearl Necklace, Del Mar Debutante, September 9, on Table Hands, and Meadowlands Cup Handicap, October 18, on Spectacular Bid.

With earnings of $2,394,734 in stake purses, he finishes second in this

* not in top 30
† includes foreign earnings

category behind Laffit Pincay. His twenty-six stakes winners put him in a tie for seventh with Sandy Hawley.

By April 20 of this year, the thirtieth anniversary of his first winner, he has reached the winner's circle more than 7,600 times.

1980

Mounts	*1st*	*2nd*	*3rd*	*Win Percentage*	*Rank (in races won)*	*Amount Won (in total purses)*	*Rank (in total purses)*
1,052	159	140	132	15%	*	$5,188,883†	6

Shoemaker wins seventeen $100,000 stake races: San Fernando Stakes, January 19, Strub Stakes, February 2, Santa Anita Handicap, March 2, LeRoy Handicap, May 18, California Stakes, June 8, Washington Park Stakes, July 19, Haskell Handicap, August 16, Woodward Stakes, September 20, all on Spectacular Bid. San Luis Obispo Handicap, February 18, on Silver Eagle, San Felipe Handicap, March 15, on Raise a Man, Native Diver Handicap, April 20, on Replant, Century Handicap, April 27, on Go West Young Man, Golden State Breeders Sire Stakes, May 24, on Rumbo, American Handicap, July 4, on Bold Tropic, Sunset Handicap, July 21, on Inkerman, Roman Handicap, August 31, on Queen to Conquer, and the Arlington-Washington Lassie Stakes, September 13, on Truly Bound.

On October 23, in a three-race challenge match at Sandown Park in England between what were said to be the ten best jockeys in the world, five from the United States and five from England, Shoemaker wins the individual championship honors and leads the United States riders to victory in the team competition.

With thirty-five stakes won, a winning stake percentage of 24%, and $2,998.034 in stake earnings for the year, he is first in all three of these categories.

* not in top 30
† includes foreign earnings

1981

Mounts	*1st*	*2nd*	*3rd*	*Win Percentage*	*Rank (in races won)*	*Amount Won (in total purses)*	*Rank (in total purses)*
878	156	117	99	18%	*	$6,122,481†	5

Shoemaker wins Arlington Million, August 30, on John Henry. (See chart)

He also wins thirteen other $100,000 stake races: Sword Dancer, July 11, Jockey Gold Cup Handicap, October 10, and Oak Tree Invitational Handicap, November 8, on John Henry, Sunset Handicap, July 20, and Man o' War, October 3, on Galaxy Libra, Beldame Stakes, October 11, on Love Sign, Alcibiades Stakes, October 17, on Apalachee Honey, Silver Bells Handicap, December 13, on Happy Guess, Citation Handicap, December 20, on Tahitian King.

On May 27, in the first race at Hollywood Park aboard War Allied, he rides his 8,000th winner, putting him 1,968 ahead of Johnny Longden. At the time, Shoemaker had won 825 stakes, and 166 races worth $100,000 or more.

In 1981 he receives two Eclipse Awards: the Award of Merit, racing's highest award for a person and the award for the top jockey of the year. Shoemaker is only the second jockey ever to be given the Eclipse Award of Merit. The citation says it is being given not only for his "extraordinary accomplishments as a jockey" but also for "being an outstanding good-will ambassador for racing." With his previous Eclipse Award of 1977, Shoemaker has been honored with three Eclipse Awards.

* not in top 30
† includes foreign earnings

1982

Mounts	1st	2nd	3rd	Win Percentage	Rank (in races won)	Amount Won (in total purses)	Rank (in total purses)
717	113	110	88	16%	*	$4,691,342†	9

Shoemaker wins twelve $100,000 stake races: Santa Anita Handicap, March 7, and Oak Tree Invitational, October 31, on John Henry, San Carlos Handicap, January 9, on Solo Guy, Blue Grass Stakes, April 22, on Linkage, Vanity Handicap, July 11, on Sangue, Del Mar Invitational, September 6, on Muttering, Golden Harvest Handicap, September 12, on Miss Huntington, California Jockey Club, December 4, on Buchanette, Santa Susana, March 14, Ashland Stakes, April 17, Kentucky Oaks, April 30, and Golden Harvest Handicap, September 12, on Blush With Pride.

In October, he is the guest of honor at a testimonial dinner in the dining room at Keeneland Race Track by the Thoroughbred Club of America, an award generally considered among the highest honors bestowed by the racing industry, recognizing a person who has made a major contribution to the sport of racing.

In winning the Santa Anita Handicap riding John Henry in March, he set another record. It was the twelfth time he has been the winning rider in that prestigious event.

In April, the Multiple Sclerosis Committee names Shoemaker National Honorary Chairman in its "Race Against MS" campaign.

In September, Shoemaker goes to England and defeats Lester Piggott in a head-to-head match race at Ascot; the event is staged as a charity to benefit the Multiple Sclerosis Society of Great Britain, and both riders donate their services. On this Charity Day, Shoemaker has two winners —Prince's Gate and Rose du Soir. On this trip, he also wins the Sandown International on Aura. These triumphs result in his being named England's Jockey of the Month, an award selected by a committee of twenty-five leading journalists and racing officials.

* not in top 30
† includes foreign earnings

In December, he visits Japan for the first time, to ride John Henry to a disappointing thirteenth-place finish in the 1982 Japan Cup at Tokyo Race Course.

In 1982, Shoemaker's total earnings go over the $90 million mark, adding up to $90,504,076 by the end of the year in this, the thirty-fourth of his riding career. His other career totals are 35,814 number of mounts, 8,194 number of winners, and his percentage of winning races is 22.9%.

1983

Mounts	*1st*	*2nd*	*3rd*	*Win Percentage*	*Rank (in races won)*	*Amount Won (in total purses)*	*Rank (in total purses)*
779	125	96	96	16%	*	$4,277,930†	9

Shoemaker adds eleven additional $100,000 stake races to his credit: Ramona Handicap, September 11, Golden Harvest Handicap, October 2, Yellow Ribbon Handicap, November 6, and The Matriarch, December 4, on Sangue, San Bernardino, April 17, Century Handicap, May 7, and California Stakes, June 12, on The Wonder, San Luis Obispo, February 21, on Pelerin, Mervyn LeRoy, May 15, on Fighting Fit; Del Mar Handicap, September 5, on Bel Bolide, and Arlington Handicap, September 18, on Palikaraki.

In 1983, he has twenty-four stakes winners and earns a total of $2,442,731 in stakes purses, to rank eighth in both the number of winners and purses won in stakes events.

The year 1983 marks the thirty-fifth year of his riding career. At the end of the year, with his astonishing figures unmatched by anyone in all racing history, his record tallies up as follows: mounts, 36,593, winners, 8,319, amount won, $94,782,006, and winning percentage, 22.7%.

* not in top 30
† includes foreign earnings

1984

Mounts	1st	2nd	3rd	Win Percentage	Rank (in races won)	Amount Won (in total purses)	Rank (in total purses)
831	108	102	96	13%	*	$4,324,667†	13

Shoemaker wins seven $100,000 stake races: Goodwood Handicap, November 4, Citation, November 24, and Native Diver Handicap, December 22, on Lord at War, Santa Anita Handicap, March 18, on Avigaition, Fall Festival Juvenile, October 6, on Michadilla, National Sprint Championship, December 1, on Lovlier Linda, and Hollywood Preview, December 5, on First Norman.

On November 13, the Meadowlands Race Track in East Rutherford, New Jersey, stages a special Bill Shoemaker Night in honor of the world's winningest jockey.

Although in 1984 he is at an age, fifty-three, when most jockeys have long since retired, Shoemaker wins twenty-one stakes events during the year with stakes-purse earnings totaling $4,341,929.

1985

Mounts	1st	2nd	3rd	Win Percentage	Rank (in races won)	Amount Won (in total purses)	Rank (in total purses)
721	80	91	83	11%	*	$4,487,095	17

Shoemaker wins eleven $100,000 stake races: San Antonio Handicap, February 17, Santa Anita Handicap, March 3, Goodwood Handicap, October 17, on Lord at War, Las Palmas Handicap, October 19, Yellow Ribbon Handicap, November 10, on Estrapade, Arcadia Handicap, March 10, on Fatih, Genesis Handicap, April 1, on Hail Bold King; Valkyr Handicap, May 7, on Shywing, Del Mar Oaks, August 31, on

* not in top 30
† includes foreign earnings

Savannah Dancer, Ramona Handicap, September 8, on Daily Busy, and Linda Vista Handicap, November 3, on Savannah Slew.

On March 5, in winning Santa Anita Handicap on Lord at War, his purse earnings pass the $100,000,000 mark. This represents his 207th triumph in a stake worth $100,000 or more and is his 917th winner of a stakes event.

On March 25, Latonia Race Track in Kentucky has an official night in honor of Bill Shoemaker.

In May, Ak-Sar-Ben Race Track, outside of Omaha, Nebraska, stages a special promotion in connection with Shoemaker's appearance.

Shoemaker, president of the Jockey Guild, joined by riders Angel Cordero, Jr., Herb McCauley, Philip Groves, and Vincent Braccia, files a lawsuit in Federal District Court in Camden, New Jersey, on September 9, challenging the recently enacted order of the New Jersey Racing Commission authorizing random drug-testing of jockeys. Shoemaker and the other jockey-plaintiffs object to the commission's order on the ground that it is an invasion of the jockeys' privacy, but the court rules against them and they get nowhere in their appeals.

In the thirty-seventh year of his riding career, he rides twenty-six winners in stakes events and earns $2,950,064 in stakes purses, to rank ninth in amount of stakes earnings, tenth in the number of stakes winners.

By year's end his lifetime totals are as follows: mounts, 38,145, winners, 8,507, amount won, $103,593,768, and percentage of winners, 22.3%.

1986

Mounts	1st	2nd	3rd	Win Percentage	Rank (in races won)	Amount Won (in total purses)	Rank (in total purses)
708	114	97	79	16.1%	*	$7,029,211	8

Shoemaker wins his fourth Kentucky Derby on Ferdinand. (See chart.) He also wins fifteen other stakes worth $100,000: Santa Anita Oaks, March 23, and Del Mar Oaks, August 24, on Hidden Lights, John Henry Handicap, May 4, on Palace Music, Nassau County Handicap, June 6, on Roo Art, Hollywood Oaks, July 6, on Hidden Light, Majorette, July 19, on Eloquack, James Iselin Handicap, August 16, on Roo Art, Chula Vista Handicap, August 23, on Fran's Valentine, Flower Bowl Handicap, September 13, on Scoot, C. F. Burke Handicap, November 3, on Louis La Grand, Hollywood Derby, November 16, on Thrill Show, Bay Meadows Derby, November 29, on Le Belvedere, Hollywood Turf Cup, December 7, on Alphabatim, Hollywood Futurity, December 14, on Temperate Sil, and Malibu, December 26, on Ferdinand.

The 1986 Kentucky Derby is the twenty-fourth time Shoemaker has ridden in America's most famous horse race. (See charts.)

In 1986, with only 708 mounts but with purse earnings over $7 million, he averages about $10,000 in earnings every time he climbed on a horse.

In September, the Birmingham Turf Club of Birmingham, Alabama, holds a Bill Shoemaker Day, honoring the man as "the greatest jockey of all time."

In 1986, at age fifty five, Shoemaker rides the winners of twenty-eight stakes events and hauls in $5,203,884 in stakes earnings, finishing sixth in both the number of stakes winners and amount won in stakes events.

His career totals by the end of the year: mounts, 38,853; winners, 8,621; amount won, $110,622,979; percentage of winning races, 22.1%.

* not in top 30

1987

*Mounts**	*1st*	*2nd*	*3rd*	*Pct.*	*Amount Won*
486	73	66	61	15%	$4,446,950

On February 3, Shoemaker undergoes arthroscopic surgery on his left knee at Centinela Hospital Medical Center in Los Angeles. His first mount upon his return is Louis La Grand and he wins the $164,000 San Luis Obispo Handicap at Santa Anita on February 16. This victory is Shoemaker's 232nd win in a race of $100,000 and over. Riding Ferdinand, he loses by a nose to Broad Brush in the Santa Anita Handicap, marking the astonishing thirty-third time he has competed in that event, with a tally of eleven wins, seven seconds, and two third-place finishes.

By mid-April, at the end of Santa Anita's winter-spring eighty-eight-day meeting, he has won eight stakes races, second only to Gary Stevens, a jockey thirty-one years his junior. In percentage of winning races, he is second to Lafitt Pincay. The highpoint of the meeting is Shoemaker's winning four races on the Santa Anita Derby Day card, just months before his fifty-sixth birthday.

In search of his fifth Kentucky Derby winner, he finishes out of the money while riding the Leroy Jolley-trained Gulch. This is the twenty-fifth appearance in the Derby for Shoemaker, more than any other rider.

In May, the Multiple Sclerosis Society presents Shoemaker with its cherished Silver Hope Chest Award, honoring him for his work on behalf of multiple sclerosis victims.

On October 4, at the formation of the California Horse Racing Hall of Fame at the California Thoroughbred Breeders Association headquarters at Arcadia, Shoemaker is one of eighteen original inductees into the California Hall of Fame. Only two other jockeys, Johnny Longden and Eddie Arcaro, are so honored.

* These figures are from January 1, 1987, through September 30, 1987. Stake race data and jockey standings information are not available.

SHOEMAKER

As of December 6, 1987, Shoemaker's total career victories in stakes races is 985. He has won 246 races with purses of $100,000 or more, including his victory on Ferdinand in the $3,000,000 Breeders' Cup Classic at Hollywood Park on November 21, 1987.

SHOEMAKER'S MAJOR VICTORIES

1949 Golden Gate Fields

ALBANY, CALIF., WEDNESDAY, APRIL 20, 1949—GOLDEN GATE FIELDS (1 MILE). Twenty-third day of forty-three-day meeting (March 17 to May 14). Pacific Turf Club, Inc. Automatic starting gate. Photo-chart Camera. Weather clear.

SECOND RACE
7 2 6 6 5
April 20-49—G.G

3-4 MILE (out of chute). (Fair Truckle, Oct. 4, 1947—1:08⅖—4—119.) Purse $2,000. 3-year-olds. Claiming. Weight, 120 lbs. Non-winners of a race since March 16 allowed 4 lbs.; in 1949, 7 lbs. Claiming price, $3,000.
Net value to winner $1,210; second, $400; third, $260; fourth, $130.
Mutuel Pool, $85,117.

Index	Horses	Eq't A	Wt	PP	St	¼	½	Str	Fin	Jockeys	Cl'g Pr	Owners	Odds to $1
(72038)	—Shafter V.	wb	110	4	5	2½	$1^{1\frac{1}{2}}$	1^{2}	$1^{2\frac{1}{4}}$	W Shoem'r*	3000	Mrs H A Guidera	9.50
(71618)	—Lady Compan'n	wb	115	10	8	7^{2}	4½	2½	2¾	R Neves	3000	Mr & Mrs A J Luke	6.30
72229[3]	—Maltese Bunny	w	113	11	2	6½	6^{3}	3^{2}	$3^{2\frac{1}{2}}$	J Westrope	3000	I Fenech	1.40
72038	Vagabond Lad	wb	113	7	10	10^{1}	8^{3}	6^{3}	$4^{1\frac{1}{2}}$	C Rallo	3000	J L Russill	86.80
67699	Sonny Hill	w	116	1	11	11^{h}	9½	8^{2}	$5^{1\frac{1}{4}}$	M Volzke	3000	Mr & Mrs P Kuntz	102.90
71981	—Miss Veloz	wb	109	5	7	4½	5^{1}	4^{1}	6^{n}	K C Fields	3000	Veloz & Yolanda	15.65
71894	—Donalyte)	w	113	3	6	$8^{1\frac{1}{2}}$	7½	$7^{1\frac{1}{2}}$	7^{2}	R Eccard	3000	M E Osborne	10.60
71978	—Life Raft	wb	113	9	12	12	11^{4}	9^{4}	8^{2}	N Combest	3000	Turk & Hack	28.90
(71978)	—Lucky Five	w	116	6	3	3^{2}	2^{h}	6^{h}	9^{1}	M Lewis	3000	Mr & Mrs H Dimpfl	4.60
71649	—Corporal Cal	wb	116	12	1	$1^{1\frac{1}{2}}$	3^{h}	10^{4}	10^{3}	B Green	3000	J A Thompson	71.05
(71649)	Alloy	w	110	2	9	9^{1}	12	12	11^{3}	S Cardiali*	3000	W C Gilmore	8.30
66652	—Sierra Breeze	w	110	8	4	5^{h}	10^{h}	11^{1}	12	J Haritos	3000	Z T Addington	123.75

Time, :23, :46⅘, 1:12. Track fast.

Mutuel Prices	$2 Mutuels Paid			Odds to $1		
SHAFTER V.	21.00	9.60	4.60	9.50	3.80	1.30
LADY COMPANION		6.20	3.80		2.10	.90
MALTESE BUNNY			2.60			.30

Winner—Ch. f, by Big V—Shasta Upper, by Snow King, trained by G. Reeves; bred by Jack Greenwell.

WENT TO POST—2:07, OFF AT 2:08 PACIFIC STANDARD TIME.

Start good from stall gate. Won ridden out; second and third driving. SHAFTER V. had good speed from the beginning, took command when ready and held her advantage. LADY COMPANION, never far back, raced wide throughout and held on well in the drive. MALTESE BUNNY, on the outside early, went to the inside nearing the stretch and finished gamely.

Scratched—72230 Accelerate, 108; 63064[3] Sideburns, 113; 72436 Dark Atom, 113; 72283 Cragie, 108.

Overweight—Maltese Bunny, 2 pounds; Sonny Hill, 3; Miss Veloz, 1; Lucky Five, 1; Sierra Breeze, 2.

1955 Kentucky Derby

SEVENTH RACE
4 7 8 5 0
May 7-55—C.D

1 1-4 MILES. (Whirlaway, May 3, 1941—2:01$\frac{2}{5}$—3—126.) Eighty-first running THE KENTUCKY DERBY. $125,000 added. 3-year-olds. Scale weights. By subscription of $100 each in cash, $250 to go through the entry box; $1,250 additional to start. $125,000 added, of which $25,000 to second, $12,500 to third, $5,000 to fourth. $100,000 guaranteed the winner. Starters to be named through the entry box the day before the race at the usual time of closing. (Owner of winner to receive a gold trophy.)

Gross value, $152,500. Net value to winner $108,400; second, $25,000; third, $12,500; fourth, $5,000. Mutuel Pool, $1,677,178.

Index	Horses	Eq't A	Wt	PP	St	½	¾	1	Str	Fin	Jockeys	Owners	Odds to $1
47153^{1}	—Swaps	w	126	8	4	1^{1}	1^{1}	1½	1½	$1^{1\frac{1}{2}}$	W Sho'aker	R C Ellsworth	2.80
46603^{1}	—Nashua	w	126	5	1	3^{1}	3^{1}	2^{1}	2^{4}	$2^{6\frac{1}{2}}$	E Arcaro	Belair Stud	1.30
46603^{2}	—Summer Tan	wb	126	10	6	4^{6}	4^{5}	3^{4}	3^{2}	3^{4}	E Guerin	Mrs J W Galbreath	4.90
47004^{1}	—Racing Fool	w	126	7	5	5^{1}	5^{1}	5^{1}	4^{3}	4½	H Moreno	Cain Hoy Stable	a-5.70
47413^{2}	—Jean's Joe	wb	126	9	9	10	8^{3}	6½	5^{2}	$5^{1\frac{1}{2}}$	S Brooks	Murcain Stable	16.20
47413^{1}	—Flying Fury	w	126	2	10	8^{3}	9^{1}	9^{2}	6½	6¾	C McCreary	Cain Hoy Stable	a-5.70
47413^{4}	—Honeys Alibi	w	126	4	2	6^{3}	6^{3}	7^{1}	$7^{1\frac{1}{2}}$	$7^{3\frac{1}{2}}$	W Harmatz	W-L Ranch Co	55.60
45834^{1}	—Blue Lem	wb	126	1	7	9½	10	10	9^{4}	$8^{1\frac{1}{2}}$	C Rogers	H C Freuhauf	23.30
47413^{3}	—Nabesna	wb	126	3	8	7^{3}	$7^{1\frac{1}{2}}$	8^{1}	8^{1}	9^{10}	J Adams	C Mooers	52.80
47153^{3}	—Trim Destiny	w	126	6	3	$2^{2\frac{1}{2}}$	2^{h}	4^{h}	10	10	L C Cook	G R White	50.90

a-Coupled, Racing Fool and Flying Fury.

Time, :23$\frac{3}{5}$, :47$\frac{2}{5}$, 1:12$\frac{2}{5}$, 1:37, 2:01$\frac{4}{5}$. Track fast.

Official Program Numbers↓

Mutuel Prices		$2 Mutuels Paid			Odds to $1		
	7-SWAPS	**7.60**	**3.40**	**2.60**	**2.80**	**.70**	**.30**
	5-NASHUA		**3.00**	**2.40**		**.50**	**.20**
	9-SUMMER TAN			**3.00**			**.50**

Winner—Ch. c, by Khaled—Iron Reward, by Beau Pere, trained by M. A. Tenney; bred by R. C. Ellsworth.

IN GATE—4:31. OFF AT 4:31½ CENTRAL DAYLIGHT TIME.

Start good. Won driving; second and third the same. SWAPS, alertly ridden, took command soon after the start, raced TRIM DESTINY into defeat before reaching the upper turn, responded readily when challenged by NASHUA during the stretch run and drew clear in the last sixteenth mile. NASHUA, well placed from the outset, was kept in hand to the last three-eighths mile, moved up boldly on the outside of SWAPS for the stretch run but was not good enough for the latter, although much the best of the others. SUMMER TAN, never far back and reserved to the last half mile, made a mild bid approaching the stretch, then faltered. RACING FOOL, in hand to the stretch, was unable to threaten the leaders when set down in the drive. JEAN'S JOE lacked early foot and was never dangerous. FLYING FURY began sluggishly and was never prominent. HONEYS ALIBI was outrun and had no mishap. BLUE LEM raced far back the entire trip. NABESNA was through early. TRIM DESTINY raced nearest SWAPS for three-quarters mile, then gave way.

1957 Belmont Stakes

SIXTH RACE
1 8 7 7 5
June 15-57—Bel

1 1-2 MILES. (Bolingbroke, Sept. 26, 1942—2:27⅗—5—115.) Eighty-ninth running BELMONT. $100,000 added. 3-year-olds. Scale weights. By subscription of $50 each, to accompany the nomination. Supplementary nominations may be made five days before the running of the race by payment of an eligibility fee of $5,000. Starters to pay $1,000 additional, with $100,000 added, of which $20,000 to second, $10,000 to third and $5,000 to fourth. Weight, 126 lbs. (The winning owner will be presented with the August Belmont Memorial Cup, to be retained for one year, as well as a trophy for permanent possession.)

Gross value, $113,350. Gross to winner $78,350. Net to winner $77,300; second, $20,000; third, $10,000; fourth, $5,000. Mutuel Pool, $409,401.

Index Horses	Eq't A	Wt	PP	¼	½	1	1¼	Str	Fin	Jockeys	Owners	Odds to $1
16969^{1}—Gallant Man	w	126	4	$4^{1\frac{1}{2}}$	4^{3}	2^{3}	2^{4}	$1^{1\frac{1}{2}}$	1^{8}	W Sho'aker	R Lowe	a-.95
17719^{2}—Inside Tract	wb	126	3	5½	6	5½	$3^{1\frac{1}{2}}$	3^{6}	2^{4}	E Nelson	D & M Stable	16.00
15400^{1}—Bold Ruler	wb	126	1	1^{1}	1½	1^{3}	1^{h}	2½	3^{9}	E Arcaro	Wheatley Stable	85
17888 —Pop Corn	w	126	5	3½	3½	4½	4^{1}	4^{2}	4^{5}	T Atkinson	Greentree Stable	29.95
17888^{1}—Lucky Dip	w	126	6	6	$5^{1\frac{1}{2}}$	6	5^{6}	5	5	P Anderson	Cain Hoy Stable	17.55
16612^{4} Bold Nero	w	126	2	2^{4}	2^{6}	3½	6	Eased.		J Choquette	R Lowe	a-.95

a-Coupled, Gallant Man and Bold Nero.

Time, :23⅖, :46⅘, 1:10⅖, 1:35⅗, 2:01⅖, 2:26⅗ (track and American record). Track fast.

Official Program Numbers↓

Mutuel Prices		$2 Mutuels Paid			Odds to $1		
	1A-GALLANT MAN (a-Entry)	3.90	2.70	....	.95	.35	....
	3 INSIDE TRACT		5.60	....		1.80	....
	NO SHOW MUTUELS SOLD.						

Winner—B. c, by Migoli—Majideh, by Mahmoud, trained by J. A. Nerud; bred by H. H. Aga & Prince Aly Khan (England).

IN GATE—4:48. OFF AT 4:48 EASTERN DAYLIGHT TIME.

Start good. Won easily, second and third driving. GALLANT MAN, away alertly and saving ground to the mile, moved up steadily thereafter and, disposing of BOLD RULER entering the stretch, drew out to win with speed in reserve. INSIDE TRACT lacked early foot, moved up boldly approaching the stretch and, closing well under punishment, was unable to reach GALLANT MAN but easily best the others. BOLD RULER began fast, disposed of BOLD NERO after five-eighths mile and set the pace to the stretch but failed to stay when challenged by GALLANT MAN, then tired badly during the last eighth mile and could not hold INSIDE TRACT for the place. POP CORN could not keep up. LUCKY DIP was never prominent and had no mishap. BOLD NERO engaged BOLD RULER to the mile, then gave way and was not persevered with after hopelessly beaten.

Scratched—17719^{1} Cohoes, 126.

1959 Kentucky Derby

SEVENTH RACE
CD - 2216
May 2, 1959

1 1-4 MILES. (Whirlaway, May 3, 1941, 2:01⅖, 3, 126.) Eighty-fifth running KENTUCKY DERBY. $125,000 added. 3-year-olds. Scale weights. By subscription of $100 each in cash, which covers nomination for both the Kentucky Derby and Derby Trial. All nomination fees to Derby winner. $250 to pass entry box, 1,250 additional to start, with $125,000 added, of which $25,000 to second, $12,500 to third and $5,000 to fourth. $100,000 guaranteed to winner. Weight, 126 lbs. The owner of the winner to receive a gold trophy. A nomination may be withdrawn before time of closing of nominations. Closed Monday, Feb. 16, with 130 nominations.

Gross value, $163,750. Gross to winner $121,280. Net to winner $119,650; second, $25,000; third, $12,500; fourth, $5,000. Mutuel Pool, $1,502,151.

Index	Horses	Eq't A	Wt	PP	¼	½	¾	1	Str	Fin	Jockeys	Owners	Odds to $1
1986Kee^{1}	—Tomy Lee		126	9	2^{2}	$2^{1\frac{1}{2}}$	1^{h}	$2^{1\frac{1}{2}}$	2^{2}	1no	W Sho'aker	Mr-Mrs F Turner Jr	3.70
1907CD^{1}	—Sword Dancer	b	126	14	$4\frac{1}{2}$	$4\frac{1}{2}$	4^{2}	$1\frac{1}{2}$	1^{h}	$2^{2\frac{1}{4}}$	W Boland	Brookmeade Stable	8.80
1925CD^{1}	—First Landing	b	126	3	7^{1}	$8\frac{1}{2}$	5^{h}	$4\frac{1}{2}$	$4^{1\frac{1}{2}}$	3^{1}	E Arcaro	Meadow Stable	3.60
1924CD^{3}	—Royal Orbit	b	126	17	$10^{1\frac{1}{2}}$	12^{3}	11^{3}	8^{2}	6^{h}	4^{h}	W Harmatz	J Braunstein Estate	46.60
1907CD^{3}	—Silver Spoon		126	4	9^{1}	9^{2}	$6\frac{1}{2}$	3^{2}	3^{h}	$5^{2\frac{1}{2}}$	R York	C V Whitney	10.80
1924CD^{2}	—Finnegan	b	126	8	6^{2}	6^{1}	$7\frac{1}{2}$	$5^{1\frac{1}{2}}$	7^{2}	$6\frac{3}{4}$	J Longden	N S McCarthy	10.60
1986Kee^{2}	—Dunce	b	126	7	$14\frac{1}{2}$	13^{2}	12^{3}	$11\frac{1}{2}$	8^{1}	$7^{1\frac{3}{4}}$	S Brooks	Claiborne Farm	f-7.30
1924CD^{1}	—Open View	b	126	13	5^{2}	5^{4}	8^{2}	6^{2}	$5\frac{1}{2}$	8^{3}	K Korte	Elcam Stable	a-17.20
2042Jam	—Atoll		126	5	$3\frac{1}{2}$	3^{h}	$3\frac{1}{2}$	7^{1}	$9^{1\frac{1}{2}}$	9no	S Boulmetis	Elkcam Stable-L Chesler	a-17.20
1924CD^{4}	—Rico Tesio	b	126	2	17	17	17	13^{2}	11^{1}	$10^{1\frac{1}{2}}$	M Ycaza	Briardale Farm	48.10
2043Lrl	—Festival King		126	15	$8\frac{1}{2}$	7^{h}	9^{2}	9^{2}	10^{h}	$11\frac{3}{4}$	W Carstens	C B Fischbach	f-7.30
1925CD^{2}	—John Bruce		126	11	$16\frac{1}{2}$	$16^{1\frac{1}{2}}$	$15\frac{1}{2}$	14^{3}	14^{1}	12no	K Church	K G Marshall	34.50
1907CD^{2}	—Easy Spur		126	6	13^{3}	10^{h}	10^{1}	$10^{1\frac{1}{2}}$	$13\frac{1}{2}$	13^{h}	W Hartack	Spring Hill Farm	7.90
1986Kee	—The Chosen One		126	16	11^{1}	14^{4}	14^{4}	$12\frac{1}{2}$	$12\frac{1}{2}$	$14^{4\frac{1}{2}}$	J Combest	Mrs S H Sadacca	f-7.30
1925CD^{4}	—Our Dad	b	126	1	$12\frac{1}{2}$	$11\frac{1}{2}$	13^{2}	15^{2}	15^{4}	15^{1}	P Anderson	Patrice Jacobs	8.00
1907CD	—Die Hard		126	12	15^{2}	$15\frac{1}{2}$	$16\frac{1}{2}$	16^{3}	16^{8}	16^{6}	J Sellers	Jacnot Stable	f-7.30
1924CD	—Troilus	b	126	10	$1\frac{1}{2}$	$1^{1\frac{1}{2}}$	$2\frac{1}{2}$	17	17	17	C Rogers	B Sharp	f-7.30

f-Mutuel field. a-Coupled, Open View and Atoll.

Time, :24⅕, :47⅗, 1:11⅗, 1:36, 2:02⅕. Track fast.

Official Program Numbers ↓

Mutuel Prices		$2 Mutuels Paid			Odds to $1		
	8-TOMY LEE	**9.40**	**4.80**	**3.80**	**3.70**	**1.40**	**.90**
	10-SWORD DANCER		**9.00**	**6.20**		**3.50**	**2.10**
	4-FIRST LANDING			**4.00**			**1.00**

Winner—B. c, by Tudor Minstrel—Auld Alliance, by Brantome, trained by F. E. Childs; bred by D. H. Wills (England). **IN GATE—4:37. OFF AT 4:37½ CENTRAL DAYLIGHT TIME.**

Start good. Won driving. TOMY LEE, snugged in off the early pace of TROILUS, moved from between horses with SWORD DANCER to assume a slight advantage at the half mile grounds, continued slightly wide to be headed on the final turn, responded to strong handling and, while drifting out and being carried in through the stretch run, proved narrowly best. TOMY LEE survived a claim of foul lodged by the rider of the runner-up for allegedly having carried that one wide from the five-sixteenths marker to the final sixteenth. SWORD DANCER moved to a contending position along the outside at once, continued wide to move readily and take command nearing the final quarter mile, was carried wide into the stretch to continue to show the way and, while lugging in, just failed to last. FIRST LANDING loomed up boldly when called upon entering the stretch but could not improve his position. ROYAL ORBIT, taken in hand when in position early, commenced to move after going three quarters to make a bold bid through midstretch but was not quite good enough. SILVER SPOON moved rapidly in the run down the backstretch to the leaders to maintain a striking position to midstretch where she could not gain under further urging. FINNEGAN appeared to have no excuse in an even effort. DUNCE was never a contender. OPEN VIEW dropped back steadily after showing early speed as did ATOLL. JOHN BRUCE lost all chance when caught between horses at the start and went to his knees. EASY SPUR was far back throughout. OUR DAD lacked his customary closing rally. TROILUS stopped badly after cutting out a swift pace for five furlongs. **Scratched—2215CD^{1} On-and-On.**

1959 Belmont Stakes

SEVENTH RACE **Bel - 2606** **June 13, 1959** **1 1-2 MILES. (Gallant Man, June 15, 1957, 2:26$\frac{3}{5}$, 3, 126.) Ninety-first running BELMONT. $125,000 added. 3-year-olds. Scale weights. By subscription of $50 each, to accompany the nomination. Supplementary nominations may be made five days before the running of the race by the payment of an eligibility fee of $5,000. Starters to pay $1,000 additional, with $125,000 added. The added money and all fees to be divided 65 percent to the owner of the winner, 20 per cent to second, 10 per cent to third and 5 percent to fourth. Colts, 126 lbs.; fillies, 121 lbs. The winning owner will be presented with the August Belmont Memorial Cup, to be retained for one year, as well as a trophy for permanent possession; trophies will be presented to the winning trainer and jockey. Closed Monday, Feb. 16, 1959, with 130 nominations. Supplementary nominations closed Monday, June 8.**

Gross value, $145,500. Gross to winner $94,575. Net to winner $93,525; second, $29,100; third, $14,550; fourth, $7,275. Mutuel Pool, $607,468.

Index	Horses	Eq't A	Wt	PP	¼	½	¾	1	Str	Fin	Jockeys	Owners	Odds to $1
2359Bel[1]	—Sword Dancer	b	126	8	7^5	7^8	5^2	2^2	2^6	$1^{3/4}$	W Sho'aker	Brookmeade Stable	1.65
2551Bel[2]	—Bagdad		126	6	2^1	2^2	2^3	1^1	1^h	2^{12}	R Ussery	H B Keck	10.45
2551Bel[3]	—Royal Orbit	b	126	7	8^9	8^7	8^{10}	6^6	3^6	3^{15}	W Harmatz	H O Braunstein	2.40
2440GS[4]	—s-Manassa Mauler		126	1	1^h	1^1	$1^{1/2}$	3^3	4^6	4^2	R Brouss'rd	E Dolce	13.35
2400GS[2]	—Scotland	b	126	4	5^2	6^6	7^6	4^1	5^h	$5^{1\,1/2}$	S Boulmetis	W M Ingraham	37.85
2568Bel[1]	—Dunce	b	126	3	$4^{1/2}$	4^h	6^h	5^6	6^6	6^{10}	M Ycaza	Claiborne Farm	9.10
2544Bel[1]	—North Pole II.	b	126	2	9	9	9	7	7	7	C McCreary	J S Kroese	94.80
2400GS[3]	—Lake Erie	b	126	9	3^4	3^5	$4^{1/2}$	Fell.			W Blum	H O H Frelinghuysen	113.30
2551Bel[1]	—Black Hills		126	5	$6^{2\,1/2}$	$5^{1/2}$	3^2	Fell.			E Arcaro	King Ranch	3.75

s-Supplementary entry.

Time, :23$\frac{2}{5}$, :46$\frac{3}{5}$, 1:10$\frac{4}{5}$, 1:37, 2:02$\frac{4}{5}$, 2:28$\frac{2}{5}$. Track sloppy.

Official Program Numbers↓

Mutuel Prices		$2 Mutuels Paid			Odds to $1		
	9-SWORD DANCER	5.30	3.00	2.30	1.65	.50	.15
	7-BAGDAD		6.00	3.30		2.00	.65
	8-ROYAL ORBIT			2.70			.35

Winner—Ch. c, by Sunglow—Highland Fling, by By Jimminy, trained by J. E. Burch; bred by Brookmeade Sta.

IN GATE—4:47. OFF AT 4:47 EASTERN DAYLIGHT TIME.

Start good. Won driving. SWORD DANCER, in hand to the mile, moved up steadily thereafter and, responding to brisk urging during the stretch run, wore down BAGDAD in the last sixteenth. BAGDAD raced nearest MANASSA MAULER to the mile, went to the front approaching the stretch and settled for the drive with a short advantage but was unable to withstand SWORD DANCER. ROYAL ORBIT, far back early and laboring in the sloppy footing, could not threaten the leaders when set down through the stretch. MANASSA MAULER saved ground while setting the pace to the mile but gave way when challenged by BAGDAD. SCOTLAND was never dangerous and had no excuse. DUNCE was through early. NORTH POLE II. began slowly and raced far back the entire trip. BLACK HILLS was moving up determinedly near the five-sixteenths mile pole when he broke down and fell. LAKE ERIE, tiring after showing early speed, was unable to avoid the prone BLACK HILLS and fell. BLACK HILLS was humanely destroyed after the mishap.

Scratched—2551Bel[4] The Irishman, 2568Bel[3] Joe's Master.

1962 Belmont Stakes

SEVENTH RACE
Bel 13370
June 9, 1962

1 1-2 MILES. (Gallant Man. June 15, 1957. 2:26⅗, 3. 126.)
Ninety-fourth running BELMONT. $125,000 added. 3-year-olds. Scale weights. By subscription of $100 each, to accompany the nomination. Supplementary nominations may be made five days before the running of the race by the payment of an eligibility fee of $5,000. $250 to pass the entry box and $1,000 additional to start, with $125,000 added, of which $25,000 to second, $12,500 to third and $6,250 to fourth. All fees to the Belmont winner. Colts and geldings, 126 lbs., fillies, 121 lbs. The winning owner will be presented with the August Belmont Memorial Cup, to be retained for one year, as well as a trophy for permanent possession and trophies will be presented to the winning trainer and jockey. Closed Wednesday, Feb. 15, 1962 with 133 nominations.

Value of race $153,300. Value to winner $109,550; second, $25,000; third, $12,500; fourth, $6,250. Mutuel Pool, $709,142.

Index	Horses	Eq't	A	Wt	PP	¼	½	1	1¼	Str	Fin	Jockeys	Owners	Odds to $1
13184GS^{1}	—Jaipur	b		126	4	$2^{1\frac{1}{2}}$	2^{1}	2^{1}	$2^{1\frac{1}{2}}$	2^{h}	1no	W Sh'mak'r	G D Widener	2.85
13184GS^{2}	—Admiral's Voyage			126	7	$1^{2\frac{1}{2}}$	1^{2}	$1^{1\frac{1}{2}}$	$1^{\frac{1}{2}}$	$1^{\frac{1}{2}}$	$2^{1\frac{1}{4}}$	B Baeza	F W Hooper	8.70
13184GS^{3}	—Crimson Satan	b		126	1	4^{h}	3^{1}	4^{3}	3^{3}	3^{6}	$3^{6\frac{1}{2}}$	M Ycaza	Crimson King Farm	3.80
13108Pim	—Decidedly	b		126	2	7^{5}	$6^{\frac{1}{2}}$	6^{5}	5^{3}	4^{2}	4^{2}	W Hartack	El Peco Ranch	4.10
13304Bel^{1}	—(s) David K.			126	8	5^{1}	7^{6}	7^{6}	6^{3}	5^{1}	5^{h}	J Sellers	Harbor View Farm	19.85
13184GS	—Vimy Ridge			126	6	$6^{\frac{1}{2}}$	$5^{\frac{1}{2}}$	5^{h}	7^{6}	$6^{1\frac{1}{2}}$	6^{4}	S Boulmetis	F E Power	6.70
13108Pim^{1}	—Greek Money			126	3	$3^{\frac{1}{2}}$	4^{1}	$3^{\frac{1}{2}}$	$4^{\frac{1}{2}}$	7^{12}	7^{14}	J L Rotz	Brandywine Stable	3.70
13344Bel^{3}	—Folk Dancer	b		126	5	8	8	8	8	8	8	R Ussery	M Newton	37.55

(s) Supplementary nominee.

Time, :24⅕, :48⅖, 1:12⅕, 1:36⅗, 2:02⅕, 2:28⅘ (with wind in backstretch). Track fast.

$2 Mutuel Prices:			
4-JAIPUR	**7.70**	**4.40**	**3.40**
7-ADMIRAL'S VOYAGE		**7.40**	**5.20**
1-CRIMSON SATAN			**3.70**

Dk. b. c, by Nasrullah—Rare Perfume, by Eight Thirty. Trainer, W. F. Mulholland. Bred by Erde Farms Co.

IN GATE—4:50. OFF AT 4:50 EASTERN DAYLIGHT TIME. Start good. Won driving.

JAIPUR, away alertly, raced in nearest attendance to ADMIRAL'S VOYAGE after the start, moved to the outside of the latter for the stretch run and, responding to strong handling, won in the last strides. ADMIRAL'S VOYAGE went to the front soon after the start and saved ground while setting the pace under light restraint responded readily when set down through the stretch but was unable to withstand JAIPUR and just missed. CRIMSON SATAN, well placed and reserved for a mile, drifted out at the stretch turn and, bearing in badly during the drive, was forced to check after taking command between calls and gave way through the final furlong. DECIDEDLY, washy during the post parade, dropped back after beginning alertly and was caught in tight quarters at the first turn, moved to the outside approaching the stretch but was unable to threaten the leaders when set down in the drive. DAVID K. and VIMY RIDGE had no mishaps and were unable to reach serious contention. GREEK MONEY, prominent until reaching the stretch, had nothing left. FOLK DANCER began slowly and was far back the entire trip.

1963 Preakness Stakes

EIGHTH RACE
Pim 16707
May 18, 1963

1 3-16 MILES. (Nashua, May 28, 1955, 1:54$\frac{3}{5}$, 3, 126.)
Eighty-seventh running PREAKNESS. Scale weights. $150,000 added. 3-year-olds. By subscription of $100 each, this fee to accompany the nomination. $1,000 to pass the entry box, starters to pay $1,000 additional. All eligibility, entrance and starting fees to the winner, with $150,000 added, of which $30,00 to second, $15,000 to third and $7,500 to fourth. Weight, 126 lbs. Supplementary entries by payment of supplemental fee of $10,000 may be made on or before Thursday, May 16, two days before the race at the usual time of closing. A replica of the Woodlawn Vase will be presented to the winning owner to remain his or her personal property. Closed Friday, Feb. 15, 1963 with 140 nominations.

Value of race $180,000. Value to winner $127,500; second, $30,000; third, $15,000; fourth, $7,500. Mutuel Pool, $538,690.

Index	Horses	Eq't	A	Wt	PP	St	¼	½	¾	Str	Fin	Jockeys	Owners	Odds to $1
16634CD[3]	—Candy Spots	b	3	126	8	6	3^{h}	3^{3}	$2^{1\frac{1}{2}}$	$1^{1\frac{1}{2}}$	$1^{3\frac{1}{2}}$	W Sh'maker	R C Ellsworth	1.50
16634CD[1]	Chateaugay		3	126	4	4	$6^{1\frac{1}{2}}$	$6^{1\frac{1}{2}}$	4^{h}	$2^{1\frac{1}{2}}$	$2^{4\frac{1}{2}}$	B Baeza	Darby Dan Farm	2.90
16634CD[2]	—Never Bend		3	126	5	1	1^{1}	$1^{1\frac{1}{2}}$	$1^{\frac{1}{2}}$	3^{5}	$3^{2\frac{1}{4}}$	M Ycaza	Cain Hoy Stable	1.80
[illegible]pt[1]	—Lemon Twist		3	126	2	7	7^{1}	7^{3}	$6^{1\frac{1}{2}}$	6^{5}	4no	[illegible] LeJeune	T D Duhl	22.00
16688Aqu[2]	—Sky Wonder		3	126	6	2	5^{3}	5^{2}	5^{1}	5^{h}	$5^{\frac{3}{4}}$	C Burr	Mrs C D Morgan	37.10
15661Pim[2]	—Rural Retreat	b	3	126	7	3	2^{h}	$2^{1\frac{1}{2}}$	3^{1}	4^{1}	6^{6}	R L Baird	W B Robinson	99.50
16634CD[4]	—On My Honor		3	126	1	8	8	8	8	7^{4}	7^{3}	P Frey	M F-J L Stein	34.50
16661Pim[7]	—Country Squire	b	3	126	3	5	$4^{1\frac{1}{2}}$	$4^{\frac{1}{2}}$	$7^{\frac{1}{2}}$	8	8	W Ch'mbers	Jacnot Stable	22.30

Time, .24$\frac{1}{5}$, .47$\frac{4}{5}$, 1.11$\frac{2}{5}$, 1.37, 1.56$\frac{1}{5}$. Track fast.

$2 Mutuel Prices:			
8-CANDY SPOTS	**5.00**	**3.20**	**2.20**
4-CHATEAUGAY		**4.40**	**2.40**
5-NEVER BEND			**2.20**

Ch, c, by Nigromante—Candy Dish, by Khaled. Trainer, Meshach A. Tenney. Bred by R. C. Ellsworth.

IN GATE—5:48. OFF AT 5:48 EASTERN DAYLIGHT TIME. Start good. Won ridden out.

CANDY SPOTS moved into contention on the first turn, followed the leaders into the backstretch while in hand, moved fast to wrest command from the outside entering the stretch and was ridden out to draw off after turning back the bid of CHATEAUGAY in midstretch. The latter, restrained off the early pace, rallied from between horses on the far turn, loomed boldly from the outside after straightening away but was no match for the winner while best of the rest. NEVER BEND, away alertly, made the pace under light restraint and while saving ground but could not keep up in the late stages. LEMON TWIST passed tiring horses. SKY WONDER raced within striking distance into the far turn but had nothing left. RURAL RETREAT raced closest to the early pace but was finished after three-quarters. ON MY HONOR was always outrun. COUNTRY SQUIRE stopped badly after showing some early foot.

1965 Kentucky Derby

SEVENTH RACE
CD 23807
May 1, 1965

1 1-4 MILES. (Northern Dancer, May 2, 1964, 2:00, 3, 126.)
Ninety-first running KENTUCKY DERBY. Scale weights. $125,000 added. 3-year-olds. By subscription of $100 each in cash, which covers nomination for both The Kentucky Derby and Derby Trial. All nomination fees to Derby winner. $500 to pass entry box, $1,000 additional to start, $125,000 added, of which $25,000 to second, $12,500 to third, $5,000 to fourth, $100,000 guaranteed to winner (to be divided equally in event of a dead heat), Weight, 126 lbs. The owner of the winner to receive a gold trophy. Closed Monday, Feb. 15, 1965, with 130 nominations.

Value of race $154,000. Value to winner $112,000; second, $25,000; third, $12,500; fourth, $5,000.
Mutuel Pool, $2,227,484.

Index	Horses	Eq't	A	Wt	PP	1/4	1/2	3/4	1	Str	Fin	Jockeys	Owners	Odds to $1
23602Kee^{1}	—Lucky Debonair		3	126	8	3^{h}	$2^{2\frac{1}{2}}$	$2\frac{1}{2}$	2^{2}	1^{3}	1^{nk}	W Sh'maker	Mrs Ada L Rice	4.30
23633Aqu^{4}	—Dapper Dan	b	3	126	1	11	11	11	7^{1}	$5\frac{1}{2}$	2^{2}	I Valenzuela	O Phipps	30.00
23507CD^{1}	—Tom Rolfe		3	126	9	7^{2}	5^{1}	$3^{1\frac{1}{2}}$	$4^{1\frac{1}{2}}$	3^{h}	3^{1}	R Turcotte	Powhatan	5.60
23507CD^{2}	—Native Charger	b	3	126	4	4^{3}	$4^{1\frac{1}{2}}$	$4\frac{1}{2}$	$3\frac{1}{2}$	4^{1}	4^{nk}	J L Rotz	Warner Stable	6.40
23633Aqu^{2}	—Hail to All		3	126	7	9^{2}	10^{2}	$9^{1\frac{1}{2}}$	8^{h}	$6^{1\frac{1}{2}}$	$5^{2\frac{1}{4}}$	M Ycaza	Mrs B Cohen	3.80
23602Kee^{3}	—Mr Pak		3	126	10	8^{2}	$8^{2\frac{1}{2}}$	7^{2}	$6\frac{1}{2}$	8^{4}	6^{h}	J Nichols	Mrs Mary Keim	53.80
23602Kee^{2}	—Swift Ruler		3	126	11	10^{h}	$9\frac{1}{2}$	$8\frac{1}{2}$	10^{2}	$7\frac{1}{2}$	7^{3}	L Spraker	E Allen	34.90
23633Aqu^{1}	—Flag Raiser	b	3	126	5	1^{2}	1^{h}	1^{h}	1^{h}	2^{h}	$8^{2\frac{1}{2}}$	R Ussery	I Bieber	17.90
23524CD^{2}	—Carp'nt'r's Rule	b	3	126	6	$6^{1\frac{1}{2}}$	7^{2}	10^{3}	11	9^{1}	$9\frac{1}{2}$	W Harmatz	P L Grissom	78.70
23524CD^{1}	—Bold Lad	b	3	126	3	5^{h}	$6^{1\frac{1}{2}}$	$6\frac{1}{2}$	5^{h}	$10\frac{1}{2}$	10^{2}	W Hartack	Wheatley Stable	2.00
23507CD^{3}	—Narushua		3	126	2	2^{h}	3^{h}	5^{2}	$9\frac{1}{2}$	11	11	T Dunlavy	J W Mecom	92.00

Time, :23$\frac{1}{5}$, :47$\frac{1}{5}$, 1:11$\frac{4}{5}$, 1:37, 2:01$\frac{1}{5}$. Track fast.

$2 Mutuel Prices:			
8-LUCKY DEBONAIR	**10.60**	**5.40**	**4.20**
1-DAPPER DAN		**26.00**	**12.60**
9-TOM ROLFE			**4.80**

B. c, by Vertex—Fresh as Fresh, by Count Fleet. Trainer, F. Catrone. Bred by Danada Farm.

IN GATE—5:00. OFF AT 5:00 EASTERN STANDARD TIME. Start good. Won driving.

LUCKY DEBONAIR broke alertly to show the way through the opening furlong, dropped back a bit when Shoemaker took a snug hold nearing the sixteenth marker, moved up again to engage FLAG RAISER midway of the first turn, continued to duel with that one while along the outside to the final quarter where he moved to the fore when sharply roused, moved off to a lengthy advantage through the upper stretch but was fully extended to turn back a belated bid from DAPPER DAN. The latter, away slowly and unhurried for six furlongs, moved up along the inside on leaving the backstretch, angled out sharply to launch his closing rally on the final turn and, responding to strong handling, was slowly getting to the winner. TOM ROLFE, in hand for a half mile, moved up boldly along the inside to engage the top flight at the half mile pole, dropped back a bit while awaiting racing room then came again while under extreme pressure and finished gamely. NATIVE CHARGER, bumped while between horses entering the first turn, quickly recovered to remain in contention while along the outside to loom menacingly on the stretch turn and finished evenly in a good effort. HAIL TO ALL, slow to begin as usual, launched a rally on rounding the second turn and finished boldly while between horses through the closing drive. MR. PAK finished well. SWIFT RULER failed to reach contention. FLAG RAISER came out soon after the start to bump with CARPENTER'S RULE but was quickly straightened away to take a clear lead in the initial run through the stretch, came to the inside thereafter to be well-rated only to weaken badly through the closing drive. CARPENTER'S RULE was bumped soon after the start and failed to reach contention. BOLD LAD, in hand while being outrun early and saving ground, was angled to the outside soon after entering the backstretch to reach a contending position at the half mile ground, then continued well to the top of the stretch where he gave way badly in the final drive. NARUSHUA showed forwardly for three-quarters and tired badly.

1967 Preakness Stakes

EIGHTH RACE **1 3-16 MILES. (Nashua, May 28, 1955, 1:54⅗, 3, 126.)**
Pim 31134
May 20, 1967

Ninety-second running PREAKNESS STAKES. Scale weights. $150,000 added. 3-year-olds. By subscription of $100 each, this fee to accompany the nomination. $1,000 to pass the entry box, starters to pay $1,000 additional. All eligibility, entrance and starting fees to the winner, with $150,000 added, of which $30,000 to second, $15,000 to third and $7,500 to fourth. Weight, 126 lbs. A replica of the Woodlawn Vase will be presented to the winning owner to remain his or her personal property. Closed Wednesday, Feb. 15, 1967, with 140 nominations and one supplemental.

Value of race $194,000. Value to winner $141,500; second, $30,000; third, $15,000; fourth, $7,500. Mutuel Pool, $621,109.

Index	Horses	Eq't	A	Wt	PP	St	¼	½	¾	Str	Fin	Jockeys	Owners	Odds to $1
31052CD^{3}	—Damascus		3	126	2	8	9^{2}	$8^{1\frac{1}{2}}$	8½	$1^{3\frac{1}{2}}$	$1^{2\frac{1}{4}}$	W Sh'maker	Edith W Bancroft	a-1.80
30709GP^{1}	—In Reality	b	3	126	4	5	7^{4}	7^{5}	6½	2^{2}	2^{4}	E Fires	Frances A Genter Stable	4.30
31052CD^{1}	—Proud Clarion	b	3	126	1	10	10	10	9^{2}	3½	3¾	R Ussery	Darby Dan Farm	4.30
31106Aqu^{3}	—Reason to Hail	b	3	126	10	9	4½	4½	7^{1}	4½	$4^{1\frac{1}{2}}$	W Blum	Patrice Jacobs	17.80
31053Pim^{6}	—Misty Cloud		3	126	8	3	5^{1}	6^{h}	3^{1}	5^{1}	$5^{1\frac{1}{2}}$	E Nelson	R S Reynolds Jr	40.40
31052CD^{2}	—(s) Barbs D'li't	b	3	126	7	6	3^{2}	3^{2}	2^{1}	6^{2}	6^{2}	W Hartack	Hueg'let Jr-Spald'g-Steele Jr	3.30
31052CD^{5}	—Ask the Fare	b	3	126	5	7	$8^{1\frac{1}{2}}$	9^{2}	10	8^{h}	7no	J Sellers	Holiday Stable	21.30
31053Pim^{3}	—Celtic Air	b	3	126	3	2	1^{h}	1^{2}	1^{1}	7^{2}	8^{1}	N Shuk	O Wilson Jr	a-1.80
31086Aqu^{4}	—Favorable Turn		3	126	9	4	6^{3}	5^{1}	4½	9^{3}	9^{10}	C Baltazar	H Allen	78.00
31044GS^{1}	—Great Power	b	3	126	6	1	2½	2^{h}	5^{1}	10	10	B Baeza	Wheatley Stable	16.50

a-Coupled, Damascus and Celtic Air (s) Supplementary nomination.

Time, :23, :46⅖, 1:10⅘, 1:36⅘, 1:55⅕. Track fast.

$2 Mutuel Prices:				
	1-DAMASCUS (a-Entry)	**5.60**	**3.60**	**2.60**
	3-IN REALITY		**4.60**	**3.60**
	2-PROUD CLARION			**3.80**

B. c, by Sword Dancer—Kerala, by My Babu. Trainer, F. W. Whiteley, Jr. Bred by Mrs. T. Bancroft (Ky.).

IN GATE—5:31. OFF AT 5:32 EASTERN DAYLIGHT TIME. Start good. Won driving.

DAMASCUS, taken under steadying restraint at the start and dropping far back of the pace being set by his running-mate, was put to hand pressure settling into the backstretch but did not accelerate appreciably until approaching the turn. Circling the field with a mighty rush, he reached the front at the quarter-pole, came in to the rail and established a command lead under the rousing of a half-dozen right-handed whip-strokes and was hand urged through the last sixteenth of a mile. IN REALITY, reserved behind the first flight and saving ground, moved through close quarters along the inside when the field bunched on the final turn, could not match the rally of the winner but responded gamely and was gaining gradually in the final stages. PROUD CLARION, taken in hand and reserved in the last place early, was guided to the middle of the track and put under pressure to remain within striking distance of DAMASCUS in the backstretch, rallied closely behind that rival around the turn but drifted and hung under heavy punishment in the straightaway. REASON TO HAIL was brought to the rail for a saving of ground at the first turn, then bested only tiring horses in the drive. MISTY CLOUD lost ground outside the leaders and weakened. BARBS DELIGHT was snugly rated just off the pace into the far turn, drew on almost even terms for the lead entering the stretch and gave way in the drive. ASK THE FARE was outrun. CELTIC AIR saved ground setting the pace under alert handling into the final turn and weakened. FAVORABLE TURN weakened. GREAT POWER was used up forcing the pace. A noseband, which was a part of his equipment, broke at the gate and was removed.

1967 Belmont Stakes

EIGHTH RACE **Aqu 31326** **June 3, 1967**

1 1-2 MILES. (Going Abroad. Oct. 12, 1964, 2:26$\frac{1}{5}$, 4, 116.) **Ninety-ninth running BELMONT. Scale weights. $125,000 added. 3-year olds. By subscription of $100 each, to accompany the nomination. Supplementary nominations may be made by Tuesday, May 30, by payment of an eligibility fee of $5,000. $250 to pass the entry box and $1,000 additional to start, with $125,000 added, of which $25,000 to second, $12,500 to third and $6,250 to fourth. All fees to The Belmont winners. Colts and geldings, 126 lbs.; fillies, 121 lbs. The winning owner will be presented with the August Belmont Memorial Cup, to be retained for one year, as well as a trophy for permanent possession and trophies will be presented to the winning trainer and jockey. Closed Wednesday, Feb. 15, 1967 with 122 nominations.**

Value of race $148,700. Value to winner $104,950; second, $25,000; third, $12,500; fourth, $6,250. Mutuel Pool, $804,153.

Index	Horses	Eq't	A	Wt	PP	¼	½	1	1¼	Str	Fin	Jockeys	Owners	Odds to $1
31134Pim^1	—Damascus		3	126	1	6^1	$5\frac{1}{2}$	6^2	3^3	2^2	$1^{2\frac{1}{2}}$	W Sh'maker	Edith W Bancroft	.80
31055WO^1	—Cool Reception	b	3	126	7	2^1	3^3	1^2	1^h	1^h	$2\frac{1}{2}$	J Sellers	Mrs W J Seitz	5.60
31107Spt^3	—G'tlem'n James	b	3	126	8	9	9	9	7^2	4^2	3^1	J Nichols	M G Phipps	28.70
31134Pim^3	—Proud Clarion	b	3	126	4	4^2	4^3	4^1	2^1	3^3	4^6	B Baeza	Darby Dan Farm	3.90
31134Pim^9	—Favorable Turn		3	126	6	3^3	$2\frac{1}{2}$	3^h	5^1	6^1	$5\frac{1}{2}$	A Cord'o Jr	H Allen	66.20
31205Aqu^2	—Gaylord's Feather		3	126	5	8^5	8^5	7^h	6^1	7^2	6no	H Gustines	J M Roebling	49.50
31134Pim^4	—Reason to Hail	b	3	126	9	5^h	6^1	$5\frac{1}{2}$	4^4	5^4	7^2	R Ussery	Patrice Jacobs	6.60
31205Aqu^1	—Blasting Charge		3	126	2	7^2	$7\frac{1}{2}$	8^5	8^4	8^8	8^{20}	J L Rotz	J M Schiff	51.30
31195Aqu^1	—Prinkipo	b	3	126	3	$1\frac{1}{2}$	1^2	$2\frac{1}{2}$	9	9	9	E Cardone	E Zantker	13.20

Time, :23$\frac{2}{5}$, :47, 1:12$\frac{2}{5}$, 1:37$\frac{2}{5}$, 1:49$\frac{4}{5}$, 2:02$\frac{3}{5}$, 2:28$\frac{4}{5}$ (crosswind in backstretch). Track fast.

$2 Mutuel Prices:				
	1-DAMASCUS	**3.60**	**2.60**	**2.40**
	7-COOL RECEPTION		**4.20**	**3.60**
	8-GENTLEMAN JAMES			**7.00**

B. c, by Sword Dancer—Kerala, by My Babu. Trainer, F. Y. Whiteley, Jr. Bred by Mrs. T. Bancroft (Ky.).

IN GATE—5:30. OFF AT 5:30 EASTERN DAYLIGHT TIME. Start good. Won handily.

DAMASCUS, in hand and saving ground to the mile, moved up fast on the outside leaving the upper turn, was set down hard in the early stretch and, after taking command from COOL RECEPTION, drew clear while under mild urging. COOL RECEPTION, away alertly, took command from PRINKIPO after three-quarters mile, held on gamely until inside the stretch but was unable to withstand DAMASCUS, then came back decidedly lame, the result of a broken right cannon bone. GENTLEMAN JAMES, far back until near the stretch, finished determinedly in a courageous performance. PROUD CLARION, reserved and saving ground while racing within striking distance of the leaders to the mile, moved up boldly approaching the stretch but faltered during the drive. FAVORABLE TURN had early speed but failed to stay. GAYLORD'S FEATHER lacked early foot and was never dangerous. REASON TO HAIL, steadied when caught in tight quarters after a mile, dropped out of serious contention during the stretch run. BLASTING CHARGE, never prominent, had no mishap. PRINKIPO began alertly but stopped before going a mile.

Scratched—Nehoc's Bullet.

1975 Belmont Stakes

SEVENTH RACE
Bel
June 7, 1975

1½ MILES. (2:24) One-hundred-and-seventh running BELMONT. SCALE WEIGHTS. $150,000 added. 3-year olds. By subscription of $100 each, to accompany the nomination; $250 to pass the entry box; $1,000 to start. A supplementary nomination may be made by payment of $2,500 at the closing time of entries, plus an additional $10,000 to start. $150,000 added, of which 60% to the winner, 22% to second, 12% to third and 6% to fourth. Colts and geldings, 126 lbs.; fillies, 121 lbs. The winning owner will be presented with the August Belmont Memorial Cup, to be retained for one year, as well as a trophy for permanent possession and trophies will be presented to the winning trainer and jockey. Closed Saturday, Feb. 15, 1975, with 211 nominations.

Value of race $193,600. Value to winner $116,160; second, $42,592; third, $23,232; fourth, $11,616. Mutuel Pool, $1,104,599. Off-track betting, $1,562,590. Exacta Pool, $544,992. Off-track betting Exacta Pool, $1,384,132.

Last Raced	Horse	Eq't	A	Wt	PP	¼	½	1	1¼	Str	Fin	Jockeys	Owners	Odds to $1
17 May 75 ^{8}Pim^{5}	Avatar	b	3	126	5	4^{1}	4^{2}	3^{1}	2^{1}	1^{1}	1^{nk}	WShoemaker	A A Seeligson Jr	13.20
17 May 75 ^{8}Pim^{2}	Foolish Pleasure		3	126	2	6^{2}	6^{2}	5^{1}	4^{3}	3^{1}	$2^{3\frac{1}{2}}$	JVasquez	J L Greer	1.30
17 May 75 ^{8}Pim^{1}	Master Derby		3	126	1	3^{1}	$3^{\frac{1}{2}}$	$2^{\frac{1}{2}}$	$1^{\frac{1}{2}}$	$2^{1\frac{1}{2}}$	3^{1}	DMcHargue	Mrs R E Lehmann	8.60
17 May 75 ^{8}Pim^{3}	Diabolo	b	3	126	4	$1^{1\frac{1}{2}}$	$1^{1\frac{1}{2}}$	1^{2}	3^{2}	4^{5}	$4^{1\frac{1}{4}}$	LPincayJr	F M McMahon	4.90
17 May 75 ^{8}Pim^{4}	Prince Thou Art	b	3	126	3	9	9	7^{h}	7^{5}	6^{2}	5^{1}	BBaeza	Darby Dan Stable	2.70
26 May 75 ^{8}GS^{1}	Singh		3	126	6	$2^{\frac{1}{2}}$	2^{1}	$4^{\frac{1}{2}}$	5^{4}	$5^{\frac{1}{2}}$	$6^{4\frac{1}{2}}$	ACorderoJr	Cynthia Phipps	11.30
17 May 75 ^{8}Pim^{9}	Just the Time		3	126	7	$7^{1\frac{1}{2}}$	7^{2}	8^{h}	8^{1}	8^{6}	7^{2}	RTurcotte	Buckland Farm	a-26.50
20 May 75 ^{7}Aqu^{1}	Nalees Rialto	b	3	126	8	6^{2}	5^{2}	6^{7}	6^{10}	7^{2}	8^{12}	DMontoya	Mrs G M Humphrey	19.00
17 May 75 ^{9}Aqu^{9}	Syllabus	b	3	126	9	$8^{\frac{1}{2}}$	$8^{\frac{1}{2}}$	9	9	9	9	JCruguet	Elmendorf	a-26.50

Coupled, a-Just the Time and Syllabus.

OFF AT 5:39 EDT. Start good. Won driving. Time, :23$\frac{4}{5}$, :48, 1:12$\frac{2}{5}$, 1:38$\frac{3}{5}$, 2:02, 2:28$\frac{1}{5}$. Track fast.

$2 Mutuel Prices:			
6-AVATAR	28.40	8.00	5.00
3-FOOLISH PLEASURE		3.20	2.60
2-MASTER DERBY			5.20

$2 EXACTA (6-3) PAID $104.40.

Ch. c, by Graustark—Brown Berry, by Mount Marcy. Trainer, A. T. Doyle. Bred by A. A. Seeligson, Jr. (Ky.).

AVATAR, away in good order, was rated along behind the leaders while racing well out in the track, continued along the outside to go after MASTER DERBY nearing the stretch, took over soon after straightening away, opened a clear lead inside the final furlong and was under pressure to turn back FOOLISH PLEASURE. The latter, unhurried early, commenced to rally nearing the end of the backstretch, came out to continue his move nearing the stretch and finished strongly. MASTER DERBY, allowed to follow DIABOLO while well in hand, moved to the fore from between horses near the three eighths pole but weakened during the drive. DIABOLO sprinted clear racing into the first turn, made the pace while racing well out from the inner rail, remained a factor to the upper stretch and gave way. PRINCE THOU ART, void of early foot, passed tired horses. SINGH, a forward factor to the far turn, tired badly. JUST THE TIME was always outrun. NALEES RIALTO, well placed until near the far turn, had nothing left. SYLLABUS showed nothing.

1986 Kentucky Derby

EIGHTH RACE
Churchill
May 3, 1986

1 1-4 MILES. (1.59⅗) 112th Running THE KENTUCKY DERBY Grade I. $350,000 Added. 3-year-olds with an entry fee of $10,000 each and a starting fee of $10,000 each. All fees will be paid to the winner. $350,000 added shall be paid by Churchill Downs Incorporated as the Added Purse. Second place shall receive $100,000, third place shall receive $50,000 and fourth place shall receive $25,000 from the Added Purse (the Added Purse and fees to be divided equally in the event of a dead heat). Starters shall be named through the entry box on Thursday, May 1, 1986, at the usual time of closing (the "Closing"). The maximum number of starters shall be limited to twenty (20) and each shall carry a weight of 126 pounds. In the event that more than twenty entries pass through the entry box at the Closing, the starters shall be determined at the Closing with preference given to those horses that have accumulated the highest earnings in graded sweepstakes, including all money paid for performance in such Graded Stakes. Should additional starters be needed to bring the field to 20, the remaining starters shall be determined at the Closing with preference given to those horses that have accumulated the highest earnings in Non-Restricted Sweepstakes. For purposes of this preference, a "Non-Restricted Sweepstakes" shall mean those Sweepstakes whose conditions contain no other restrictions other than that of age or sex. In the case of ties resulting from preferences or otherwise, the additional starter(s) shall be determined by lot. An "also eligible" list will not be maintained and in no event will starters be added or allowed to run in the race which are not determined to be starters at the Closing. The owner of the winner for the race shall receive a gold trophy.

Value of race $784,400; value to winner $609,400; second, $100,000; third, $50,000; fourth, $25,000. Mutuel Pool, $5,350,857. Exacta Pool $814,262.

Last Raced	Horse	Eq't A	Wt	PP	¼	½	¾	1	Str	Fin	Jockey	Odds to $1
6Apr86 $^{5}SA^{3}$	—Ferdinand	3	126	1	15^{hd}	16	$11^{1\frac{1}{2}}$	5½	1^{1}	$1^{2\frac{1}{4}}$	Shoemaker W	17.70
24Apr86 $^{7}Kee^{3}$	—Bold Arrangement	3	126	4	14^{hd}	11½	7½	2½	3½	2¾	McCarron C J	9.10
19Apr86 $^{8}Aqu^{1}$	—Broad Brush	3	126	9	$7^{1\frac{1}{2}}$	6½	$6^{1\frac{1}{2}}$	1^{hd}	2^{hd}	3^{nk}	Bracciale V Jr	14.40
19Apr86 $^{9}OP^{1}$	—Rampage	3	126	8	$11^{1\frac{1}{2}}$	$10^{1\frac{1}{2}}$	9^{1}	7^{2}	6^{3}	$4^{1\frac{1}{2}}$	Day P	9.00
5Apr86 $^{10}Hia^{1}$	—Badger Land	b 3	126	10	9½	9½	8^{1}	3½	4^{3}	5^{4}	Velasquez J	2.60
19Apr86 $^{9}OP^{2}$	—Wheatly Hall	3	126	11	8½	7½	$5^{1\frac{1}{2}}$	6^{1}	5^{hd}	$6^{1\frac{1}{2}}$	Stevens G L	47.70
19Apr86 $^{9}GS^{1}$	—Fobby Forbes	3	126	16	12^{hd}	12½	14^{hd}	$10^{1\frac{1}{2}}$	7½	$7^{3\frac{1}{4}}$	Romero R P	f-16.00
24Apr86 $^{7}Kee^{4}$	—Icy Groom	3	126	5	10^{hd}	$13^{1\frac{1}{2}}$	12^{1}	9½	8^{3}	8^{2}	Maple E	f-16.00
12Apr86 $^{7}Kee^{1}$	—Wise Times	b 3	126	3	13½	15½	$15^{1\frac{1}{2}}$	$11^{1\frac{1}{2}}$	10^{hd}	9^{nk}	Allen K K	f-16.00
19Apr86 $^{8}Aqu^{2}$	—Mogambo	3	126	2	16	14½	16	14^{5}	$11^{2\frac{1}{2}}$	$10^{3\frac{3}{4}}$	Vasquez J	8.80
6Apr86 $^{5}SA^{1}$	—Snow Chief	b 3	126	12	4^{5}	4^{6}	3^{hd}	4^{1}	9^{hd}	11^{nk}	Solis A	2.10
19Apr86 $^{9}GS^{2}$	—Zabaleta	b 3	126	15	2^{1}	$2^{1\frac{1}{2}}$	$2^{1\frac{1}{2}}$	8½	$12^{3\frac{1}{2}}$	12^{3}	McHargue DG	f-16.00
12Apr86 $^{8}Pim^{5}$	—Southern Appeal	b 3	126	6	6½	$5^{1\frac{1}{2}}$	10^{hd}	13½	13^{2}	$13^{8\frac{1}{2}}$	Davidson J	f-16.00
24Apr86 $^{7}Kee^{1}$	—Bachelor Beau	b 3	126	13	3^{1}	3½	4^{2}	12^{hd}	14^{6}	14^{11}	Melancon L	60.00
19Apr86 $^{8}GG^{1}$	—Vernon Castle	3	126	7	5^{hd}	8^{3}	13^{hd}	16	15^{2}	$15^{7\frac{1}{2}}$	Delahoussaye E	12.20
19Apr86 $^{8}Aqu^{3}$	—Groovy	3	126	14	1^{1}	1^{1}	1^{hd}	15^{2}	16	16	Pincay L Jr	57.30

f-Mutuel field.

OFF AT 5:40, Start good, Won driving. Time, :22⅕, :45⅕, 1:10⅕, 1:37, 2:02⅘. Track fast.

$2 Mutuel Prices:			
1-FERDINAND	37.40	16.20	8.60
3-BOLD ARRANGEMENT		9.40	6.80
6-BROAD BRUSH			9.20

$2 EXACTA 1-3 PAID $385.00.

Ch. c, by Nijinsky II–Banja Luka, by Double Jay. Trainer Whittingham Charles. Bred by Keck H B (Ky.).

FERDINAND, bothered following the start, dropped well back while lacking room along the inside racing to the first turn, came out while beginning to advance after entering the backstretch, moved through inside the leaders after splitting horses through the upper stretch and drew away under left-handed pressure. BOLD ARRANGEMENT, outrun early, rallied while racing well out in the track approaching the end of the backstretch, loomed boldly between horses leaving the far turn and continued on with good courage to gain the place. BROAD BRUSH, reserved into the backstretch, made a bold bid between horses nearing the stretch but wasn't good enough in a long drive. RAMPAGE, steadied along early, was moving well when blocked behind a wall of horses nearing the stretch, was checked again when unable to find room inside SNOW CHIEF approaching the final furlong, then finished well after angling out for room. BADGER LAND lacked room after the start, moved boldly around horses approaching the stretch but weakened during the drive. WHEATLY HALL moved up approaching the far turn, remained a factor to the stretch and tired. FOBBY FORBES failed to be a serious factor while racing very wide during the late stages. ICY GROOM angled over shortly after the start tightening it up on FERDINAND, MOGAMBO and WISE TIMES, then failed to be a serious factor. WISE TIMES, forced to steady soon after the start, was always outrun. MOGAMBO lacked room after the start and was never close. SNOW CHIEF, allowed to follow the early leaders, gained a brief advantage approaching the five-sixteenths pole, moved to the inside leaving the far turn and gave way readily under pressure. ZABALETA prompted the pace into the backstretch, reached the front briefly when GROOVY gave way suddenly at the far turn, then was bothered along the inside while tiring after entering the stretch. SOUTHERN APPEAL tired. BACHELOR BEAU raced forwardly to the far turn and had nothing left. VERNON CASTLE was finished early while saving ground. GROOVY saved ground while showing speed to the far turn and stopped suddenly.

Owners— 1, Keck Mrs H B; 2, Richards A J; 3, Meyerhoff R E; 4, Reed Mr-Mrs H J; 5, Hatley & Lukas & Lukas; 6, McKinnon J; 7, Due Process Stable; 8, Fleming W; 9, R L Reineman Stable Inc; 10, Brant P M; 11, Grinstead & Rochelle; 12, Riordan M D; 13, Bender H M; 14, Waterfield & Tafel; 15, Paulson A E; 16, Ballis J A.

Trainers— 1, Whittingham Charles; 2, Brittain Clive E; 3, Small Richard W; 4, Thomas Gary A; 5, Lukas D Wayne; 6, Van Berg Jack C; 7, Garcia Carlos A; 8, Ramer Sam T; 9, Gleaves Philip; 10, Jolley Leroy; 11, Stute Melvin F; 12, Gosden John H M; 13, Moncrief Marvin L; 14, Hauswald Philip; 15, Sullivan John; 16, Crowell Howard.

ABOUT THE AUTHOR

Barney Nagler has been a renowned sports columnist for fifty years. He has produced and written television shows for NBC and ABC and covered sports events throughout the world. His articles have appeared in major national magazines. He has written four books and currently writes the column "On Second Thought" for *Daily Racing Form.*